COUNSELING ACROSS AND BEYOND CULTURES

Exploring the Work of Clemmont E. Vontress in Clinical Practice

Edited by Roy Moodley and Rinaldo Walcott

Multicultural counseling is a dynamic field, one that continually changes to reflect shifting social norms and to serve an increasingly diverse and globalized population. There is a growing need for counselors and psychotherapists who are sensitive and inclusive not only in regard to race, culture, and ethnicity, but also in matters related to gender, age, sexual orientation, disability, and class.

Inspired by the pioneering work of Clemmont E. Vontress, the contributors to *Counseling across and beyond Cultures* trace the evolution of multicultural counseling and discuss remaining challenges for practitioners. Essays include personal reflections by Vontress himself, assessments of developments in multicultural counseling, evaluations of Vontress's influence in Canada and the United Kingdom, and African and Caribbean perspectives on his work. Throughout, the volume offers historical, philosophical, and critical analysis of Vontress's accomplishments in the light of the changing epistemologies of multicultural counseling and psychotherapy.

ROY MOODLEY is a professor of counseling psychology at the Ontario Institute for Studies in Education at the University of Toronto.

RINALDO WALCOTT is a professor of sociology and equity studies at the Ontario Institute for Studies in Education at the University of Toronto.

Counseling across and beyond Cultures

Exploring the Work of Clemmont E. Vontress in Clinical Practice

Edited by Roy Moodley and Rinaldo Walcott

UNIVERSITY OF TORONTO PRESS
Toronto Buffalo London

Toronto Buffalo London
www.utppublishing.com
Printed in Canada

ISBN 978-0-8020-9781-1 (cloth)
ISBN 978-0-8020-9535-0 (paper)

Printed on acid-free, 100% post-consumer recycled paper with vegetable-based inks.

Library and Archives Canada Cataloguing in Publication

Counseling across and beyond cultures : exploring the work of Clemmont E. Vontress in clinical practice / edited by Roy Moodley and Rinaldo Walcott.

Includes bibliographical references and index.
ISBN 978-0-8020-9781-1 (bound). ISBN 978-0-8020-9535-0 (pbk.)

1. Vontress, Clemmont E., 1929–. 2. Cross-cultural counseling. I. Moodley, Roy II. Walcott, Rinaldo, 1965–

BF636.7.C76C68 2010 158'.3 C2010-903999-8

Financial support from the Ontario Institute for Studies in Education at the University of Toronto for this book is gratefully acknowledged.

University of Toronto Press acknowledges the financial assistance to its publishing program of the Canada Council for the Arts and the Ontario Arts Council.

University of Toronto Press acknowledges the financial support for its publishing activities of the Government of Canada through the Book Publishing Industry Development Program (BPIDP).

Contents

Foreword

My journey in the profession of counseling began when I started my master's program in counseling two years after I graduated from college in the early seventies. The first person I met was Dr Clemmont Vontress, the professor who was assigned to be my adviser. I vividly remember my first meeting with him; sitting in his office and looking around, I was absolutely in awe of him and incredibly intimidated. That feeling carried over to the next semester, when I took my first class with him, and for a while longer. I was about halfway through my master's program when he looked at me during an advising session and said, 'Well, of course you're going on for a doctorate, aren't you?' I thought that if this man, who was so well known and published, thought I could complete a doctorate, then I guess I could. Now I look back on those days and laugh. I am proud that Clemmont Vontress has been my professor, adviser, mentor, and friend for over thirty years now. He influenced my thinking, education, practice, and involvement in the American Counseling Association (ACA). And I know that he is as proud of me as I am of him.

Over the ensuing years I have been a school counselor, a supervisor, a state-level administrator, and, now, a counselor educator. I have also become very involved with the ACA and some of its entities. As I reflect upon the profession and the practice of counseling from these viewpoints, I am astounded at how much has changed in that time. Yet, at the same time, some things need to continue to evolve. One of the areas in which I have become quite interested is ethics. One of the measures of a profession is its code of ethics. The *ACA Code of Ethics* outlines both the musts and shoulds of professional behavior and suggests ways in which counselors might examine their own attitudes, values, and beliefs and reflect upon how those areas affect their practice. Codes of ethics are revised periodically to reflect changes, particularly in society, in technology, and in the scope and practice of counseling. The 2005 *ACA Code of Ethics*[1] incorporates major changes from previous iterations of the code – but reflects concepts that Dr Clemmont Vontress has been writing about since the 1960s. One might say that the profession has finally embraced his thinking. Several of these concepts are outlined below. Readers will find a more comprehensive discussion of these concepts in the chapters of this book.

Central to Vontress's writing is the importance of culture. Everyone has a culture, and is in fact multicultural. Clients must be understood in terms of their culture. The preamble to the 2005 *ACA Code of Ethics* begins with the assertion that 'members must recognize diversity and embrace a cross-cultural approach in support of the worth, dignity, potential, and uniqueness of people within their social and cultural contexts' (2005, p. 3). Multicultural and diversity issues were infused into this code, instead of being a separate section, and the section on diagnosis cautions the reader to view problems within a cultural context. These changes further support the need to view counseling in a cultural context. The concept of family must also be viewed from a cultural context; in many cultures family includes many more people than those to whom one is biologically connected. This concept is reflected in the change from the term family to 'support network' in the code, thus acknowledging the reality of our clients' worlds. Over the past thirty years these concepts have moved from being part of a required class in most master's programs to becoming integral to everything we do as counselors.

A second focus of Vontress's work, particularly his early work, concerns the issue of the marginalization of minorities and the role of counseling in perpetuating this societal oppression. For years counselors had recognized these ideas, but little was done to address them. Over the past decade or so the social justice movement has gained increasing traction and support among counselors, the profession, and the association. Social justice recognizes that behaviors that may have previously been viewed as dysfunctional, symptoms of mental illness, or inappropriate may be the rational response to an unjust situation. Social justice requires that counselors confront oppressive systems to promote the

1 American Counseling Association. (2005). *ACA Code of Ethics.* Alexandria, VA: Author. Retrieved 15 November 2008 from http://www.counseling.org.

empowerment and positive change of the client. Advocacy, a related movement in counseling, has also taken on increased importance. Counselors are expected to work on behalf of their clients to change systems, obtain services, and support the client in new ways. The work of counselors now goes beyond just meeting with clients individually and in groups to include working outside the session to change the status quo.

There are still areas where counseling needs to continue to evolve. As the United States becomes more diverse, many people are choosing to retain their language, customs, and beliefs. Second, we are becoming a global society. Counseling has become international and an important force across the world, but it may be practised in a way that looks very different from traditional counseling. Some of Vontress's recent work concerns traditional healing and looking at incorporating healing modalities into counseling practice. This is a very different way of looking at counseling, and one which only some in the profession embrace. The changed role of the counselor, that is going beyond 'genuineness' to truly sharing one's self, is still in its infancy. While the new code of ethics changed the language from 'dual relationships' to 'beneficial and harmful relationships,' as a profession we still struggle with what our role should be with our clients and when we should go beyond the scheduled appointment time.

We must also understand the importance of the concepts of individualism and collectivism, about which Vontress writes. In mainstream American culture, the wants and needs of the individual are paramount. The focus of counseling has been on helping individuals, independent of others, with their decisions, wants, and needs. In many cultures the needs of the individual are not more important than those of the group to which the client belongs. This is a hard concept for many to grasp, but will be increasingly important for counselors to understand as our clientele becomes more diverse. Lastly, Vontress writes about death as being an inevitable part of life. While the profession is beginning to look at the role of counselors in helping clients, there is still more work to be done. These are some of the areas where counseling is just beginning to change, and it must continue to evolve if we are to be relevant to and effective with our clients.

As one reads this book, I hope the reader will be struck by the tremendous impact Dr Clemmont Vontress has had on so many leaders and practitioners in our field. The book takes us on a journey from his birth and early years in Kentucky, through experiences which shaped his early work, and on to his evolution as an existentialist. Along the way he influenced many luminaries, students, and colleagues in the field both in the United States and internationally. The names of many of the authors are instantly recognizable to any professional: Drs Courtland Lee, Patricia Arredondo, Roy Moodley, Rinaldo Walcott, and Paul Pedersen. All the authors are well known within the field of cross-cultural counseling. Whether directly, through his teaching and presenting, or indirectly, through his scholarship, Dr Clemmont Vontress has impacted counseling in numerous ways. The chapters of this book reflect the influence he has had on these individuals and their work. Each one takes the reader on a journey of self-reflection and growth as a result of the author's experience with Vontress. And each of these individuals, in turn, has influenced numerous others.

No discussion of Vontress's work would be complete without referencing his work in existentialism and its application to cross-cultural counseling and to our world. His work recognizes the commonality of human beings and our ability to relate to others through those commonalities. I was struck by this thought as I listened to President Obama's inauguration speech, in which he suggested that the ways in which we are the same are more important than the ways in which we are different. As our country and the world become more diverse, this is an important message to remember. Years ago many of us could not imagine a world where an African American became president of the United States. For the first time in many years, a sense of hope and excitement grips the country for the promise of change. I would like to think that the work of Dr Clemmont Vontress has contributed to a world where people are beginning to think differently about race and culture. In recognition of his life time accomplishments, Dr Vontress became a Fellow of the American Counseling Association and was recognized with a Presidential Award on 21 March 2010.

Lynn E. Linde
President, American Counseling Association, 2009–10

Acknowledgments

Our sincere thanks go to Clemmont Vontress for making it possible to analyze and interpret his work in the way that all the contributors of this book did. He offered us his time, and valuable assistance during the long process of developing this book. Our deepest gratitude and appreciation to you, Clemmont Vontress.

This book actually began at the second Critical Multicultural Counselling Conference, at OISE / University of Toronto in 2004, at which Clemmont Vontress was awarded the first Lifetime Achievement Award for Multicultural and Diversity Counselling Psychology by the Honourable Alvin Curling (Speaker of the Ontario Legislature). Our appreciation and thanks go to Alvin Curling. We would also like to thank the graduate students – Carla Grey, Linda Green, Deanne Edwards, Michael Goldman, and others – in the Department of Adult Education and Counselling Psychology who organized this conference. Our special thanks to Drs Sharon Mier and John Wright (Cornell University) and Professors Lana Stermac and Charmaine Williams (University of Toronto) for their support before, during, and after the conference.

We sincerely thank all the expert contributors to this book for sharing their insight and clinical understanding of Clemmont Vontress's work: Patricia Arredondo, Nancy Arthur, Niyi Bojuwoye, Sandra Collins, Deone Curling, Jessica Diaz, Lawerence Epp, Farah Ibrahim, Courtland Lee, Lynn Linde, Ronald Marshall, Paul Pedersen, Tracy Robinson-Wood, Patsy Sutherland, Val Watson, and Carmen Braun Williams.

We are pleased to acknowledge the support of the Ontario Institute for Studies in Education (OISE) at the University of Toronto for its support in this project. Special thanks go to Denise Makovac-Badali and

Norman Labrie. Our thanks to Virgil Duff, our editor at University of Toronto Press. Finally, a 'big thank you' to the people closest to us for their patience and understanding during the editing of this book: Roisin, Maya, Tara, Zina, Daniel, Anissa Talahite, and Abdi Osman.

COUNSELING ACROSS AND BEYOND CULTURES

Exploring the Work of Clemmont E. Vontress in Clinical Practice

Introduction

ROY MOODLEY AND RINALDO WALCOTT

> It is not I who make a meaning for myself, but it is the meaning that was already there, pre-existing, waiting for me ... waiting for that turn of history ... I am a potentiality of something.
>
> Frantz Fanon, 1952

> That all my life I had been looking for something
> and everywhere I turned
> someone tried to tell me what it was ...
> I was looking for myself and asking everyone except myself,
> questions which I and only I could answer ...
> that I am nobody but myself
> but first I had to discover that I am
> an invisible man
>
> Ralph Ellison, 1952

The invisible man in Ralph Ellison's quintessential American novel is in search of a personal identity that is beyond the racialized and ethnicized constructions of subjectivity, consciously and unconsciously imposed 'by that turn of history.' It is Frantz Fanon's return to that history through 'the fact of blackness' in *Black Skin, White Masks* (1952) that turns it around by offering us the 'potentiality of something' ... perhaps something visible, visual, tactile, and material. Fanon enter this space of the politics of identity, declaring: 'I am wholly what I am' (p. 135), and in so doing attaches a material reality of race and ethnicity as central to his subjectivity. The invisible man, however, can only arrive at this juncture through a transcendence of race to discover his humanity, while at the same time paradoxically holding on to the transcended object. Yet, in its attachments as transitional objects, race, culture, and ethnicity are localized, since 'we speak from a particular space, out of a particular history, out of a particular experience, ... We are all, in that sense, ethnically located and our ethnic identities are crucial to our subjective sense of who we are' (S. Hall, 1992, p. 258). The politics of this race and cultural identity, as Stewart Hall sees it, is a crucial determining factor in constructing the subject; and this has been the reality for Clemmont E.Vontress, one of the pioneers of cross-cultural counseling.

The radical prose of Fanon and the contrapuntal rhythms of Ellison's narrative epitomize Vontress's personal and professional manner. Vontress's own search for a subjective identity beyond race and ethnicity has led him to become one of most significant figures in the culture and counseling movement. And yet, being a cross-cultural counselor in the West, especially in the United States, has been a culturally wounding experience for Vontress. Perhaps the very notion of cross-cultural counseling itself is a wounding experience for those who engage with it, either as therapists or as clients. Vontress has become culturally wounded (healed) and made invisible, or rather, as a result of being invisible he has become wounded culturally. Throughout his forty years of putting culture into counseling he maintained a strong position of working therapeutically with clients in a way that transcends race, culture, and ethnicity, so that their subjectivities can reclaim their universal humanity. As Vontress says, 'Counselors must concern themselves with the human condition in general before addressing the specifics of the client's culture because people are more alike than they are dissimilar' (1985, p. 28). 'Counselors and clients share something in common, the universal culture' (1988, p. 76).

In his attempt to include culture as part of therapy, Vontress has invariably interrogated and critiqued the foundations of Euro-American theories of counseling and psychotherapy for being ethnocentric, individualistic, and directive. The face-to-face challenge with Carl Rogers on client-centerd therapy in which he argued for a culture-centered approach is one of the many ways in which Vontress can lay claim to putting culture into counseling.

Clemmont Vontress's ideas and writings have been part of the changing world of.multicultural counseling: from its early beginnings in the 1960s with its emphasis on culture, throughout its development towards a multicultural focus, and currently through its paradigmatic evolution into diversity counseling. This has been seen in the name of cross-cultural counseling changing over time to become transcultural, then intercultural and multicultural counseling (although not strictly in this order), and then critical multicultural counseling before entering the space of diversity. Vontress, of course, as one of the pioneers of the culture in counseling movement held steadfastly to the origins of culture-centered counseling, questioning any deviation from this path, especially multicultural counseling and its latest version of diversity counseling.

The Changing Faces of Culture and Counseling

During the four decades the culture and counseling movement has evolved in various ways (as mentioned above), a variety of nomenclatures have been used to define and redefine the changes taking place in the context of its client groups. These are: cross-cultural (Vontress, 1962, 1963, 1976, 1979, 1982, 1986, 2003, 2008), transcultural (d'Ardenne & Mahtani, 1989), culturally different (Sue & Sue, 1990), culture-centered (Laungani, 1999), intercultural (Karem & Littlewood, 1992), and multicultural (Pedersen, 1991; Pope-Davis & Coleman, 1997) counseling. These approaches emphasized culture and ethnicity as key variables in therapy with Black and ethnic minority clients, while other forms, such as Afrocentric (W.A. Hall, 1995), Black feminist (Pankhania, 1996), and 'race' and culture (Carter, 1995; Lago & Thompson, 1996) focus on 'race' as a major construct. As an extension of the race-focused approach, other practitioners have constructed 'race' and racial identity models as a way of making counseling more relevant to minority clients (see, for example, Atkinson, Morten, & Sue, 1993; Cross, 1971, 1978, 1991; Helms, 1984, 1986, 1990; Ponterotto, 1988; Sabnani, Ponterotto, & Borodousky, 1991), or cultural competency models (see Sue & Sue, 1990; Sue, Arrendondo, & McDavis, 1992).

In essence, all these approaches deconstruct the racial, cultural, and ethnic identities of clients from minority communities (McLeod, 1993). Taking account of the 'race' and ethnic identity of the client and contextualizing it within particular socio-political experiences seems to be crucial in counseling the culturally diverse (Lago & Thompson, 1996). While it may be ideal to examine racial, cultural, and ethnic identities in counseling minority clients, it proves more difficult in actual practice. Carter (1995) suggests that issues of 'race' are less conspicuous in counseling because practitioners are more comfortable in considering cultural and ethnic issues than in addressing racial issues. However,

Vontress and his allies in the cross-cultural counseling movement agree that counseling minority clients is most effective when the client's presenting problems are understood within a culturally sensitive process. As the ethnic and cultural demographic landscape has changed through migration and immigration, the culture and counseling movement has also responded.

The consequences of all the micro- and macro-level changes in the culture and counseling movement has transformed counseling from a monocultural paradigm to one that espouses the concept of multiculturalism. In the meantime, Vontress (1979, 1982) too has been making a concerted effort to connect cross-cultural counseling with mainstream ideas in counseling psychology, that is, integrating existentialism and cross-cultural counseling. This became Vontress's second area of research and theorizing.

Therefore, cross-cultural counseling has been changing, moving beyond its own boundaries and limitations to be more inclusive of issues that involve more than just race, culture, and ethnicity. And, in the last two decades, a cultural shift began to emerge – first, the inclusion of gender alongside race, culture, and ethnicity promoted chiefly by Black women feminists and/or womanists. Towards the middle of the 1990s, sexual orientation as a construct became possible within the culture and counseling movement, taking center stage alongside race and gender. Thus, the LGBTQ (lesbian, gay, bi-sexual, transgendered, and queer) movement was incorporated into multicultural counseling. Then disability emerged as a critical issue, followed shortly by age and religion, to complete the inclusion of the Big 7 socio-cultural identities (race, gender, class, sexual orientation, disability, age, religion) as key variables in multicultural counseling and psychotherapy (see Moodley & Lubin, 2008, for discussion). In addition, the post-structuralist's view of the client as a dynamic blend of multiple identities, constructed through discursive practices of the social and cultural, has the potential to offer a comprehensive and sophisticated understanding of the client's subjectivity. Consequently, any form of psychotherapeutic intervention will need to take into account the following: (a) complex multiple and intersected social identities, for example, race, gender, class, sexual orientations, disability, age, religion; (b) clients' illness representations and presentations in therapy, for example, the 'network of personal meanings' of health and illness experienced throughout life; (c) clients' cure-seeking strategies in relation to race, culture, and ethnicity involving, for example, traditional healers and healing, or complementary and alternative forms of medicine; and, (d) clients' historical and cultural experiences of racism, sexism, homophobia, classism, etc. Increasingly, many clinicians have become more aware of the need to emphasize context, the importance of subjective meanings, language, and discourse (as opposed to reductionism), complex interacting particulars (as opposed to universals), and holistic perspectives rather than use narrow viewpoints and descriptors (Moodley & Lubin, 2008). However, the process of accommodating and integrating these various marginalized multiple identities in therapy has not been clearly set out in the theory and practice of multicultural counseling, resulting in much confusion in the profession (Moodley, 2007; Sue, 1997).

Four decades ago, around the same time that Clemmont Vontress began his culture and counseling movement, Wrenn (1962) coined the term 'culturally encapsulated counselor' to critique the universal approach to mental health care of ethnic minority communities. Since then, many conceptual and theoretical meanderings have been attempted to destabilize the notion of the culturally encapsulated counselor, and to bring into consciousness the subjective ways in which clients generate meanings for their 'psychological distress.' Since a 'close correlation exists between a patient's cultural beliefs about his/her illness and between his/her understanding of the treatment of such distress' (Moodley, 2000a, 2000b, 2000c, p. 163), it seems critical that counselors and psychotherapists establish a treatment process that takes into account the equilibrium between culture, illness, and cure. This notion is articulated succinctly by Good and Good when they say, 'The meaning of illness for an individual is grounded in – though not reducible to – the network of meanings an illness has in a particular culture' (Good & Good, 1982, p. 148). Clients will be able, if given the opportunity to receive different cures (for example, talking therapy and traditional healing), to organize systematically the expression of their problem into the discourse of the healer, thus 'presenting their subjective distress to each therapist appropriately ... Competing and contradictory cures can be held alongside or in tandem with each other without necessarily creating conflict in the patient' (Moodley, 2000c, p. 164). This theorizing reinforces the view that a culture's specific meanings are still at the root of an individual's network of meanings, just as Vontress had understood throughout the forty years of his career in psychology.

Clearly, Vontress through his culture-centered focus has been instrumental in bringing to consciousness the critical value of infusing culture, race, and ethnicity into counseling theory and practice. For

Vontress the notion of culture is at the heart and soul of all counseling relationships, and as such it must be at the center of therapy, rather than something to be considered exotic or specialized. And it is this philosophy that has motivated Vontress to develop the field of cross-cultural counseling psychology, and connect it to areas such as existentialism in counseling, traditional healing, and issues related to men and masculinities, particular Black men in the United States. These are the areas that Clemmont Vontress has been preoccupied with in his research and writings; and it is for this canon of work that he was the first recipient of the Achievement Award for Cross-Cultural and Diversity Counseling Psychology and Psychotherapy from OISE/UT (Ontario Institute for Studies in Education at the University of Toronto) in June 2004. The award was offered in recognition of Vontress's outstanding scholarship, research, and practice and to celebrate a lifetime of distinguished professional contribution to the theory, research, and practice of cross-cultural and multicultural counseling psychology and psychotherapy. The citation read as follows:

> For his outstanding contribution to the field of counseling psychology, particularly to cross-cultural and multicultural counseling in North America, and the rest of the world. Clemmont E. Vontress's creative and inspiring insights into the human spirit have been provocative and challenging to the orthodoxy of traditional counseling theory and practice. Clemmont Vontress is a remarkable counselor, psychotherapist, teacher, mentor, and leader. His innovative research and writings on culture and counseling has [*sic*] been the hallmark of his work. Vontress's work has always been about integration, synthesis and collective healing. It exemplifies an integrated, multilevel, and universal response to the ways in which we can understand and solve the big questions of life: this has led him to make connection between cross-cultural counseling and existentialism. As reiterated throughout his articles, books, and numerous interviews, Vontress's ideas in the field of counseling and psychotherapy has [*sic*] contributed in bringing together cultural studies, the social sciences, education, the arts and the humanities.

The Lifetime Achievement Award for Cross-Cultural and Diversity Counseling and Psychotherapy is awarded by the Centre for Diversity in Counseling and Psychotherapy (CDCP) at the Ontario Institute for Studies in Education at the University of Toronto (OISE/UT). The peer-nominated winner has a full-day symposium dedicated to his/

her work, at which leading scholars and researchers in this field reflect on, critically examine, and celebrate the winner's scholarship, research, and pioneering work, as well as identify its future potential. In all his research and publications – more than 100 articles, chapters, and monographs on counseling culturally different clients – Vontress has emphasized the critical interplay of culture and ethnicity as key variables in the process of empathy and healing. Given the current complexities of race, culture, and ethnicity as competing and problematic discourses in the modern world, it seems crucial to engage Vontress's work and to critically examine and analyze, as well as celebrate, many of his theories and pronouncements regarding the future of psychology, counseling, and psychotherapy.

The symposium held to honour Clemmont Vontress generated a high level of scholarship and critical debate, eventually resulting in this collection of essays. This volume also contains chapters that were solicited by the editors from scholars who were not present at the symposium but were connected to Vontress. The book brings together some of the most celebrated and highly respected scholars and researchers in the world of cross-cultural counseling and psychotherapy, and multicultural psychology. Through their divergent views on cross-cultural, multicultural, and diversity counseling, and their critical analysis of Clemmont Vontress's work, the various chapters in this book explore the dynamics of culture and its relationship to counseling.

How the Book Is Organized

This book was brought together to do the following: (a) analyze and critically examine the work of Clemmont Vontress, and by doing so highlight the complexities, confusions, and challenges that are confronting culture and counselling today; (b) celebrate the life and work of Vontress as a pioneer of cross-cultural counseling; (c) produce a historical record of the culture and counseling movement; and, finally (d), present a range of theoretical and empirical accounts of the issues facing students in training, professional counselors, psychotherapists, social workers, and others who use counseling and psychotherapy as part of their professional engagement. The aim was to understand better the nature of current shifts in professional and clinical practice in the field of counseling psychology. Therefore, the ideas presented in this volume tend to form a critical interrogation of the dominant discursive regimes of conventional counseling theories and their applications in terms of difference and diversity.

The book begins (in chapter 1) with Clemmont Vontress offering a personal reflection of his life and work. He discusses his life experiences and intersects this with his research and writings over the forty years that he has been instrumental in the field of cross-cultural counseling. Through a critical analysis and, at times, some very personal narratives, Clemmont Vontress takes the reader into the historical, social, and cultural history of the United States. This opening chapter also provides insight into the various components of Vontress's work; for example, he talks about culture and its relationship with counseling, his research on cross-cultural counseling, his views on integrating existentialism with cross-cultural counseling, and, of particular note, his work with African traditional healers and healing. In chapter 2, Vontress is in conversation with Roy Moodley 'In the Therapist's Chair.' Here, Vontress shares his biography, reflecting on his early life – about his great-grandfather who was killed by the Ku Klux Klan, his father who was a sharecropper, and his escape from the farm to attend school, eventually achieving a PhD in counseling psychology. He talks about his sweetheart, his son and his son's early death, and his historical, cultural, and spiritual connection with his grandchildren. Throughout this personal conversation we get to know Clemmont E. Vontress the man, the cultural being, and the human being whose life experiences have had a major impact on his research and writings in culture and counseling. Finally, Vontress reflects on life, death, and life after death. In chapter 3, Rinaldo Walcott uncovers and discovers a theory of apprehension through the work of Vontress and Fanon. He juxtaposes their writings to question and challenge the ways in which the complexity of cultural identity is reduced to fix notions of race, culture, and ethnicity.

Part 2 explores Clemmont Vontress's role as a mentor and elder of cross-cultural counseling. The section begins with Patricia Arredondo (chapter 4), talking about how, as a counseling student in the 1970s, she felt fortunate to find some of the early contributions of Vontress in the *Personnel and Guidance Journal* critical to her understanding of cross-cultural counseling. She shows how Vontress's work has contributed to the developments in multicultural counseling. In chapter 5, Farah Ibrahim highlights the impact of Vontress's work on her own understanding of cross-cultural counseling, as well as on the field of culture and counseling. Farah talks about her 'adoption' of Vontress as a revered elder and a mentor. She draws from his work to present a case for the concept of multiple identities. Lawrence Epp, a past student and now a colleague of Clemmont Vontress, follows this discussion in chapter 6 by sharing his understanding of his personal relationship with Vontress, and showing how Vontress's work has led to his research and writings in the field of culture and counseling. He explores particularly Vontress's work in relation to cross-cultural counseling and existentialism. In chapter 7, Paul Pedersen considers Vontress's work across a historical time span, from 1976–2007. Paul uses this thirty-year-old framework to offer a critical analysis of current counseling across cultures. He argues that in some ways we have not progressed far over this period in finding answers to the problems we face. However, in other ways, he suggests, our understanding of the problems themselves has become much more accurate and informed.

Part 3 looks at the influences on, and challenges to, the international multicultural scene that Clemmont Vontress's work has had. In chapter 8, Courtland Lee and Jessica Diaz highlight the seminal work of Vontress within the context of the growth of the discipline of multicultural counseling in the United States in the last half of the 20th century. The chapter begins with the historical and social context of the United States from the end of the Second World War to the beginning of the 21st century. Through this discussion Courtland and Jessica focus critically on how the work of Clemmont Vontress has impacted multicultural theory and practice. This is closely followed by Canadians Nancy Arthur and Sandra Collins (chapter 9), who consider the work of Vontress in relation to Canadian multicultural counseling. They discuss how he identified many core ideas in the 1980s that continue to inform and incite debate. The chapter reviews key contributions of his work, how he alerted the field to the work that needed to be done, and how well his core ideas stand as a foundation for guiding multicultural counseling in the early years of this century. In positioning Vontress in a Canadian context Nancy and Sandra show how the culture and counseling movement in Canada has also developed its own culture-infused counseling approach. In chapter 10, Val Watson, basing her work on practitioner experience and reflection, identifies the ways in which the work of Vontress has contributed to and influenced counseling training and practice in the United Kingdom. The significance of Black counsellors' understanding of their cultural heritage and how they may actively use this in the context of the counseling relationship is considered with reference to current debates in the United Kingdom about the expression of 'culture,' the reality of ethnicity, the notions of 'multicultural[ism]' and anti-racism, and how these are affecting relationships. Chapter 11, by Niyi Bojuwoye, discusses Clemmont Vontress's work in relation to African traditional healing methods. He argues that despite his passion for African cultural practices, Vontress is a Westerner, with a Western cultural-value perspective in his evaluation of the different phenomena he came across during his African visits, including the responses he got to his inquiries and the ways he chose to describe events and the people he studied. Niyi's chapter provides an African perspective on Clemmont's works, especially with regard to the social, cultural, and historical contexts in which African traditional healing practices occur. Finally, in chapter 12, Ronald Marshall and Deone Curling look at counseling psychology in the Caribbean and illustrate how Vontress's work has influenced the counseling movement there. Ronald and Deone discuss the psychological surrender of clients in the counselling process to show the difficulties that disadvantaged people have in surrendering themselves psychotherapeutically. In an attempt to establish good practice in counselling in the Caribbean, Vontress's work is examined for useful clinical strategies, skills, and competencies.

Part 4 explores the current preoccupation of the multicultural counseling field – issues of multiple identities and their varied and diverse pathways. These meditations are placed in the context of the early writings of Clemmont Vontress. In chapter 13, Roy Moodley discusses the work of Vontress and its place in the evolving and critical world of culture and counseling. The chapter examines the crisis that presents itself in this field, with its numerous nomenclatures and interest groups. It also explores Vontress's work in relation to the problematic of multicultural and diversity counseling. In chapter 14, Tracy Robinson-Wood looks at the intersections between racial, ethnic, sexual, class, ability, disability, cultural, and gender identities. With Vontress's work at the center of the culture and counseling movement, Tracy explores what it means to privilege multiple and shifting, evolving identities in current therapy practice. In chapter 15, Carmen Braun Williams examines the philosophical orientation of the work of Clemmont Vontress from a womanist perspective that integrates racial and feminist ideologies. The chapter explores shifts in culture and counseling, with a focus on African American women and other women of color. Carmen argues that African American women live as people for whom race and gender – and a host of additional sociopolitical variables – intersect. The chapter discusses Vontress's work as foundational to cross-cultural counseling, but suggests that it has some shortcomings in its omission of an analysis of the interaction of race and gender. Carmen adds that this shortcoming, as Vontress himself has said, does not make a theory misguided, only incomplete. Carmen builds on Vontress's work by considering its application to African American women. Patsy Sutherland and Roy Moodley examine the ideas of Clemmont Vontress in chapter 16, which explores the intersection of religion, spirituality, and traditional healing in his work. The chapter also examines Vontress's quest for spirituality and traditional healing as a personal and existential journey. And to conclude, chapter 17 presents Tracy Robinson-Wood's interviews with Vontress, which took place on 27–28 July 2008 at George Washington University and concluded at Vontress's home, in his study. Tracy says, 'My time with this peaceful, generous, and dynamic man represents a highlight of my career. The purpose of this interview was to capture his personal reflections on culture and counseling and to include his wisdom in this text that pays homage to his vision for humanity, and his counseling scholarship over the decades. His critique of the profession is unfettered and yet deliberate.'

In closing, we need to acknowledge that the task undertaken in this book is not without certain limitations. It has been many years since the idea was originally discussed, in Toronto, at Clemmont Vontress's Lifetime Achievement Award event. Since then much has changed in counseling psychology, and also nothing has changed, depending on which lens one uses. Many of the issues concerning race, culture, and ethnicity still stand, and many will for many years to come if practitioners and researchers do not act to engage in social justice and diversity issues in the profession. We hope that this book, while celebrating the life and work of one pioneer, Clemmont Vontress, will also, in some small way, provide the impetus for another breakthrough in counseling psychology.

REFERENCES

Atkinson, D. R., Morten, G., & Sue, D. W. (Eds.) (1993). *Counseling American minorities: A cross-cultural perspective* (4th ed.). Dubuque, IA: Brown & Benchmark.

Carter, R. (1995). *The influence of race and racial identity in psychotherapy.* New York: Wiley.

Cross, W. E. (1971). Towards a psychology of liberation: The negro-to-black conversion experience. *Black World, 20*, 13–27.

Cross, W. E. (1978). The Thomas and Cross models of psychological nigrescence: A review. *Journal of Black Psychology, 5*, 13–31.

Cross, W. E. (1991). *Shades of black*. Philadelphia: Temple University Press.

Cross, W. E., Parham, T. A., & Helms, J. E. (1991). The stages of black identity development: Nigrescence models. In R. L. Jones (Ed.), *Black psychology* (3rd ed., pp. 319–338). Los Angeles: Cobb & Henry.

d'Ardenne, P., & Mahtani, A. (1989). *Transcultural counselling in action*. London: Sage.

Ellison, R. (1952). *The invisible man*. New York: Vintage.

Fanon, F. (1952). *Black skin, white masks* (C. L. Markmann, Trans.). New York: Grove Press, reprint 1967.

Good, B. J., & Good, M.-J. D. (1982). Towards a meaning-centred analysis of popular illness categories: 'Fright-illness' and 'heat distress' in Iran. In A. J. Marsella & G. M. White (Eds.), *Cultural conceptions of mental health and therapy* (pp. 141–166). Dordrecht: Reidel.

Hall, S. (1992). New ethnicities. In J. Donald & A. Rattansi (Eds.), *'Race,' culture and difference* (pp. 252–259). Buckingham: Open University Press.

Hall, W. A. (1995). Counselling Black Students. In R. Moodley (Ed.), *Education for transformation* (pp. 53–57). Leeds: Thomas Danby Publications.

Helms, J. E. (1984). Towards an explanation of the influence of race in the counseling process: A black-white model. *Counseling Psychologist, 12*, 153–165.

Helms, J. (1986). Expanding racial identity theory to cover counseling process. *Journal of Counseling Psychology, 33*, 62–64.

Helms, J. (1994). How multiculturalism obscures racial factors in the therapy process: Comment on Ridley et al. (1994), Sodowsky et al. (1994), Ottavi et al. (1994), and Thompson et al. (1994). *Journal of Counseling Psychology, 41*, 162–165.

Helms, J. (Ed.) (1990). *Black and white racial identity: Theory, research and practice.* Westport, CT: Greenwood Press.

Helms, J., & Richardson, T. Q. (1997). How 'multiculturalism' obscures race and culture as differential aspects of counseling competency. In D. B. Pope-Davis & H. L. K. Coleman (Eds.), *Multicultural counseling competencies* (pp. 60–79). Thousand Oaks, CA: Sage.

Ivey, A. E., d'Andrea, M., Ivey, M. B., & Simek-Morgan, L. (2002). *Theories of counseling and psychotherapy: A multicultural perspective* (5th ed.). Boston: Allyn & Bacon.

Kareem, J., & Littlewood, R. (Eds.) (1992). *Intercultural therapy: Themes, interpretations and practice*. Oxford: Blackwell.

Lago, C., & Thompson, J. (1989). Counselling and race. In S. Palmer & G. McMahon (Eds.), *Handbook of Counselling* (pp. 285–302). London: Oxford University Press / Routledge.

Lago, C., & Thompson, J. (1996). *Race, culture and counselling*. Buckingham: Open University Press.

Laungani, P. (1999). Client centred or culture centred counselling? In S. Palmer & P. Laungani (Eds.), *Counselling in a multicultural society* (pp. 133–152). London: Sage.

McLeod, J. (1993). *An Introduction to Counselling*. Buckingham, UK: Open University Press.

Moodley, R. (2000a). Counselling and psychotherapy in a multicultural context: Some training issues, part 1. *Counselling, Journal of the British Association for Counselling, 11*, 154–157.

Moodley, R. (2000b). Counselling and psychotherapy in a multicultural context: Some training issues, part 2. *Counselling, Journal of the British Association for Counselling, 11*, 221–224.

Moodley, R. (2000c). Representation of subjective distress in black and ethnic minority patients: Constructing a research agenda. *Counselling Psychology Quarterly, 13*, 159–174.

Moodley, R. (2007). (Re)placing multiculturalism in counselling and psychotherapy. *British Journal of Guidance and Counselling, 35*(1), 1–22.

Moodley, R., & Lubin, D. B. (2008). Developing your career to working with diversity. In S. Palmer & R. Bor (Eds.), *The practitioner's handbook*. London: Sage.

Pankhania, J. (1996). Black feminist counselling. In M. Jacobs (Ed.), *Jitendra – lost connections: In search of a therapist* (pp. 55–72). Buckingham: Open University Press.

Pedersen, P. (1991). Multiculturalism as a fourth force in counseling. *Journal of Counseling and Development, 70*, 4–250.

Pedersen, P. (Ed.) (1985). *Handbook of cross-cultural counseling and therapy*. New York: Praeger.

Ponterotto, J. G. (1988). Racial consciousness development among white counselors' trainees: A stage model. *Journal of Multicultural Counseling and Development, 16*, 146–156.

Pope-Davis, D. B., & Coleman, H. L. K. (Eds.) (1997). *Multicultural counseling competencies: Assessment, education and training, and supervision*. Thousands Oaks, CA: Sage.

Sabnani, H. B., Ponterotto, J. G., & Borodousky, L. G. (1991). White racial identity development and cross-cultural counselor training: A stage model. *The Counseling Psychologist, 19*, 76–102.

Sue, D. (1997). Multicultural training. *International Journal of Intercultural Relations, 21,* 175–193.

Sue, D., Arrendondo, P., & McDavis, R. J. (1992). Multicultural counseling competencies and standards: A call to the profession. *Journal of Counseling and Development, 70,* 477–486.

Sue, D. W., & Sue, D. (1990). *Counseling the culturally different: Theory and practice.* New York: John Wiley & Sons.

Vontress, C. E. (1962). Patterns of segregation and discrimination: Contributing factors to crime among Negroes. *Journal of Negro Education, 31,* 108–116.

Vontress, C. E. (1963). The Negro against himself. *Journal of Negro Education, 32,* 237–252.

Vontress, C. E. (1976). Racial and ethnic barriers in counseling. In P. Pederson, W. J. Lonner, & J. G. Draguns (Eds.). *Counseling across cultures.* Honolulu, HI: University Press of Hawaii.

Vontress, C. E. (1979). Cross-cultural counseling: An existential approach. *The Personnel and Guidance Journal, 58,* 117–122.

Vontress, C. E. (1982). Social class influences in counseling. *Counseling and Human Development, 14,* 1–12.

Vontress, C. E. (1985). Existentialism as a cross-cultural counseling modality. In P. Pedersen (Ed.), *Handbook of cross-cultural counseling and therapy* (pp. 207–212). New York: Praeger.

Vontress, C. E. (1986). Social and cultural foundations. In M. D. Lewis, R. Hayes, & J. A. Lewis (Eds.), *Introduction to the counseling profession.* Itasca, IL: Peacock.

Vontress, C. E. (1988). An existential approach to cross-cultural counseling. *Journal of Multicultural Counseling and Development, 16,* 73–78.

Vontress, C. E. (2003). On becoming an existential cross-cultural counselor. In F. D. Harper & J. McFadden (Eds.), *Culture and counseling.* Boston: Allyn & Bacon.

Vontress, C. E. (2008). Existential therapy. In J. Frew & M. D. Spiegler (Eds.), *Contemporary psychotherapies for a diverse world.* Boston: Houghton Mifflin / Lahaska Press.

Vontress, C. E., Johnson, J. A., & Epp, L. R. (1999). *Cross-cultural counseling: A Casebook.* Alexandria, VA: American Counseling Association.

Wrenn, C. G. (1962). The culturally encapsulated counselor. *Harvard Educational Review, 32,* 444–449.

PART ONE

Clemmont E. Vontress – The Culturally Wounded Healer in Cross-Cultural Counseling

1 Culture and Counseling: A Personal Retrospective

CLEMMONT E. VONTRESS

Although my great-grandfather was only a teenager when the Civil War in the United States started in 1861, his father went off to war and left him in charge of the family plantation in Warren County, Kentucky. For five years he supervised the planting and harvesting of the crops, raising farm animals, and the nearly one hundred slaves the Vontress family owned. While his father was gone, he cohabitated with a mulatto slave girl who worked in the 'big house.' Out of that relationship came three children, two girls and a boy. The boy was my grandfather. At the end of the war, his father never came home. He was among the more than 300,000 soldiers who lost their lives during the conflict.

During the *Reconstruction*, the term generally used to refer to the postwar era from 1865 to 1877, Night Riders (now referred to as the Ku Klux Klan) began to criss-cross the South, terrorizing blacks, in order to get them to return to their prewar social status. When they discovered that my great-grandfather had taken a former slave as his common-law wife, they killed him. Although many former slaves fled the plantation, my grandfather retained ownership of the land. The farm remained in the Vontress family until the Great Depression in 1929, the year I was born. The national economic collapse and the ensuing widespread destitution forced my father to sell the property in order to support his family. We were obliged to become sharecroppers on the land that had been in the Vontress family for almost a hundred years. Consisting of my parents and seven boys and two girls, our family was a living example of the large, destitute, and servile Black sharecropper families that Du Bois (1903) described at the beginning of the 20th century.

Our life as sharecroppers was miserable. We lived in a two-room shack with holes in the walls. It was difficult to protect ourselves from the wind, rain, and snow. The house was heated by a single pot-bellied wood stove that stood in the middle of the main room. Our food consisted of wild animals and foul, plants, chicken, pigs raised in the front yard, and vegetables that we cultivated in the fields. My mother canned enough food in the summer to get us through the winter. When everything ran out, my father went to the country store to buy food and supplies on credit to last us until the growing season. One essential that he brought back was cloth that my mother made into pants, shirts, overalls, and quilts for the family.

Water for cooking, washing, and bathing came from a cistern in the front yard, a pond, or a nearby creek. My mother prepared breakfast before daybreak, so that all members of the family except little children could be in the field by sun-up. After breakfast, she prepared lunch and took it to us in the field, so that we would not lose too much time eating. After we ate, she took the utensils back to the house and started preparing dinner for us to eat when we came home at sundown (see Vontress, 2005b). Back at the house, we had 'supper' (called 'dinner' today) and went to bed, in order to be ready for the next day. On Sunday morning, after each of us had taken a bath in a round tin tub, the entire family loaded into the horse-drawn wagon to go down the country road to the plantation church at the fork of the roads. We remained at the church for evening services, then we went home to prepare for another day in the fields.

When we did not have to work on the farm, some of us went to the one-room schoolhouse down the road and across the field. The building was heated by a pot-bellied stove in the center in which grades one through eight were taught alternately by the same teacher. Usually, the teacher was someone from outside the community. Therefore, he or she had to live with a family near the school. The teacher resided with a family for two or three weeks, before moving on to another home. Even so, students were not spared the rod when they needed to be whipped for behavior the teacher deemed unacceptable. Occasionally, walking to and from school was anxiety-producing. Often, we encountered adolescent white boys on the road. Sometimes, they would rape the elementary schoolgirls in our group. Fearing for our lives, we Black boys would run into the woods to hide until the rapists left. The girls and their parents were afraid to report such assaults to local authorities, because they feared that the victims would be accused of provoking the rapes.

Even though my father was the nominal head of the family, the landowner made the important decisions that affected our lives. For example, when my father agreed that I would go to high school, he had to convince the landowner that I had to go in town to look after my invalid aunt. I went to the county seat, where the only 'colored' high school was located. I roomed and boarded with families in that community for four years until I finished high school in 1948. When I went to college, I learned that the way of life we had experienced in the first half of 20th century in the United States should be referred to as *culture.*

After going off to college in 1948, I only went home to visit my folks on Sundays. My father told me that the landowner would make me remain and work in the fields with the family crew if he found out that I was home. Therefore, during the summer months, I worked on campus. When I graduated from college in 1952, I got a scholarship to work on my MA degree at the University of Iowa. However, my studies in French and English literature were interrupted after one year, when I was drafted into the US Army, which had just become racially integrated. Not accustomed to associating with whites, I felt uncomfortable being the only Black in my company. However, my uneasiness lifted when I was assigned to a unit in Germany, where I served until I was discharged. On periodic furloughs, I traveled throughout Europe. The exposure to various cultures and languages and the respite from racial oppression enabled me to see the world and its people in a different light. I experienced bursts of insight that I had never had before. In retrospect, I appreciate Frankl (1962), who demonstrated that out of indescribable personal suffering often come significant meaning in life and immeasurable understandings of human existence. Over fifty years ago, Parsons and Shils (1954) pointed out that a theory or conception of any human behavior is necessarily influenced by the culture or environment that socializes or otherwise contributes to the formation of the concept builder. Informed by this observation, in this chapter I will discuss some of my views about culture and counseling that I have expressed throughout my five-decade-long professional career. They are presented under the following headings: culture, cross-cultural counseling, existential therapy, and traditional healing.

Culture

Although I received my BA degree in French and English from Kentucky State University and completed one year toward the MA degree in French and Spanish at the University of Iowa, while abroad

I developed an interest in culture and cultural differences. In France I encountered African American expatriates and blacks from other parts of the world. In Germany I studied German and fraternized with Germans in their homes and at social events. I also got to know my white American comrades as human beings. Some were eager to know and to accept me as an equal; others were not. My closest friend was a white Southerner and recent fellow college graduate. We spent much time discussing racial issues. I learned that he knew much less about Black people than I did about whites. I knew why. It is always in the best interest of the oppressed to understand their oppressors. It seems tenable to conclude that individuals who suffer most think most about the human condition.

I returned to the United States in 1955 and enrolled in Indiana University in Bloomington, to work on the MA degree in counseling. A year later, I was accepted into the PhD program in counseling, with minors in psychology and sociology. It was in my sociology classes that I was offended by lectures in which professors declared that some Americans were 'culturally deprived' or 'culturally disadvantaged.' I found such views coming from respected scholars incredible. How could anyone be without a culture? Culture is a way of life. Everyone has a way of life; therefore, everybody has a culture.

I began to write a series of articles in which I made the case that African Americans have a different way of life, because they are segregated in their native country. The segregation and the different way of life engender a host of predictable consequences. In the sixties, crime and delinquency were inordinately high in the Black community, as they are today. I pointed out how segregation and discrimination contribute to deviant behavior (Vontress, 1962). I wrote articles in which I discussed dimensions of the Black personality, many of which reflected the racist attitudes of the general American society (Vontress, 1963a, 1966a). It was understandable that blacks might internalize these attitudes and hate themselves because they are Black. When I was director of a large all–Black urban high school in Indianapolis, I observed how demoralized parents, administrators, teachers, and students were. Each group blamed the other for the lack of achievement of the students. I wrote an article in which I analyzed the source of the demoralization (see Vontress, 1963b). Again, I pointed an accusatory finger at the larger community that neglected to provide support and encouragement for Black students in the same way it did for their white counterparts.

Near the end of the 1960s, American society began to show signs of racial change. One major change was the movement of blacks from inner cities to suburbs. I took note of this phenomenon and posited some implications of the negro suburban retreat (see Vontress, 1966b). One of the effects of the residential shift of the 'Black bourgeoisie,' as E. Franklin Frazier (1957) called them, was the leadership void it left in the Black ghettos. As blacks moved to white communities and attended white schools and churches, some of the distinguishing differences that set them apart from whites started to disappear. One of these was their speech pattern, as I pointed out (Vontress, 1967b). By the late 1960s and early 1970s, blacks were TV news anchors in many parts of the country. It was no longer possible to identify racial identity by the sound of a speaker's voice. I maintained that in the Black community, speech pattern could be used as an index of assimilation into the larger society.

As my interest in culture grew, I conceptualized a view of culture designed to help psychotherapists more effectively relate to, diagnose, and intervene on behalf of all clients. Two writers contributed significantly to my understanding of the context in which people develop and solve personal problems. The first was W.E.B. Du Bois, the great African American scholar. I read his classic, *The Souls of Black Folk* (Du Bois, 1903). Although I took several courses in sociology and social theory in graduate school, none of my professors ever mentioned his name, even though he was one of the country's greatest social philosophers. I understood why. American sociology was infused with a European way of thinking and being deeply rooted in Greco-Roman and Judeo-Christian heritage. During the 17th, 18th, 19th, and 20th centuries Western powers spread across the world, influencing how people in other lands thought about themselves and their culture (Calhoun, 2006). In the middle of the 20th century, few if any white American academicians considered very important the views of African American scholars.

In *The Souls of Black Folk*, Du Bois described the way of life that had developed in the American South forty years after President Abraham Lincoln (1809–65) signed in 1862 the Emancipation Proclamation that would free the slaves in 1863. Albeit nominally liberated from bondage, blacks remained socially and psychologically chained to their former masters. As slaves, they had to know the thoughts and ways of their masters in order to serve them without incurring their immediate wrath. Simultaneously, they remained aware of their history of oppression. Their nominal freedom did not change their need to be on guard against whites who generally considered them to be subhuman. The recently freed slaves had to strategize to survive in a hostile land. From that strategy evolved a Black culture that existed alongside and incorporated much of the culture of their oppressors. Du Bois (1903) referred to this phenomenon as double-consciousness.

The second person who contributed to my conceptualization of culture was Ludwig Binswanger (1881–1966), a Swiss psychiatrist who applied the principles of existential phenomenology to psychiatry. I learned about his work while attending a conference in Wiesbaden, Germany, in the summer of 1972. On my flight back to Washington, I read two of Binswanger's (1962, 1963) books. I was fascinated by three constructs that he had coined in German to describe the parameters of human existence. The first is the *Umwelt*, or natural environment, which consists of all elements that support life. People cannot survive without air, water, food, and many other essentials. The second is the *Mitwelt*, or the social environment, which is basic to individual and collective existence. Neonates enter a world already prepared by current and previous generations of human beings. The third is *Eigenwelt*, or the self-world of the individual. Although a part of the group, each person is a unique essence.

By the 1970s, I was ready to posit my view of culture (see Vontress, 1971a, 1971b, 1971c, 1972, 1974, 1979). Enlightened by Du Bois's (1903) notion that African Americans are torn internally by two competing cultures, one Black and one white, I argue that most human beings are molded by five concentric cultures: (1) universal, (2) ecological, (3) national, (4) regional, and (5) racio-ethnic (see Vontress, 1986b; Vontress, Johnson, & Epp, 1999). The human being is at the core of these cultures, which are neither entirely separate nor equal. The first and most external layer is the *universal culture*, or the way of life that is determined by the physiology of the human species. People are conceived in a given way, they consume nourishment to live, they grow into adulthood, they contribute to the group, and they grow old and die. These and other ways of life are invariable dimensions of human life. During the course of the social development of the species, people learn to play a variety of roles basic to survival. These are internalized and transmitted from one generation to another. It seems important that counselors recognize themselves and their clients as members of this culture that is common to all humanity. The recognition helps counselors to identify with and assist all clients, regardless of their cultural or socioeconomic heritage (Vontress, 2008a).

Human existence is also shaped by the ecosystem where people live. Climatic conditions, indigenous vegetation, animal life, seasonal changes, and other factors determine how people interact with nature and themselves. People who use dog sleds to go to the grocery store experience life differently than those who need only to gather foodstuff from the trees and plants in their backyard. Inhabitants of Arabian deserts wear loose body coverings with ample headgear that protect them from dangerously hot sun rays. The way of life that people develop in order to survive in a specific geographical area of the world may be called the *ecological culture*, the second layer of culture.

The third environment that molds human beings is the *national culture*. It is reasonable to conceptualize a national culture for several reasons. Most people are born in a particular nation. In general, each country has a national language, basic institutions, a form of government, a way of seeing the rest of the world, and values and attitudes about themselves and their fellows. Individuals born in the confines of a country are usually socialized to adjust to the rules and regulations of that country. They learn to fit into the prevailing way of life. People first start learning to fit into the national social order in the home and continue their socialization in school and other settings. Although there may be several national subcultural groups, they cannot escape the influence of the overarching national culture (Vontress, 2008a).

A fourth influence on the lives of people is *regional culture*. In many countries, people identify not just with the national culture, but also with a specific part of the country. For example, Americans who live along the Mexican border may feel as Mexican as they do American. They often speak Spanish and enjoy the food, music, and way of life common to Mexico. Regional cultures are evident in many African countries. In the north of Nigeria, where the country borders Niger, the Housas, one of the country's largest ethnic groups, straddle the border, thereby causing a regional culture to exist in each country.

The final cultural layer is *racio-ethnic* (Vontress, 1986). It is based on the recognition that racially or ethnically different groups often reside in countries separate from the dominant racial or ethnic group. People inhabiting racial or ethnic enclaves usually develop and maintain a culture unique to the community in which they live. Although a part of the national culture of the country in which they live, they may also identify strongly with their racial or ethnic culture. For example, because of their slave heritage, African Americans have developed and maintained a culture that is in many ways differ from the national culture.

However, it should be emphasized that there is not a single way of life that can be defined as 'African American.' Since the 1960s, blacks have increased their participation in and identification with the national culture. Today, there are four categories of blacks, based on their perception of being a part of the total society. First, *mono-culturally white blacks* see themselves as Americans, period. They are apt to be offended when others place them in categories based on race or ethnic identity. A second group may be referred to as *equicultural,* in the sense that they are equally comfortable around whites and blacks. Third, there are *biculturals,* who appear to prefer one racial group to the other but who can function between both. Finally, some blacks only feel comfortable in their own racial enclave. These may be called the *monoculturally blacks.*

The fivefold concentric conception of culture indicates that people are the product of several influences over which they have little control. They should not be considered members of a single national, racial, or ethnic culture. Individuals are more alike than they are different. Counselors who recognize the commonalities that humans share are apt to be more effective in helping all clients than those who focus on perceived cultural differences. Universal and ecological cultures unify the human group more than regional, national, or racio-ethnic differences separate the species.

Instead of participating in a Eurocentric-Afrocentric cultural debate, I argue that culture is influenced by multiple factors. I maintain that humans are culturally different and similar at the same time, as Wiredu (1996) points out. Cultures evolve to meet specific needs of people at a time and place in history. In a global society, individuals become cultural vagabonds, constantly moving from one country or continent to another. Although socialized in one culture, they are able to adjust to other cultures as needed. Therefore, it is not useful to engage in protracted discussions about whether a culture peculiar to a continent is superior to that of another. My model of culture aims to transcend such polemics. Globalization suggests an increased appreciation of the universal culture. The recognition of the oneness of humankind is basic to the future of cross-cultural counseling.

Cross-Cultural Counseling

As Harper and McFadden (2003) indicate, there are many descriptors currently used to capture succinctly the nature of the relationship of culture to counseling. Since the 1960s, *multicultural counseling, cross-cultural counseling, intercultural counseling*, and other labels have been used interchangeably to describe psychotherapeutic dyads in which one or both of the participants is presumed to be culturally different. I have pointed out that real differences should be differentiated from perceived differences (Vontress, 1976, 1988b). Differences are problematic when they are perceived to be an impediment to counseling. Counselors should not assume that each relationship in which the client is gay, of the other gender, lower-class, physically challenged, or of another race is cross-cultural. Cultural differences are often in the eye of the beholder. Illustratively, an adolescent Black American client, who was the adopted son of a white New England family, entered the white counselor's office. She immediately wanted to know if he was one of the students bused in from the inner city. In order to avoid making such gaffes, my colleagues and I suggest that counselors ask each client to write a brief cultural autobiography before they start a counseling session (Vontress, Johnson, & Epp, 1999).

The conception of culture posited in this chapter suggests that it is not productive to think of culture in racial terms. As I have already discussed (Vontress, 1967a, 1967b, 1982), it is influenced by human physiology, geography, nationality, regionalism, and racio-ethnic identity. Therefore, it is tenable to conclude that physical, social, spiritual, and psychological problems that humans encounter during their existence should be understood and treated in a multi-layered cultural context. This is why cross-cultural counseling is important in a global society. It is a psychotherapeutic interaction in which at least one of the participants is perceived to be culturally different from the other (Vontress, 2003). Perceived differences are as crucial to the outcome of the association as are real differences (Vontress, 1971c, 1979, 1988b). It is for this reason, among others, that counseling across cultures is so challenging to most counselors.

Early in my career, I pointed out cultural barriers to counseling African Americans, mainly because I had developed in graduate school a passion for understanding culture. The great interest was triggered by my sociology professors who talked about people being deprived of culture (see Vontress, 1971a, 1971c, 1974). I make the argument that everybody has a culture, even though it may differ in some ways from one group to another. Culture is basic to human existence. It affects everything that people do, including counseling. I have tried to show how cultural differences influence the counseling relationship, diagnosis, treatment plans, and intervention.

Around the middle of the 20th century, Carl Rogers (1958, 1962) argued that the interpersonal relationship is the core of counseling. *Empathy*, which he defined as one individual feeling as if he or she were the other, is basic to the therapeutic encounter. I questioned whether counselors socialized in a racist society such as the United States could achieve a common feeling with African Americans whom they considered to be their inferiors (see Vontress, 1971b). That question was in my mind when Rogers came to Indiana University to keynote a state counseling conference in the 1960s. I was one of the four graduate students selected by professors to share the dais to ask questions. After Dr Rogers's address, in which he outlined the ingredients of a therapeutic relationship, I asked him how empathy, positive regard, and congruence would enhance rapport with angry inner-city clients. He responded that such clients needed to perceive the qualities in the counselor, in order for them to have the desired effect. Although in awe of Dr Rogers, I was not entirely satisfied with his response, because I had not been effective using his approach with disgruntled ghetto adolescents (Vontress, 2004). That was the day I started a life-long search for a supplement to the Rogerian theory of counseling.

During the same historical period, *self-disclosure* was considered important for establishing an effective psychotherapeutic relationship. Recognizing the seminal work of Jourard (1959, 1964) on self-disclosure, I argued that Black Americans, because they are socialized in a culture in which they learn to distrust whites in general, are often reluctant to self-disclose to white American counselors. *Resistance*, another psychotherapeutic concept often discussed in the psychological literature, is related to self-disclosure. It suggests that clients refuse to accept or submit to the goals of counseling. Its opposite is *psychotherapeutic surrender*, a concept which I offered to explain why many minorities are resistant to counseling. This, too, is related to the fear and distrust that the oppressed often feel toward their perceived oppressors (see Vontress, 1971a, 1975, 1976).

Two other constructs are also related to culture. They are *transference* and *counter-transference*. When transference first entered the psychological literature, it usually referred to clients' responding to counselors as if they were someone else in their history. I posited that in the case of blacks in the United States, persons in their experience are apt to be all white Americans. Therefore, I conceptualized *cultural transference* to suggest another reason why Black clients may respond negatively to white counselors. Similarly, I conceptualized *cultural counter-transference*. Counseling is a professional enterprise that cannot be divorced from the general culture, which is visible and invisible, conscious and unconscious, and cognitive and affective. If the culture is shot through with racism, then counselors are infected with it. Therefore, in dyads and groups in which the counselor is white and the clients are blacks, negative counter-transference may be explained by the impact of the general culture on the counselor (see Vontress, Johnson, & Epp, 1999).

About ten years ago, a colleague and I (Vontress & Epp, 1997) conceptualized *historical hostility*, designed to help counselors understand why it is often difficult to establish productive cross-racial counseling dyads in the United States. In the case of Black Americans, it is the tendency to feel angry toward and to seek to inflict harm on a person or group perceived to be the source of their multi-generational frustration. Usually unconscious, it is often not perceived or understood in counseling and may influence negatively one or more of the psychotherapeutic elements discussed above.

Diagnosis is the process of defining the client's presenting problem, its manifestations, and etiology. In cross-cultural counseling, it is one of the most difficult aspects of helping, because often counselors are expected to make judgments about the states and traits of clients from cultural backgrounds unfamiliar to them. They also are supposed to establish a cause-and-effect relationship of behavior that occurs in a culturally different context. They have no yardstick or standard for measuring the extent to which clients deviate from established social and psychological norms.

When the American Counseling Association was formally organized in 1952, counselors relied heavily on measures obtained from objective standardized tests to diagnose clients. Usually these instruments were written in the idiom and expectations of middle-class white Americans. The psychometric research showed that most of the tests that counselors used for diagnosing their clients were culturally biased. That is why I recommended that cross-cultural counselors use a clinical approach in diagnosing their clients (see Vontress, 1988b). It consists of the diagnostician's using a mix of procedures including psychometric devices, observations, and clinical interviews. Later, my colleagues and I suggested that counselors add a cultural autobiography (see Vontress, Johnson, & Epp, 1999). Counselors benefit from knowing where their clients were born, the language spoken at home, how long they have lived in the United States, their parents' level of education, and other such information that helps to ascertain their level of acculturation to the American society.

During the last five decades, counselors have been studying and using the same theories, procedures, and diagnostic tools that other psychotherapeutic professionals use. The main diagnostic tool that they rely on is the *Diagnostic and statistical manual of mental disorders* (DSM), published by the American Psychiatric Association (APA, 1994). In recent editions of the manual, the APA advises users to consider cultural differences in making diagnoses. In spite of this advice, few counselors seem to know how to culturally modify their psychological judgments (Vontress, Johnson, & Epp, 1999). Since insurance companies and health management organizations require a DSM code for reimbursement, most therapists use the same criteria and codes for all clients, regardless of their cultural background.

Vontress, Woodland, and Epp (2007) urge therapists to recognize that psychological problems may result from people moving to a new culture or may be a product of stressors experienced in their native culture. It is untenable to assume that a single set of criteria can be used to measure the well-being of all clients, regardless of their cultural background. Minimally, counselors need to take an extensive cultural history of clients, in order to discover how significant others in their identifying immediate culture view various feelings and behaviors considered abnormal. Clients from countries in which people believe that most problems in life result from a hex or spell placed on them by a malevolent source may challenge a Western counselor's diagnostic skills.

Although a crucial aspect of cross-cultural counseling, intervention is the psychotherapeutic function that needs a great deal of attention. It is action taken by the counselor or therapist to influence or modify the client's situation. To make a difference in an individual's life, counselors should know not only what corrective measures to introduce, but also their likely results if applied. The effective cross-cultural counselor understands the cultures already discussed in this chapter. First, counselors should recognize the impact of the universal culture on human beings. People are more alike than they are different. Second, helpers need to be aware of the unique character of any racio-ethnic culture that impacts directly the client's existence. Throughout my career, I have discussed numerous barriers to cross-cultural intervention (see Vontress, 1986b, 1988). Language differences and family support are two of them (Vontress, Johnson, & Epp, 1999).

Over thirty-two years ago, I posited language as a barrier in cross-cultural counseling (see Vontress, 1976). It may be especially problematic in intervention. Language differences are most often associated with social class (see Vontress, 1986b). Class differences affect not only the clarity of communication, but also the inclination of the client to follow through. For therapeutic intervention to be effective, clients must be able and willing to apply the measures agreed upon in counseling. Unfortunately, many lower-class individuals may not be socialized to be assertive and self-reliant. Living in a culture where other people make decisions and take actions that affect their lives, they become accustomed to being other-directed. Further, in many racio-ethnic groups, the most dominant member of the family makes decisions for everybody else in the unit. This is why I recommended that cross-cultural counselors involve the client's significant others when they develop treatment plans (Vontress, 1971b). Positive changes in a client's life are most apt to occur when they are supported by significant family members.

Cross-cultural counseling is a by-product of the Civil Rights Movement of the 1960s (Vontress, 2002). African Americans protested the legally sanctioned second-class citizenship they endured in their own country. Spurred on by the momentum of the movement, a Black caucus at the annual convention of the American Counseling Association in 1969 demanded that the organization recognize and organize to meet the special needs of Black clients. Out of the demands emerged the Association for Multicultural Counseling and Development. Soon afterwards, other groups such as gays, women, seniors, and the physically challenged also petitioned the association to recognize and respond to them as being culturally different and therefore in need of special counseling considerations (Vontress, 2008b). In universities, cross-cultural courses that used to be taught by minority professors are now taught by any interested faculty member. The content of the courses varies from one university to another, depending on the interest, knowledge, and skills of the professor.

Cross-cultural counseling is at a crossroads. Culture, having been appropriated by people external to traditional social sciences, has been redefined. For example, some homosexuals, although socialized in the same family and community as their siblings, are presumed by some people to be culturally different simply because of their sexual preference. African American adoptees of white parents, although socialized in an all-white community, may be considered culturally different from their parents. Individuals who suffer a physically debilitating are often perceived to be to culturally different.

Since the founding of the American Counseling Association in 1952, counseling has also taken on different meanings for professionals who offer services defined as counseling. In some cases, service providers perceive themselves as guidance workers, similar to their colleagues of over 50 years ago. Others see themselves as psychologists. Understandably, cross-cultural counseling, a composite of two rather ambiguous concepts, is an enterprise that eludes precise definition. This is why it is at a crossroads in need of an identity and direction. Unless a mission and clientele are defined, its future is uncertain. If the implied mission is to prepare all counselors to be cross-cultural therapists, because every client is culturally different, then perhaps we are on the right course. However, such a mission and general clientele presuppose a counselor training curriculum that provides more training in the social and psychological sciences. If everybody is culturally different, then nobody is culturally different. Counselors must be experts in recognizing, measuring, and encouraging differences among all clients.

Existential Counseling

Focused on a universal culture, my existential approach to counseling recognizes the commonality of human beings. People are more alike than they are different. At base, they share a common environment and destiny. After being exposed to some of the ideas of Jean-Paul Sartre and Simone de Beauvoir in the 1950s, I read the works of many American and European existentialists. However, few of them discussed culture, even tangentially, as it impacts human existence. Ludwig Binswanger (1962, 1963) was an exception. I have been inspired by his description of the three existential environments, the *Umwelt*, *Mitwelt*, and *Eigenwelt* (Vontress, Johnson, & Epp, 1999; Vontress, 2008a). I also incorporated ideas about human existence embodied in writings from many other parts of the world. My existential approach to cross-cultural counseling is more philosophical than it is psychological. It grew out of the recognition that humans are physical, social, psychological, and spiritual creatures. Even though people are influenced by all of these forces, some societies emphasize one over the others. For example, Africans generally believe that the spirits of their departed ancestors impact significantly their existence. On the other hand, Americans and Westerners in general believe that individuals are influenced significantly by psychological forces. Variations in world views affect perceptions of well-being, the causes of problems in living, who should treat them, and the most effective methodology for restoring people to productive and harmonious existence.

My colleagues and I (Vontress, Johnson, & Epp, 1999) maintain that humans are products of their genetic endowments and life experiences, which are filtered though five cultural layers – the universal, ecological, national, regional, and racio-ethnic. Throughout their lives, individuals are distillates of the cultural filters. Simultaneously, they are embodiments of four existential worlds – the *Eigenwelt*, *Mitwelt*, *Umwelt*, and *Uberwelt*. The *Eigenwelt* is the very private self that cannot be experienced or completely understood by another person. The *Mitwelt* is the individual's world with others or the social environment. The *Umwelt* is the natural environment which sustains and supports all life. Finally, the *Uberwelt* or the spirit world connects people with all other humans who have come and gone via memory, genetic contributions, and cultural indoctrination (Vontress, 1996).

Culture should not be considered separate from the rest of human existence. Neither should it be viewed apart from counseling. Problems that people encounter during their life take place within a cultural context. Each society recognizes and endorses its helpers. Theories and procedures used to modify or alleviate problems are also products of culture. Understandably, cross-cultural counseling is challenging. However, the challenge is lessened when counselors see clients as human beings not unlike themselves. I recommend that this perception of our fellows infuse the existential counseling relationship, diagnosis, and methodology.

As compared to other theoretical approaches, the existential therapeutic encounter is relatively devoid of psychological ritual, posturing, and pretension. It is a deep fellowship based on authentic sharing. The counselor and client relate to each other as one human being to another. From my perspective, therapists should not be concerned about constructs, such as transference, counter-transference, empathy, sympathy, and resistance. Rather, the existential counseling relationship is undergirded by basic philosophical concepts that suggest the oneness of humanity. These include death, authenticity, and responsibility, which contribute to the feeling of sameness between counselors and their clients.

I recommend that counselors use well-known existential constructs as diagnostic measures of well-being. Self-knowledge, authenticity, courage, meaning in life, harmony, and responsibility are among the yardsticks that can be used to assess mental health. People who do not know themselves are apt to be the same ones who do not know what to do with their existence. They often are *stuck* in place, not knowing which road to take in life. That is why such individuals may fall prey to others who pretend to know the way. Individuals devoid of self-knowledge are inauthentic, because they are unable to live in accordance with personal dictates they do not know. Authenticity is related to courage. People who hide behind a false face usually lack the courage to accept the challenge of human existence. I have also pointed out that meaning in life is basic to mental health. A person without meaning in life is probably someone who can be characterized as despondent, sad, and often neurotic. Harmony is also a diagnostic yardstick. People are most happy to be alive when they feel as one with the forces of nature, others, the self, and other known and unknown forces that impact existence. Realizing that they cannot stop the world to get off, they go with the flow of life. Finally, I maintain that responsibility is basic to the cohesiveness of the human group. We need to feel responsible for ourselves and others close to us. Responsibility contributes to a sense of purpose, strength, security, and self-protection. Individuals derive happiness, fulfillment, and a sense of purpose in life to the extent that they manifest responsibility in the interdependent roles they play (Vontress, 1988a; Vontress, Johnson, & Epp, 1999).

Existential counseling as I conceive it is not a science. Therefore, there is no precise way of doing it that can be codified and memorized. Rather, it is a natural human-to-human encounter in which one person helps another person to cope with existence.

Since each individual is endowed with a unique essence, therapeutic methodologies should meet the needs of each client. I see existential counselors as philosophical companions, not people who repair psyches. This is why I have not pretended to offer a 'technique' for counseling. Instead, my colleagues and I recommend that counselors initiate a *Socratic dialogue* with their clients (see Vontress, 2008a; Vontress & Epp, 2001). It is a conversation in which the therapist helps clients to identify personal problems and to find solutions to them. The counselor is an intellectual midwife who facilitates clients' understanding of what is best for them, in view of their circumstances. Clients give birth to the knowledge that they already possess. Counselors who try to impose their own solutions on clients may do harm to them, because at base each life is externally inscrutable. The best counselors are ones who are patient and wise enough to let clients give birth to themselves. They resist the temptation to 'fix' others.

Existential counseling has a promising future. Existentialism, its supporting philosophy, is becoming increasingly acceptable to the lay public. Motivational speakers, religious leaders, TV talk show personalities, and others often sprinkle their presentations with ideas that could be labeled existential. In attempting to help clients cope with the malaise and the frequent sense of hopelessness of modern society, many counselors use aspects of existential counseling to supplement their usual therapeutic styles. Existential counseling is especially suited to helping diverse clients, because it transcends cultural boundaries to focus on the overarching human condition (Vontress, 2008a).

Traditional Healing

My curiosity about traditional healing in Africa parallels my interest in culture, cross-cultural counseling, and existential therapy. I learned a great deal about the work of healers from my African graduate students at George Washington University. One of them encouraged me to visit his country, Côte d'Ivoire, where, according to him, some of the most powerful healers in the world live and work. Intrigued by his reports, I launched into extensive background research on the topic. I interviewed many African students in the United States and France, in order to learn about their experiences in consulting healers. I read books and articles on African philosophy, medical practices, and the various categories of healers. After I felt reasonably informed on the subject, I planned trips to Africa, to interview patients and some of their healers. I decided to visit Côte d'Ivoire, Senegal, and Burkina Faso, because they were countries in which my former students and their families lived. They were valuable contacts, guides, and interpreters. Generally, I travelled to remote villages far from urban areas. Although educated Westernized Africans often report that they believe in and often use traditional healers, they do not resort to them to the extent that villagers do. It is also in the villages where the most powerful healers live and practice.

My field trips began in the 1980s and ended in 2000. I made six trips to sub-Saharan Africa and several to France. When I first stepped onto African soil at the airport in Abidjan in Côte d'Ivoire, West Africa, I was surrounded by a sea of Black people. My eyes filled with tears not because of the throng that engulfed me in the hot sun. Rather, I experienced an immense and indescribable spiritual fulfillment that I had never felt before. Even today, I tear up each time I recall my first emotional reaction to Africa. That initial contact with Africans and their transcendental spirit enhanced my ability to understand, relate to, and appreciate the people and their way of life.

I found that beliefs and attitudes about healing are related to culture. What people believe about the etiology of physical, psychological, social, and spiritual illness, healers, and methods of healing all emerge from cultural context. Understanding the culture of Africa is challenging for several reasons. First, it is one of the world's largest continents, second only to Asia. Second, it contains more countries than any other continent. Third, it is the home of the earth's largest desert, the Sahara. Fourth, the longest river, the Nile, is located there. Fifth, its people speak over 1000 ethnic languages. All these factors contribute to the diverse culture of the continent. Each layer of culture discussed in this chapter is clearly evident in Africa. Therefore, healing in Africa should be considered with its cultural multifariousness in mind. In my writings about healing, I have made several general observations about the practice (see Vontress, 1991, 1999, 2003, 2005a; Vontress & Naiker, 1995). They appear to transcend ecological, national, regional, and racio-ethnic cultural boundaries in sub-Saharan Africa.

Animism is the Weltanschauung, or world view, underpinning traditional healing in Africa. It is the idea that the entire universe is unified and animated by a single spirit, soul, or energy (see Vontress, 2005a). The universal spirit inhabits animate and inanimate objects alike. Trees, rivers, rocks, the wind, animals, and humans all embody the same spirit. The spirit is eternal, powerful, and curative. Although it resides in each person, at death, it departs the body and returns to its original source. In many African families, it is believed that the spirits of ancestors remain close by to hover over, protect, and direct the lives of their relatives. People who experience illness, failed crops, and death often blame such misfortunes on the spirit of an ancestor displeased with the behavior of one or more of their relatives in the material world.

African healers are people who have the ability to tap into, channel, focus, or otherwise manipulate the universal soul, spirit, or energy to help individuals and groups solve physical, psychological, social, and spiritual problems. This approach to healing is not new. It resembles many ancient medical beliefs and practices reported throughout human history (Myss, 1996). In the United States, some lay and religious leaders are often characterized as being charismatic or inspired by God.

From time to time, there are reports of miraculous cures achieved by ministers who 'lay hands on' believers. Although nonbelievers may express doubt, such beliefs and practices widespread in many parts of the world suggest that there is a powerful curative force or energy that can flow from an unknown source through one human being to another. In any case, this is the basis of most traditional healing in Africa.

According to Elungu (1984) and Bon (1998), the universe is perfect and harmonious. Its creatures are reflections of the perfect order. However, from time to time, humans encounter or experience disharmony in their existence. Endowed with the ability to manipulate, channel, or focus the universal spirit, traditional healers can restore harmony and well-being to their clients. Throughout sub-Saharan Africa, they are known by different names, depending on their ecological, national, regional, and racio-ethnic culture. In my research, I define six groups of healers. The definitions are based on their interest, focus, methodology, or specialty (see Vontress, 1991, 1999, 2005a). First, *herbalists* rely on barks, roots, and leaves to cure their patients. They boil or grind herbs and give them to their patients to drink as a tea or to apply to their body as a polish. Second, the *fetish person* sells objects to wear around the neck or to be placed in one's environment. The objects are embodiments of universal spirit, power, or energy that may effect a cure, bring the wearer good fortune, or ward off danger. Third, *mediums* are individuals who can summon the spirits of departed ancestors, so that they may remedy problems of the living members of their families. The visiting spirit inhabits the medium's body, in order to speak to the living. Fourth, there are *spiritual healers* who rely on scriptures to help clients. Muslim clerics may write passages from the Koran on pieces of paper and boil them and require the patient to drink tea from the brew. Christian ministers may place their hands on patients to cure their symptoms. Fifth, many Africans believe that *sorcerers* can manipulate 'the power' to hurt or punish people. That is to suggest that individuals who can channel a power to heal can also use it to hurt others. Finally, I define a general category of *healers*. They are often found in remote villages. Their neighbors recognize them as people to consult when someone in their family is sick or 'out of their head.' Usually, the healer does not know how or why he or she is able to heal. The universal power just seems to work though his or her body. Some of the healers told the researcher that there has always been someone in their family who 'had the power.'

During the last few years, traditional healing has gained respectability in the United States and the West in general. Many universities in

North America and Europe offer courses in various departments on healing modalities in developing countries. Books, articles, and newspaper stories on the topic are being published in many parts of the world. In Africa, several governments have established in their medical schools departments of traditional healing (Vontress, 1991, 1999, 2005a). In France, Nathan (1993, 1994) encourages Western therapists to incorporate the insights and procedures of traditional healing into their psychotherapeutic practice, especially in treating immigrants from developing countries. Interest in traditional healing is expected to grow in the years ahead.

Conclusion

Culture is the foundation of counseling. All human problems and their solutions occur within a cultural context and are time-related. What is problematic for us today was not necessarily a concern to our forebears in the last century. Culture is also multifaceted, as I have pointed out in this chapter. This fact means that all clients are alike in some ways and different in others. Counselors need to be serious students of culture, in order to be effective helping clients from divergent cultures. Cultural knowledge and sensitivity to cultural differences are necessary for diagnosing and solving presenting problems. Counselors need to be able to distinguish between universal and culturally specific behaviors. It is advisable that they meet and greet all clients as fellow human beings, instead of immediately focusing on perceived social differences. Existential challenges often transcend traditional cultural lines of demarcation. Concerns pertaining to death, self-knowledge, authenticity, courage, becoming, existential anxiety, meaning in life, spirituality, and responsibility supersede ecological, national, regional, or racio-ethnic cultures. Counselors socialized in societies in which science is valued over spirituality need to appreciate that such a valuation may be inverse in other parts of the world. Values determine perceptions of reality, which in turn determine what a problem is, who to consult for help in solving it, and what is a socially acceptable way to restore a client to an expected condition. Although the universal and ecological cultures are rather constant, national, regional, and racio-ethnic cultures are dynamic as the world becomes progressively globalized. That is why I developed an existential counseling model designed to meet the needs of clients on the move in a geographically shrinking world. Counselors should appreciate the work of traditional healers in Africa and appropriate any of their techniques that may be useful to them in their work with culturally different clients.

REFERENCES

American Psychiatric Association. (1994). *Diagnostic and statistical manual of mental disorders* (4th ed.). Washington, DC: Author.

Binswanger, L. (1962). *Existential analysis and psychotherapy*. New York: Dutton.

Binswanger, L. (1963). *Being-in-the-world: Selected papers*. New York: Basic Books.

Bon, D. (1998). *L'animisme: L'âme du monde et le culte des esprits* [Animism: The universal soul and the spirit cults]. Paris: Éditions de Vecchi S. A.

Calhoun, C. (Ed.). (2006). *Sociology in America: A history*. Chicago: University of Chicago Press.

Du Bois, W. E. B. (1903). *The souls of black folk: Essays and sketches*. Chicago, IL: McClurg & Co.

Elungu, P. E. A. (1984). *L'éveil philosophie africain* [The emerging African philosophy]. Paris: Édition L'Hamattan.

Frankl, V. E. (1962). *Man's search for meaning: An introduction to logotherapy*. New York: Simon & Schuster.

Frazier, E. F. (1957). *Black bourgeoisie* (trans. of *Bourgeoisie noire*). Glencoe, IL:Free Press.

Harper, F. D., & McFadden, J. (2003). *Culture and counseling: New approaches*. Boston: Pearson Education, Inc.

Jourard, S. M. (1959). Healthy personality and self-disclosure. *Mental Hygiene, 43*, 499–509.

Jourard, S. M. (1964). *The transparent self*. Princeton, NJ: Van Nostrand.

Myss, C. (1996). *Anatomy of the spirit*. New York: Three Rivers Press.

Nathan, T. (1993). Ethnopsy 93 [Ethnopsychiatry 93]. *Nouvelle Revue d'Ethnopsychiatrie, 20*, 7–14.

Nathan, T. (1994). L'influence qui guérit [Healing influence]. Paris: Éditions Odile Jacob.

Parsons, T., & Shils, E. A. (Eds.) (1954). *Toward a general theory of action*. Cambridge, MA: Harvard University Press.

Rogers, C. R. (1958). The characteristics of a helping relationship. *The Personnel and Guidance Journal, 37*, 6–16.

Rogers, C. R. (1962). The interpersonal relationship: The core of guidance. *Harvard Educational Review, 32*, 416–429.

Vontress, C. E. (1962). Patterns of segregation and discrimination: Contributing factors to crime among negroes. *Journal of Negro Education, 31,* 108–116.
Vontress, C. E. (1963a). The negro against himself. *Journal of Negro Education, 32,* 237–252.
Vontress, C. E. (1963b). Our demoralizing slum schools. *Phi Delta Kappan,* 77–81.
Vontress, C. E. (1966a). The negro personality reconsidered. *Journal of Negro Education, 35,* 210–217.
Vontress, C. E. (1966b). The negro suburban retreat and its implications. *The Chicago Jewish Forum, 25,* 18–22.
Vontress, C. E. (1967a). Counseling negro students for college. *Journal of Negro Education, 16,* 22–28.
Vontress, C. E. (1967b). The negro speech pattern: Index of assimilation. *The Chicago Jewish Forum, 25,* 267–270.
Vontress, C. E. (1971a). The black male personality. *The Black Scholar, 2,* 10–16.
Vontress, C. E. (1971b). *Counseling negroes.* Boston: Houghton Mifflin.
Vontress, C. E. (1971c). Impediments to rapport. *Journal of Counseling Psychology,18,* 7–13.
Vontress, C. E. (1972). The black militant as a counselor. *The Personnel and Guidance Journal, 50,* 574–580.
Vontress, C. E. (1974). Barriers in cross-cultural counseling. *Counseling and Values, 18,* 160–165.
Vontress, C. E. (1975). Counseling: Racial and ethnic factors. In H. J. Peters & R. F. Aubrey (Eds.), *Guidance: Strategies and techniques* (pp. 456–472). Denver, CO: Love.
Vontress, C. E. (1976). Racial and ethnic barriers in counseling. In P. Pederson, W. J. Lonner, & J. G. Draguns (Eds.), *Counseling across cultures* (pp. 42–64). Honolulu: University Press of Hawaii.
Vontress, C. E. (1979). Cross-cultural counseling: An existential approach. *The Personnel and Guidance Journal, 58,* 117–122.
Vontress, C. E. (1982). Social class influences in counseling. *Counseling and Human Development, 14,* 1–12.
Vontress, C. E. (1986). Social and cultural foundations. In M. D. Lewis, R. Hayes, & J. A. Lewis (Eds.), *Introduction to the counseling profession* (pp. 215–250). Itasca, IL: Peacock.
Vontress, C. E. (1988a). An existential approach to cross-cultural counseling. *Journal* of *Multicultural Counseling and Development, 16*(2), 73–78.
Vontress, C. E. (1988b). Social class influences on counseling. In R. Hayes & R. Aubrey (Eds.), *New directions for counseling and human development* (pp. 346–364). Denver, CO: Love.

Vontress, C. E. (1991). Traditional healing in Africa: Implications for cross-cultural counseling. *Journal of Counseling and Development, 70* (1), 242–249.

Vontress, C. E. (1996). A personal retrospective on cross-cultural counseling. *Journal of Multiculural Counseling and Development, 24*(3), 156–166.

Vontress, C. E. (1999). Interview with a traditional African healer. *Journal of Mental Health Counseling, 21*(4), 326–333.

Vontress, C. E. (2002). Foreword. In P. B. Pedersen, J. G. Draguns, W. J. Lonner, & J. E. Trimble (Eds.), *Counseling across cultures* (5th ed.). Thousand Oaks, CA.: Sage.

Vontress, C. E. (2003). On becoming an existential cross-cultural counselor. In F. D. Harper & J. McFadden (Eds.), *Culture and counseling* (pp. 20–30). Boston: Allyn & Bacon.

Vontress, C. E. (2004). Foreword. In R. Moodley, C. Lago, & A. Talahite (Eds.), *Carl Rogers counsels a Black client* (pp. i–v). Ross-on-Wye, UK: PCCS Books.

Vontress, C. E. (2005a). Animism: Foundation of traditional healing in sub-Saharan Africa. In R. Moodley & W. West (Eds.), *Integrating traditional healing practices in counseling and psychotherapy* (124–137). Thousand Oaks, CA: Sage.

Vontress, C. E. (2005b). Uncharted waters: Autobiographical notes. In R. K. Coyne & F. Bemak (Eds.), *Journeys to professional excellence* (pp. 7–18). Alexandria, VA: American Counseling Association.

Vontress, C. E. (2008a). Existential therapy. In J. Frew & M. D. Spiegler (Eds.), *Contemporary psychotherapies for a diverse world* (pp. 141–176). Boston: Houghton Mifflin / Lahaska Press.

Vontress, C. E. (2008b). Foreword. In P. B. Pedersen, J. G. Draguns, W. J. Lonner, &J. E. Trimble (Eds.), *Counseling across cultures* (6th ed.). Los Angeles: Sage.

Vontress, C. E., & Epp, L. R. (1997). Historical hostility in the African American Client: Implications for counseling. *Journal of Multicultural Counseling and Development, 25*(3), 170–184.

Vontress, C. E., & Epp, L. R. (2001). Existential cross-cultural counseling: When hearts and cultures share. In K. J. Schneider, J. F. T. Bugental, & J. F. Pierson (Eds.), *The handbook of humanistic psychology: Leading edges in theory, research, and practice* (pp. 371–388). Thousand Oaks, CA: Sage.

Vontress, C. E., Johnson, J. A., & Epp, L. R. (1999). *Cross-cultural counseling: A Casebook.* Alexandria, VA: American Counseling Association.

Vontress, C. E., & Naiker, K. S. (1995). Counseling in South Africa: Yesterday, today, and tomorrow. *Journal of Multicultural Counseling and Development, 23*, 149–159.

Vontress, C. E., Woodland, C. E., & Epp, L. (2007). Cultural dysthymia: An Unrecognized disorder among African Americans? *Journal of Multicultural Counseling and Development, 35,* 130–141.

Wiredu, K. (1996). *Cultural universals and particulars: An African perspective.* Bloomington and Indianapolis: Indiana University Press.

2 'In the Therapist's Chair' Is Clemmont E. Vontress: A Wounded Healer in Cross-Cultural Counseling

ROY MOODLEY

Clemmont E. Vontress has been an intellectual force in the field of cross-cultural counseling. His research has had a significant impact on multi-cultural counseling theory, research, and practice, influencing numerous counseling academics, researchers, and students, as well as the many counselors and psychotherapists working in clinical practice (see, for example, Vontress, 1962, 1971, 1979, 1982, 1991, 1999, 2005, in press). For nearly fifty years, he has written on five main themes: self-hatred, cultural difference, existential counseling, historical hostility, and traditional healing (Vontress, 1996, p. 157). His ideas are growing in significance in counseling psychology as scholars, researchers, and practitioners search for new paradigms to represent the complexity with which clinical practice would need to engage in a dynamic multicultural society. Clemmont Vontress's work has been instrumental in providing the starting point for many discussions around cultural diversity, diaspora, immigration, class, sexual orientations, and disability.

Clemmont Vontress's personal and professional life has been epitomized by the radical prose of Frantz Fanon's *Black Skin, White Masks* (1952) and the contrapuntal rhythms of Ralph Ellison's *The Invisible Man* (1952). In Ellison's quintessential American novel the protagonist is in search of a personal identity that is beyond the racialised and ethnicised constructions of subjectivity, consciously and unconsciously imposed by American history. In 1952, at the time that Fanon was writing *Black Skin, White Masks*, Vontress was graduating from college, perhaps experiencing Fanon's very thoughts: 'It is not I who make a meaning for myself, but it is the meaning that was already there, pre-existing, waiting for me ... waiting for that turn of history ... I am a potentiality of something' (Fanon, 1952, p. 135). In an interesting turn of history,

Vontress was sent to Europe when he was drafted into the US army; based in Germany, he also spent time in Paris, where he could have sat at the same café as Fanon, listening to Jean-Paul Sartre – each being so close but never physically meeting. In the collective unconsciousness there may have been a meeting of the mystical and the spiritual parts of themselves. Indeed, Clemmont Vontress's own search for a subjective identity beyond race and ethnicity has led him to become one of most significant figures in the culture and counseling movement. And yet, being a cross-cultural counselor in the West, especially in the United States, has been a culturally wounding experience for Vontress. Perhaps the very notion of cross-cultural counseling itself is a wounding experiencing for those who engage with it, either as therapists or clients. Vontress has become culturally wounded (as a healer) and made invisible, or rather as a result of being made invisible he has become wounded culturally. Throughout his forty years of infusing culture into counseling he maintained a strong position of therapeutically working with clients in a way that transcends race, culture, and ethnicity, so that their subjectivities can reclaim their universal humanity. As Vontress says, 'Counselors must concern themselves with the human condition in general before addressing the specifics of the client's culture because people are more alike than they are dissimilar' (1985, p. 28). 'Counselors and clients share something in common, the universal culture' (1988, p. 76).

Clemmont Vontress's inclusion of culture, ethnicity, and race in counseling has always been part of the changing world of multicultural counseling, from its early beginnings in the 1960s to the current version of diversity which adds the 'big 7 issues' (Moodley & Lubin, 2008, p. 156) – race, gender, class, sexual orientation, disability, religion, and age – as part of multicultural counseling development. Indeed, throughout this period his colleagues have been acknowledging his work in this field. For example, Ivey, D'Andrea, Ivey and Simek-Morgan (2002) note that 'Clemmont Vontress has long been a proponent of multicultural counseling and therapy ... He was drawn to the concepts of empathy and positive regard of his colleague Carl Rogers but expanded on his approach by focusing in even more depth on the therapeutic relationship as an expression of intimacy, openness, and real human exchange' (Ivey et al., 2002, p. 253).

As an existentialist, Clemmont Vontress believes that the self is not predetermined by culture, but that the material base of society (past and present history, socio-economic conditions, religious and political processes, etc.) determines the construction of culture, which in turn determines the self. It is this Sartrian philosophy of existentialism that has permeated Vontress's analysis of multicultural counseling, as indeed it would given the connection between Vontress and Sartre in the Paris cafés of the 1950s where, as a young man, Vontress heard Sartre give talks and hold discussions regarding 'the commonality of human beings,' people being 'more alike than they are different,' and sharing 'a common destiny' (Vontress, in press). Deeply influenced by these ideas, Vontress continued to explore existentialism on his return to the United States. As he says, 'After being exposed to some of the ideas of Jean-Paul Sartre and Simon de Beauvoir in the 1950s, I read the works of many American and European existentialists. However, few of them discussed culture, even tangentially, as it impacts human existence' (ibid.).

During the last twenty years, Clemmont Vontress has reflected on his theoretical views and research in many different interviews. For example, in 1987, with Morris Jackson, Vontress reflected on his ideas on culture and counseling , and discussed the genesis, status, and future direction of cross-cultural counseling. In 1994, in conversation with Courtland Lee, he spoke as a pioneer of the cross-cultural counseling movement, and reflected on his (at that time) long and distinguished career and the evolution of multicultural counseling as a professional discipline. He also attempted to map out the historical and cultural shifts in the field of cross-cultural counseling. In 1998, Lawrence Epp, a past student and now a colleague of Vontress, interviewed him to explore in particular the dynamics of existentialism and cross-cultural counseling. In an interview with Paul Pedersen (see chapter 7, this volume), Vontress spoke about some of the most challenging difficulties he faced: 'Perhaps the most difficult thing in my profession life was remaining true to my beliefs,' maintaining '[a] recognition and appreciation of individual differences'and 'recogniz[ing] the realities of living with others' so as to 'empathize with the other, without compromising ... authenticity. It is a delicate balance.' Following a July 2008 interview, Tracy Robinson-Wood (chapter 17, this volume) said: 'My time with this peaceful, generous, and dynamic man represents a highlight of my career. The purpose of this interview was to capture his personal reflections on culture and counseling and to include his wisdom and pay homage to his vision for humanity, and his counseling scholarship over the decades.' Given the current complexities of race, culture, and ethnicity as competing and problematic discourses in the modern world, it seems crucial to engage Clemmont Vontress's work and to critically examine and analyse, as well as celebrate, many of his theories and pronouncements regarding the future of psychology, counseling, and psychotherapy.

In the interview presented below, Clemmont Vontress shares personal details of his life experiences and thereby situates his research and scholarship. Given this personal background readers will be better able to understand the relationship between Vontress's writings and his motivations, desires, and articulations of multicultural counseling. Moreover, his personal history reveales the wounding he experienced as an African American man and the healing process that resulted from his research and writing. His personal wounding seems closely tied up with the public wounding (through slavery, racism, sexism, and homophobia) of African Americans in the United States. Clemmont Vontress's journey to wellness was a long road to freedom and becoming a healer himself. It was towards the latter part of this journey that Vontress, the wounded healer, was invited to be 'In the Therapist's Chair' to talk about his life and work.

In the Therapist's Chair Interview

Roy Moodley (RM): Dr Clemmont Vontress, thank you for agreeing to be in the therapist's chair. It has been a long, intense, exciting, challenging, and creative day so far. You heard the various speakers review and critique your work, research, and practice. You have had the opportunity to hear your work talked about, not only in the context of multicultural counselling, psychotherapy, and psychology, but also in the context of Canadian multiculturalism. How has the day been for you?

Clemmont Vontress (CV): It is always flattering to hear one's self and work being discussed, whether the commentary is good or bad. It is also interesting to hear discussed the ideas that I have posited over the years. It was so long ago that I wrote some of my articles, chapters, and books that I have forgotten some of the things I wrote or the exact language that I used in expressing my ideas. However, today, when I heard them discussed, they returned immediately to mind. Indeed, I am excited and honored to be here.

RM: And I guess this event opens up all sorts of memories for you.

CV: I think that you have heard of selective forgetting and selective recall. Some of what I heard today in referring to my work has been more interesting than others. Sometimes I regret what I said or wrote many years ago. Sometimes, I do not. Then again, I may forget that I ever said something. Perhaps this is normal, considering the many years that I have been writing about culture and cross-cultural counseling.

RM: Sure. Maybe what's important is to get the work out there. Indeed, what evolves from it could be very different from what you have done or should have done.

CV: Yes. I think when you write something, and it is out there – and you can't recall it – it is the same when you say something. You have said it. It is hard to deny what has been said. There has to be a certain amount of courage involved in whatever you write or say.

RM: You put yourself on the block today – with your research and practice. And that requires a particular kind of courage. Where do you think this comes from?

CV: I don't know. Perhaps it comes from the recognition of the reality of human existence. It is important to be aware of what it means to be present, here in the world in the moment. We are in a world from which there is no escape. None of us will get out alive. Once this fact is recognized and accepted, there is no reason to be afraid of life or death, what I call existential twins. You cannot have one without the other. That is why I often talk about existential courage. It takes courage to live. Death is a given, since people die whether they want to or not.

RM: In terms of this sense of challenging the fear of death – and it takes courage to live – is there a sense that it comes from your early childhood? Do you have memories of being courageous as a boy?

CV: Not really. As a young boy, my life evolved around and was influenced by my parents and my family. I just let it be, because I was unable to analyse what was happening to me at the time. Although I was influenced by others, I was unaware of the influence. That is to say, as a child I was socialized without knowing that I was being socialized. Things just happened to me, and I believe that this is so with human beings in general. Few of us can tell others why things happen to us. They just do, and we respond to them.

RM: And the childhood days were with other siblings – other brothers and sisters. Tell us about them.

CV: At home, there were many siblings, constantly in motion in and around the house. Even though we were very poor, I felt a great deal of peacefulness. In spite of our poverty, we somehow managed to survive. We kept struggling ahead one day at a time. In looking back, it is still difficult to realize just how difficult it really was. We were poor, but did not know that we were poor. Like most human beings in any situation, we got used to it and took it for granted. My family and I saw our way of life normal and acceptable, even though it was hard.

RM: ... and the people I guess who knew about things were your mum and dad at the time. I imagine that neither you nor your siblings understood what, in fact, all of you were going through.

CV: I am not sure that my family or I understood the people or forces that shaped our existence. We were oppressed. Often oppressed people are unable to perceive the source of the oppression. It is so normal. So usual. It was a part of the human condition, at least as we knew it. Therefore, it was hard for us to realize how oppressed we were. And I think that this may be true of human beings in general. At least, this is the conclusion that I have come to as a result of my travels in various parts of the world. I see this especially in Third World countries. That is, as an outsider, I see how poor the people are. However, I am not sure that the people themselves see their situation the same way. I think that people who suffer the most are the same ones who are unable to see or understand their own suffering. Whether your situation in life is deplorable depends on how you perceive that situation. It depends on what standards you use to measure how deplorable your situation is.

RM: In your biography [Vontress, 2005] you talk about how the situation changed for you in terms of your early childhood experiences. Your mum and dad were critical to this. Tell us about your dad.

CV: I have forgotten exactly what I said about my father. My father was a person whose father and grandfather had experienced a great deal of unpleasantness in growing up. First of all, my family is a product of the period of history surrounding the Civil War. It was the end of slavery and its aftermath. It was during Reconstruction that the Ku Klux Klan started roaming the countryside, trying to restore the racial status quo. It was during this period that they killed my great-grandfather for cohabiting with a 'mulatto girl.' When I was a little boy, my grandfather told me and my siblings this story. It remains to this day etched in my mind. He and my father always told us to beware of people who pretend to represent God. My father saw them as hypocrites, because the people who killed my great-grandfather were the local minister and church deacons wearing white sheets. So my father taught us to believe in a supreme being, but to question the motives of people who pretend to represent Him. Because of what my father taught me, even today I find it difficult to buy into traditional religion. I am especially suspicious of the so-called 'Religious Right' in the US today, who are often hurtful in terms of what they say and do. To this day, I think that what my father taught me as a child is true. It has always stayed with me.

RM: It must be very painful to know that your great-grandfather was killed by the Ku Klux Klan, because we usually think of these things as happening a long time ago.

CV: Yes, you are right. He was killed by the Klan because he had violated the social norm back then. Although there were strong views against racial mixing, it went on all the time. White men cohabitated with black women almost as often as they did with whites. Therefore, my great-grandfather had entered the relationship with my great-grandmother without considering it unusual. He was an adolescent, and the girl was a 'mulatto' who worked in the 'big house.' So when the Klan learned that he had cohabitated with a slave girl, they killed him. Although white men raped black women with impunity, they were not expected to set up household with them as equals. That was just the way it was. It is the dark side of American history.

RM: How has this awareness, this knowledge of this complex history, affected you?

CV: Well, they made me see human beings as they really are. Human beings can be good and bad at the same time. And people grow up and are expected to adhere to whatever social order exists. So it was in the South. Historically, whites had developed a social order to meet their own needs. Blacks were a part of that system, even though they were slaves and considered inferior creatures. They, the whites, did not or could not consider how their social order was damaging to blacks. They saw themselves as being the center of their world. They saw the world from their perspective, not that of blacks. That was the way things were. And we must always be aware of people as they are. As psychologists, we see people as they really are, not as we want them to be.

RM: It seems to me that the pain that you experienced in your youth caused you to be fully aware of the reality of life, that you were able to see all of your clients objectively and honestly, regardless of their race or ethnic background. I guess the same can be said of your research and writing on culture and counseling.

CV: Yes, you are right. I could cry about the past, but that would not change things in the future. Whatever you do, it is important to always keep focused on the future. I could have cried about the pain of my past, but that would not have done any good. You have to keep focused on the future as best you can.

RM: Why do you say that it would not have done you any good to cry about the past? Why not cry?
CV: You have heard the expression 'Don't cry over spilled milk.' One should learn as much about the past as possible and then move on to the future. That's what life is all about. That is a requirement of life.
RM: But away from the metaphor – not crying over spilt milk – and more in terms of Clemmont, the man and the issue of not wanting to cry about the past. Being able to let go – to shed tears, so to speak. Are you saying that you haven't done that?
CV: No. I've cried. It's not been about the past. It's been about the present. For example, when I first went to Africa. I arrived at the airport and went outside and saw all the black people. It was an overwhelming experience; and I cried.
(*Silence. Tears flow down from Vontress's eyes. He takes a glass of water.*)
RM: A very touching moment for you!
(*Silence. A very emotional moment for Clemmont Vontress, and for Roy Moodley. And for the audience … who empathized with his feelings.*)
RM: I wonder if Africa represents the place of both the pain and the healing in your life now. As you research spirituality in Africa and when you talk about yourself as the wounded healer – is there something there about the past and, like you said, your 'journey in the turbulent sea to get to the other side' (Vontress, 2005, p. 7)? Is this part of the past for you and the community – the pain, the tears, and the healing that come with this reflection on Africa and spirituality?
CV: When I arrived in Africa, I mourned thousands of common ancestors who were abducted from the continent, enslaved in America, and abused, killed, and oppressed in the USA through the centuries. Even today, people of African descent in the United States still experience or relive the wounds of slavery, the wounds of their ancestors, now come and gone. Although blacks and whites all experience the wounds of the past, they deal with them differently. For blacks, the wounds constitute scars that make us stronger. Although you recognize your wounds, you guard against your scars making you so callous that you are unable to feel anymore. Perhaps that is why I have made so many trips to Africa. As a wounded healer, I am pulled back to the land of my ancestors in search of the authenticity, equality, freedom, humanity, and the pride which Africans exhibit. I feel connected to Africa and its people. I am a part of them.
RM: In your paper [Vontress, 2005] you talk about your mother being the rock of Gibraltar. I was fascinated with this idea, this metaphor.

Gibraltar connects Africa to Europe. And your work constitutes the two strands also – the existentialism of Europe and the spirituality of Africa. I am just wondering if it was your mother or what she represented that made the connection for you between Africa and Europe. The feminine is the spiritual rock that makes it possible for the wounding to be healed. And your mother or the mother in you has made you the wounded healer. Tell us about your mother.

CV: She had nine children. She would have a child one day and be up the next. When people asked her why she was up so soon, she would reply, 'I am not sick. I just had a baby.' She felt that her main responsibility was to look after her family. When I started making field trips to Africa, I met women who reminded me of my mother, in terms of how they looked after their family. My eldest sister was also a mother to me. In large families, the first often looks after the last. That is, older children become parents to their younger siblings. For example, when my sister went away to college, she encouraged my younger siblings and me to follow in her footsteps. She encouraged me to obtain my master's and PhD degree. When my mother died, she became the matriarch of the family.

RM: In your work you talk about your mother and sister giving you strength, courage, empathy, and perseverance that informed your work.

CV: Yes. I think that courage and perseverance are very important. I am sure that I got a little bit of both from my mother and sister. My mother demonstrated these qualities and my sister articulated them. My father was so busy taking directions from the white landowner that he had little time for the direct socialization of the children. He therefore relinquished that responsibility out of necessity to my mother and sister. Many such family practices were passed down from the days of slavery. For example, back then, the slave owner often gave orders directly to the mother rather than the father, because he felt closer to black women than men, probably because some of them were his concubines. As the head of a sharecropper family, my father was head in name only. In a way, being unable to make decisions that affected his family must have assaulted his manhood. For example, if he wanted us to go to school instead of working in the fields, he had to first consult the landowner for permission. For the landowner it was important that we all stayed there and worked his land.

RM: And the women in your family?

CV: My sister went away to college. As a woman, she could get away to college. She had to get me out – took place in the middle of the night – I had to escape. And once I escaped I could not go back because the landowner might reclaim me for the land. You see; it was that difficult. It was like this after the Civil War, and it continued into the 1920s and the 1940s. Just before World War II, African Americans started escaping the South into the North; some fled to Canada or any place where they would no longer be oppressed. So going off to college was an escape for me. While in college, I married my childhood sweetheart. It was a shotgun wedding. One day my sweetheart's father called me into the living room and said, 'You have knocked up my daughter! What are you going to do about it?' Can you imagine how I as a nineteen-year-old kid felt? There was only one thing to do: get married. That was the way it was back then. Of course, today things are different. However, my marriage would eventually fail. After all, it was a shotgun wedding. Shotgun weddings seldom ever worked out even with the support of the families on both sides. We had a little boy. I finally graduated from college and went to graduate school, only to be drafted into the US Army a year later. Being in the military took me away from my family. So my son grew up without me being around much. So when he went to high school he began to have social and academic difficulties that are often associated with children from single-parent families. He started drinking and got hooked on drugs while in high school. Even so, he got married and fathered three sons by two different women, and died at an early age, leaving me three grandsons. It is interesting how forces seem to move your life in ways that seem to be beyond your control.

RM: Do you connect with your grandchildren?

CV: Yes, we have a good rapport. I am especially close to my youngest grandson, with whom there seems to be a spiritual connection. Recently, he wanted to know about my youth and his father, my son, whom he never knew, since he was an infant when he died. I told him about my early years and about his father when he was a child. Afterwards, he said that he understood himself better. He recognized where he got some of his personality traits. Yeah. I have a spiritual connection with him.

RM: Do you think that this connection has something to do with the notion of spiritual transmission? In view of your research on traditional healing in Africa, you are somewhat of a Shaman yourself now. Do you think there is a kind of transmission of a family-related spirituality down through the generations?

CV: Yes, I do think there is a spirituality that is passed from one generation to the next. Nobody knows how it is passed from one life to another. Some people suggest a genetic transmission. The genes are imbued with all sorts of qualities that can be passed from person to another. We know that the genes can be imbued with mental health qualities. If psychological traits can be transmitted, then it is reasonable to consider the possibility that spiritual qualities can also be passed on. I feel that my grandson and I are on the same spiritual wavelength. To a lesser extent I also feel it with my other two sons.

RM: It's interesting that you said 'my other two sons,' referring to your grandsons. You must be missing your son very much.

CV: Yes. I was very hurt when I attended his funeral. It is especially hurting for relatives to attend funerals of family members who are younger than they are. I think about this when I attend funerals of my former students. People often say, 'I did not expect my child to die before me.' It is very hurting to hear that. However, I think that life is like a terminal: people are coming and going all the time. Some leave before others; others leave on schedule, at the time expected. A few may have a long wait. However, they all eventually leave. We have no control over this fact. I often say to my students that they should not have come into the world if they did not want to leave it.

RM: As we reflect on life and death, tell us more about your sense of death and life after death.

CV: I think that all life is recycled. To live is to die. Everything that lives eventually dies and returns as new life. All life lives out its cycle. The seed is planted. It sprouts, grows to full potential, attains its destiny, and dies, only to rise again. In this sense, there is always life after death.

RM: Do you think of death often?

CV: Not really. No more than I think about going to sleep. I think that it is the same. Humans have no control over it. They get tired and need to rest and sleep. It is the same with death. You go to sleep, but you never wake up. Birth and death are the two most important events in human existence. Although we experience neither personally, our significant others usually celebrate them. There is no reason to fear death, since you have no control over it. It can come any time, anywhere, and often unannounced.

RM: We have fantasies about many things in life. One thing we are not often asked about is – What would you like written on your tombstone?

CV: I used to think about that. However, I now believe that tombstone poetry and prose are motivated by vanity. On the other hand, I understand that remaining relatives need to soothe the pain associated with losing someone close to them. For me, it is sufficient to write my name, birth date, and date of death on the headstone. Just spell my name correctly.

RM: Clemmont E. Vontress, thank you for talking to us today. In conclusion and on a lighter note, can I engage you in a fantasy? If you were exiled to, stranded on, or otherwise offloaded to a deserted island and given only three things to take with you – a book, a piece of music, and one other item. What would you want? Let's start with the book.

CV: I cannot give you the name of a book. However, I can say that if I were on a desert island, I would assume that there is natural vegetation or foodstuff. So I would want a book that tells me what is safe to eat. I just want a book to tell me what is safe on the island to eat. I want the most recent book on the subject.

RM: And the piece of music?

CV: I enjoy music that has a beat, something that approximates the human heartbeat. Ravel's *Bolero* is a beautiful piece of music that I have always loved, since I learned to appreciate music. It has a great beat that finally reaches a crescendo. African and Hispanic music are noted for powerful drumbeats that invigorate and stimulate the body and spirit.

RM: It engages the body, the senses.

CV: Yes. It makes you feel alive. It makes you want to live into the future to enjoy again and again the music.

RM: Frees the spirits.

CV: To be sure!

RM: And the last item?

CV: Well, if I were on a deserted island and had forgotten to take matches with me, I would want some rocks or something to rub together to make a fire.

RM: Okay. We will send all these items with you. Enjoy your trip and your desert island. Dr Clemmont Vontress, thank you for being 'In the Therapist's Chair.'

CV: Thank you!

This very personal, and at times emotional, conversation with Clemmont Vontress has remained one of the most significant moments of my academic and clinical career. It is very rare to see a fellow academic share his or her personal narrative with such intensity, openness, and authenticity. Indeed, the 50 minutes that we talked appeared to be like a lifetime of experiencing personal, historical, and cultural events. In our conversation Clemmont Vontress transported me (and hopefully the audience at the conference) to a past which is often written about but seldom spoken of at such a personal and private level by an academic. His words and emotions brought his ancestors (both black and white of the deep South) into the context of a Canadian space, and all that it represented in the post-modern imagination. His psychic journey to that turbulent and tumultuous time of US history (the killing of his white great-grandfather by the Ku Klux Klan) and the memory of this event and its consequent wounding led Clemmont Vontress to take a particular journey along his own long walk to freedom. From then on, and even before he was born, these events constructed a specific and challenging path for Vontress to follow, one that affirms Frantz Fanon's words: 'It is not I who make a meaning for myself, but it is the meaning that was already there, pre-existing, waiting for me ... waiting for that turn of history.' Indeed, the subsequent events in his personal life, especially his son's death at an early age, reshaped his path even further, such that the linear narrative of his life story, going back, comes full circle. His regular trips to West Africa (on the coast from which the slave ships left for America) to research traditional healers and healing serve as the entry point into his own collective unconscious, thereby 'healing' his consciousness of the current US socio-cultural context within which he finds himself located personally and professionally. This truly is a 'back to the future narrative,' in which the past, present, and future are unified, such that Clemmont Vontress becomes the wounded healer in cross-cultural counseling and psychotherapy.

REFERENCES

Ellison, R. (1952). *The invisible man*. New York: Vintage.

Epp, L. R. (1998). The courage to be an existential counselor: An interview of Clemmont E. Vontress. *Journal of Mental Health Counseling, 20*(1), 1–12.

Fanon, F. (1952). *Black skin, white masks* (C. L. Markmann, Trans.). New York: Grove Press.

Ivey, A. E., D'Andrea, M., Ivey, M. B., & Simek-Morgan, L. (2002). *Theories of counseling and psychotherapy: A multicultural perspective* (5th ed.). Boston: Allyn & Bacon.

Jackson, M. L. (1987). Cross-cultural counseling at the crossroads: Dialogue with Clemmont E. Vontress. *Journal of Counseling and Development, 66*, 20–23.

Lee, C. C. (1994). Pioneers of multicultural counseling: A conversation with Clemmont E. Vontress. *Journal of Multicultural Counseling and Development, 22,* 66 –78.

Moodley, R., & Lubin, D. B. (2008). Developing your career to working with diversityand multicultural clients . In S. Palmer & R. Bor (Eds.), *The practitioner's handbook.* London: Sage.

Pedersen, P. (in press). Counseling across cultures: Clemmont Vontress from 1976–2007. In R. Moodley & R. Walcott (Eds.), *Counseling across and beyond cultures: Exploring the work of Clemmont E. Vontress in clinical practice.* Toronto: University of Toronto Press.

Robinson-Woods, T. (in press). Paving the path of culture and counseling: A conversation with Clemmont E. Vontress. In Moodley & Walcott (Eds.), *Counseling across and beyond cultures.*

Vontress, C. E. (1962). Patterns of segregation and discrimination: Contributing factors to crime among negroes. *Journal of Negro Education, 31,* 108–116.

Vontress, C. E. (1971). Counseling negroes. Boston: Houghton Miffin.

Vontress, C. E. (1979). Crosscultural counseling: An existential approach. *The Personnel and Guidance Journal, 58,* 117–122.

Vontress, C. E. (1982). Social class influences in counseling. *Counseling and Human Development, 14,* 1–12.

Vontress, C.E. (1985). Theories of counseling: A comparative analysis. In R. J. Samuda & A. Wolfgang (eds.), *Intercultural Counseling and Assessment* (pp. 19–31). Toronto: C.J. Hogrefe.

Vontress, C. E. (1988). An existential approach to cross-cultural counseling. *Journal of Multicultural Counseling and Development, 16,* 73–78.

Vontress, C. E. (1991). Traditional healing in Africa: Implications for cross-cultural counseling. *Journal of Counseling and Development, 70,* 242–249.

Vontress, C. E. (1996). A personal retrospective on cross-cultural counseling. *Journal of Multicultural Counseling and Development, 24,* 156–166.

Vontress, C. E. (1999). Interview with a traditional African healer. *Journal of Mental Health Counseling, 21,* 326–333.

Vontress, C. E. (2005). Uncharted waters: Autobiographical notes. In R. K. Conyne, & F. Bemak (Eds.), *Journeys to professional excellence* (pp. 7–18). Alexandria, VA.: American Counseling Association.

Vontress, C. E. (in press). Culture and Counseling: A personal perspective. In Moodley & Walcott (Eds.), *Counseling across and beyond cultures.*

3 A Theory of Apprehension? Fanon, Vontress, and Cultural Identity; or, How Not to Get Stuck There

RINALDO WALCOTT

The fundamental concern of Clemment Vontress and Frantz Fanon is the question of culture. Therefore, the question mark in my title is neither a caution nor an attempt to signal a coming problem. Rather, my question mark is meant to signal apprehension with a movement forward. The intent is not to apprehend Clemment Vontress, Frantz Fanon, or even cultural identity (all of which this chapter takes up), but even more to speak to the apprehensions that any engagement with the work of Vontress and Fanon and cultural identity should produce in the reading, thinking, desiring subject. I am therefore suggesting that apprehension might be a symptom of a healthy psychic condition and social life. I am further suggesting that apprehension is a method by which subjects might pause and think about what we know and believe, so that something else might enter our consciousness and our unconscious: apprehension allows us to move towards questioning. I am indebted to Fanon for what I will call a theory of apprehension.

By such a theory I mean to point to the moment when a certain stillness allows for thought to occur and for thought to become action. Such stillness in action allows for thought with movement in mind, movement meant to engage the past and the present simultaneously as the force that might constitute a future not yet known but desired. In this conception of apprehension that I am offering I assume a future is desired that is substantively different from the present and the past. It is a future conceived within the context of constantly negotiated and shifted notions of justice and freedom. It is my contention that Fanon and Vontress have provided us with blueprints and other signposts to move towards a different conception of freedom than that which presently, and partially, organizes human life.

Apprehension allows us to think about the place of the psychoanalytic concept of 'working through' as it presents itself in the work of Vontress and Fanon. Often the desire for knowable identities does not allow for adequate acknowledgment of the complexities, contradictions, and complications of the interior lives of the racialized. Thus, while neither Fanon nor Vontress makes any explicit claims to psychoanalytic theory in their work, I find some moments of psychoanalysis useful for reading their work. A theory of apprehension seeks to move with and through the ways in which Fanon and Vontress allow us to grapple both with the promise of contemporary cultural identity claims and their stalled desires and, simultaneously, to grapple with the evidentiary stakes of identities constantly in flux, shift, and change.

This chapter is a complementary (not comparative) reading and interpretive exercise in the ideas of Fanon and Vontress. Their contributions to thinking about contemporary Human life allow us to make better sense of cultural identities in North America specifically, and the wider Western world generally. Fanon and Vontress can be seen as providing scholars with access to rethinking the category of the Human in an effort to produce more livable possibilities for all of us.

This chapter has five sections: (1) Culture as a Whole Way of Life, (2) Fanon? (3) Vontress? (4) Cultural Identity? and (5) Diagnosis in Black. These sections set out to demonstrate the ways in which Fanon and Vontress converge, and how they both offer us ways out of the morass of modernity without recourse to a romantic notion of a 'before.' Rather their engagement is with the urgency of the here and now. Significantly, what is striking is how both Fanon and Vontress come full circle on one of the most pressing issues of Black cultural identity – Africa. It is my contention that we cannot make light of either man's return to Africa and its potential working through for Black diasporic reparation and thus healing.

Culture as a Whole Way of Life

I come to the work of both Fanon and Vontress through the circuitous route of what is in university-generated discourse called cultural studies (Readings, 1997). Embedded in some of the theoretical moves of cultural studies is a cautious, but necessary nod to the workings of psychoanalytic theory (Hall, 1996). The grandfather of cultural studies Raymond Williams strongly suggested that culture was 'a whole way of life.' Williams made this claim on behalf of the British or English working class – a white working class, that is. By culture he meant 'a whole way of life, not only as a scale of integrity, but as a mode of interpreting all our common experience, and, in this new interpretation, changing it' (Slack and Whitt, 1992, p. 576). In Williams's definition of culture is a wink or, more modestly, an opening to psychoanalytic possibilities or, at least, the space for such possibilities to enter the conversation. Thus, working through culture is a kind of interpretive psychological/psychoanalytic method. This idea of culture as a whole way of life proposed taking as primary to 'culture' all the different claims concerning what it means to be human, whether biological, psychic, material, economic, political, or social. To make a leap here, for Black peoples or peoples made Black, as well as other subordinated peoples, culture is definitely imbued with a range of ingredients similar to what is suggested by Williams's definition – culture is indeed a whole way of life. Thus I am not surprised that for Fanon and Vontress culture is the very foundation of their interventions.

Thus, in the face of making artificial separations between the interior life and the exterior life, Black peoples and other subordinated peoples have long refused to separate the two. Historically, scholarship on Black peoples has tended to focus on exteriority or the social, and thus the material poverty of their life has been one of the enduring ways of assessing Black peoples' health. This focus was not unwarranted given the clear material deprivation of Black life in the diaspora and on the African continent. Black life came to be located in the lower realms of material access and privilege – this is now especially true for continental Africa.

However, the artificial separation between exteriority, read as material poverty, and interiority, which came to be read as Black cultural poverty, pointed to the necessary fallacy in making such separations. It is in fact at exactly the site of culture, in this case cultural expression, that Black and other subordinated peoples demonstrate that material poverty is not correlative with cultural poverty. The cultural expression of Black peoples and other subordinated peoples demonstrates how such expression is indicative of a desiring subject forged in the context of multiple conflicting environmental factors. It is, in fact, I would argue at the site of culture that a theory of apprehension should make its first appearance. Culture as a whole way of life must force those of us interested in making sense of suffering, survival, and healing to address the ways in which subordinated peoples continue to make pleasurable, livable lives in ongoing contexts of various forms of degradation.

Let me give an example of my claim. In the late nineteenth century and early twentieth only two racially identified groups made significant inventions for human civilization: Jews and Blacks. Jews, or Freud, invented the theory of psychoanalysis and Blacks in the United States invented jazz, while the only twentieth-century instrument, the Steel Pan, was invented in the Caribbean. These new inventions, I would argue, are symptomatic of the social, cultural, and psychic position that these groups had been asked to occupy in their given geopolitical environments. As inventors of jazz and psychoanalysis Blacks and Jews have proffered another story of modernity. It is a story fraught with racial conflict that references both interiority and exteriority. Black and Jews have represented how culture as a whole way of life is filled with the political, the psychic, the material, and the social. Before I go any further, part of the claim I am making here is that while the science of psychoanalysis is a claim of interiority, its invention can or might in fact be read as reacting to claims of exteriority. Thus, Freud's contributions to understanding interiority are crucially linked to explaining the sociocultural exteriority of being a Jew in modern Europe. Jazz is a music of expressive interiority. The principle theorist of Black interiority with all his flaws is Frantz Fanon. Both Fanon and Vontress are motivated by the ways in which culture sits at the root of human suffering.

Fanon?

Fanon concludes *Black Skin, White Masks* with the statement 'O my body, make of me always a man who questions!' (Fanon, 1967, p. 232). In short, Fanon concludes his landmark book with an apprehension and thus movement. Fanon's desire to be a questioning subject plays itself out most forcefully in what is his most influential book, *The Wretched of the Earth* (1963). However, in *Black Skin, White Masks* Fanon, who was trained as a psychiatrist, launches an attack on colonial culture and its workings. To achieve poignancy in his attack he draws a number of archetypes, which sometimes come quite close to being an analysis of given types. But I think it important to state that Fanon clearly does not believe in the ontological validity of something called Black and something called white. However, he is less interested in a theory of explanation for individual behavior than he is in diagnosing what ails us collectively, or put another way, what is wrong with the culture of humanity.

Thus, Fanon tells readers very early in *Black Skin, White Masks*:

> Reacting against the constitutionalist tendency of the late nineteenth century, Freud insisted that the individual factor be taken into account through psychoanalysis. He substituted for phylogenetic theory the ontogenetic perspective. It will be seen that the black man's alienation is not an individual question. Beside phylogeny and ontogeny stands *sociogeny*. (ibid., p. 11, emphasis added)

I want to suggest that sociogeny opens up a whole new arena of diagnosis, analysis, and prognosis. If we read Fanon's sociogeny alongside Jung's collective unconscious, numerous interesting possibilities arise for thinking about the contexts of what we might call culture, and thus healing within culture.

In Fanon's final prayer to be made a man who always questions is the desire for a rethinking of the category of the Human. For me, this signal of the desire to rethink the category of the Human lies in Fanon's claim that 'the architecture of this work is rooted in the temporal' (p. 12), and I believe that the claim is fully achieved in the famous chapter 5, 'The Fact of Blackness.' Before I turn to chapter 5, let me state that Fanon's language in *Black Skin, White Masks* does not solidify anything related to the category of race. He is always aware of racial claims of difference as positioned within a network of power and its exercise and of acquiescence to powerful authorities. Fanon writes:

> This work represents the sum of the experiences and observations of seven years; regardless of the area I have studied, one thing has struck me: The Negro enslaved by his inferiority, the white man enslaved by his superiority alike behave in accordance with a neurotic orientation. Therefore I have been led to consider their alienation in terms of psychoanalytical classifications. (ibid., p. 60)

Fanon's claim in this statement is a refusal of calcified racial categories in favor of a language that references the ways or practices of behavior on the part of both whites and Blacks. Thus, one of the central features of chapter 5 is that what is claimed on behalf of blackness and whiteness are practices that are changeable over time. We can recover from these categories if we begin the process of apprehending them and working through them. Thus, Fanon's insistence on the temporality of the work is not an invalid claim. Very early in *Black Skin, White Masks*

Fanon articulates a common but different humanity for both whites and Blacks. For both it is a flawed humanity. And thus, I would argue that Fanon is fundamentally concerned with offering us an analysis that might produce 'new forms of human life,' as Sylvia Wynter puts it in her reading of Fanon's sociogenetic invention and intervention (Wynter, 1995).

'The Fact of Blackness' is the diagnosis, and refusal, of a set of universals about blackness. In Fanon's refusal of the objectifying of blackness and its attendant history of internalized shame with regard to slavery and Africa he states, 'For not only must the black man be black; he must be black in relation to the white man' (Fanon, 1967, p. 110). This classic analysis of how identities are constituted through each other allows Fanon to further articulate his 'new' humanist vision. Thus, Fanon later tells us, 'The Negro is not. Any more than the white man' (ibid., p. 231). He is intent on unraveling the facts of blackness in an effort to remake the category of the Human something more encompassing than it currently passes for.

The Wretched of the Earth is Fanon's explication of sociogeny. If we read *Wretched* as a text meant to diagnose, analyze, and offer a possible prognosis, and even healing, of the colonial rupture and trauma, then it functions as a sociogenetic analysis. Up until now I have not attempted to suggest what sociogeny might mean. What is at stake in articulating sociogeny or the sociogenetic is an attempt to think the group and the individual at once. But the group takes primacy in this particular analysis. Additionally, sociogeny recognizes, or more strongly refuses, the mind-body split. Wynter defines it in part this way:

> The proposal here is that Fanon's thesis, that besides phylogeny and ontogeny stands sociogeny, reveals that the 'qualitative mental states' (such as the aversive reaction of white Europeans and of blacks ourselves to our skin color and physiognomy), are states specific to the modes of subjective experience defining what it is like to be human within the terms of our present culture's conception of what it is to be human; and, in the terms of the sociogenic principle ... they are states defining what it is to be the lived expression of a species-specific genomic principle. (Wynter, 2001, p. 46)

And in fact *Wretched* is the text where Fanon most forcefully reconnects mind and body in their social and political contexts, offering us an analysis of the stakes of rethinking the category of the Human. In *Wretched* Fanon's critique of the national elites who abort the revolution in service to particular material, social, and political advantages of proximity to European-ness makes the case for both the continued colonial project and the elites' complicity with it.

Let me suggest a number of general points about the sociogenetic explication of Fanon in *Wretched*. *Wretched* diagnoses coloniality in a very different register from *Black Skin*. In *Wretched* we get a possible answer toward recovery. Read most popularly for Fanon's discourse on violence, *Wretched* in my view offers an analysis that complicates the assertion of a very specific and contextual use of violence in the colonial situation. In *Wretched* Fanon articulates most forcefully his new humanism. If we take the colonial situation as in effect an ongoing trauma, with obviously vastly different consequences for colonizer and colonized, but as a trauma nonetheless for both, Fanon's prognosis offers us a new universalism from the vantage point of the subordinated. He writes: 'This new humanity cannot do otherwise than define a new humanism both for itself and for others' (Fanon, 1963, p. 246). Embedded in the conflict that is the struggle between the colonizer and the colonized is a struggle over culture. Once both groups are liberated from a flawed way of life, something else might become possible – a whole way of life.

It is crucially important to note that Fanon's *Wretched* is as much a text about the potential liberatory effects of the violent overthrow of the colonizer as it is a text about the remaking of culture and cultural expression as simultaneously the exterior and interior of the colonized and the colonizers' lives. This observation is important for rethinking how *Black Skin, White Masks* works to refuse the limits and constraints of history as a shame of slavery and Africa. Thus, it was in Africa, in particular Algeria, that Fanon found both a practice of a new self and the potential for the ushering in of a new humanism that might change the world from the bottom up. His return to Africa can be read as an attempt to grapple with exigencies of recovery beyond a narrative of a history of injustice, to reach a history of how to rethink the ongoing global formations of how to live cultural differences within a reconfigured Human experience as the first instance.

Vontress?

Clement Vontress is hailed as one of the fathers of cross-cultural or multicultural counseling. But when reading his work one is faced with a sense that he is uncomfortable with such a configuration. Such discomfort is not dissimilar from his refusal of Afrocentrism (Vontress, 1996, p. 164) and Fanon's discomfort with Negritude . Vontress states: 'I do not question the need for counselors to become more professionally proficient in the area of cross-cultural counseling. I am simply raising questions about the most efficient means to accomplish the goal' (Jackson, 1987, p. 22). Vontress is therefore concerned that cross-cultural counselors do not 'focus more on the racio-ethnic layer of culture than they do on either the national or the universal. That is, they are often more influenced by the race of the client than they are by the fact that the person is a human being, first of all' (ibid., p. 22). Both Fanon and Vontress are interested in something larger –the category of the Human. Therefore, both men are interested in resignifying what Human means. In fact, it might be argued that Vontress's project shares much in common with Fanon's call for a new humanism.

There are many convergences between Fanon and Vontress. Their time in Paris, encounters with Sartre, the fact of being Black men, intellectual lives, and so on. But what is most germane to our interests is that both men have or held a focus on the place of culture in Human healing. Vontress writes that after his doctoral work 'I devoted my career to exploring the effects of culture on counseling' (Vontress, 1996, p. 157). By focusing on culture both Fanon and Vontress have had to address the difficult issue of self-hatred. In fact, I would claim that self-hatred is one of the keys to bringing these two thinkers together. Self-hatred is an interesting dynamic because it is immediately indicative of exteriority and interiority, thus erasing any separation between the two states of life. By this I mean that self-hatred can both be seen in particular practices or behavior and is, as well, an internalized dynamic. Self-hatred is thus a flawed way of living a life and experiencing the world.

The schema of four worlds (self, others, the natural environment, and forces greater than ourselves) of diagnosis that Vontress offers for existential counseling are all in service of a common humanity – as he puts it 'en route to the same destination, death' (Vontress, 1996, p. 161). Fanon too understands death as a common denominator in the struggle to produce a whole self; the idea of violence in his writing is exemplary of the claim that violence comes as both opposition to the oppressor and as the modus operandi of the dominator. Thus, not all violence is the same and some forms of violence work to produce new relation to the self both individually and collectively. But importantly, self-hatred is its own unique kind of violence. So how does one recover from all these violences? Let's turn to Vontress's practice for a while.

When Vontress describes his practice something interesting happens. He also here tends to step away from the label 'existential' while holding on to it. In this instance, his method of counseling reminds me of jazz, where improvisation is an anti-method born of evading various violences. What Vontress describes as 'interactive dialogue' is like improvisation. A dynamic relationship between the individual and the group is relayed and played. Vontress, like a jazz musician, has a technique-less technique. It is this kind of skillful movement across a range of concerns that makes cross-cultural counseling apprehend racial and cultural difference in the service of producing a whole Human being. What Vontress's practice is able to achieve, much like the jazz musician, is to take traces, essences, and bits and pieces that are both recognizable and not, and reassemble them into a whole that is both simultaneously new and recognizable, and thus a whole for which relation is possible in numerous ways.

Improvisation as a method is only possible through the interiorization of the elements necessary to draw on in the moment of creation or articulation. If we follow the jazz trope through to the making of identities, then the bits and pieces from which we assemble identities only become meaningful and workable in the context of recognizing those pieces in others and having them recognized in us. Importantly, such forms of recognition can move cultural identities and clams of singular identities into encounters with other similar claims and, in the process, a deeper recognition of human-ness. It is in part my argument that state multiculturalism's inattention to the interior life limits the desire for deeper human connection.

Vontress's project then is in concert with Fanon's refusal to be reduced to the 'nigger' of the European imagination and the brute-force attempt to make him into a non-human. Instead, Vontress offers us a model of counseling that provides the necessary avenues for a reconnection to parts of the self submerged and discredited in the social, the historical, the political, and the cultural. His method provides for a reintegration at the same time that it allows for both individual and collective renewal and re-creative possibilities. Such a generative model both demands an accounting of the ways in which individual and collective culture have become deeply meaningful and at the same time views culture as a transitory practice on the way to being something else. Thus, for example, Vontress's model recognizes something called Black culture, but is not limited by a set of preconceived notions of what that Black culture would be or is. Instead, it allows for the historical and the contemporary to co-mingle in the service of producing a different present in the immediacy of a situation and a new look towards the future. In such fashion then Vontress's model both enables some forms of multiculturalism and simultaneously undermines those forms that produce culture and identity as static and unchanging qualities.

Cultural Identity?

In this section I turn to a brief discussion of the complications of cultural identity and its modes of practice as singular. This discussion is meant to demonstrate how Fanon and Vontress can pedagogically inform the stakes of contemporary human life in which identity becomes the foundation upon which human possibilities are erected. Cultural identity as a conceptual claim and a practice often relies upon the singularity of a claim to distinguish it from some other identity. What is significant is that claims to the singularity of cultural identity do not secure those identities as fundamentally different forms of being human, despite the claim of difference. My argument is that often cultural identity claims in multicultural counseling often do not grapple seriously with the interior life of oppressed others. Instead, the appeal to cultural identity becomes stuck in past or present injustices and does not allow for the kinds of productions of human-ness that both Fanon and Vontress envision in their thinking and writing.

Multicultural counseling is by and large a discourse meant to put into play a notion of the whole Human being too, even if an oppressed form of human. But such a form of human is quite different from Vontress's and Fanon's Human, wherein culture and the past are a gateway to something else. A belief that the past fundamentally frames us has become crucial to multicultural counseling in North America. By this I mean that ideas of cultural identity put in place a set of practices for counseling around cultural difference that paradoxically legitimize the terrible histories of the making of cultural difference, and therefore simultaneously position cultural difference as an ongoing problem for the still colonized and or the oppressed person's healing. I want to insist on the paradox of cultural identity because it both is a potentially liberating force and, at the same time, can be a place in the past to be stuck in, from which little or no recovery is possible. In making such a claim I am not suggesting that cultural identities are not meaningful, useful, or play a role in human life; rather I am pointing to the exaltation of cultural identity as the beginning and end of what it means to be Human. When cultural identity is exalted as the beginning and the end, how it works in everyday life is often overlooked.

Both Fanon and Vontress offer us in their work scripts for taking all of human culture as our own. In each of these thinkers accounts of how one heals from or resists the continuing effects of racism, colonialism, and cultural relativism point to cultural identity as a moment of apprehension. Cultural identity in their articulations offers partial insight and perspective, but does not provide the entire picture. In their view cultural identities can and often are woven out of the same ideas and practices that produced the context of colonial encounter and racism. Thus, to lodge one's self there and only there is to give into the very context one hopes to escape from, if not defeat. In this sense, then, both Fanon and Vontress are highly aware of the ways in which the stereoptype can be and often is internalized and how such internalization must be worked against.

Take, for example, what is called Black on Black crime in North America. This phenomenon has largely been understood as some kind of Black pathology. However, on closer inspection this alleged Black on Black crime is a result of failed initiatives of racial inclusion and the inability of North American institutions to effectively incorporate the experience, histories, and thus individual and collective identities of these young Black men and their families into the fabric of society. Paradoxically, many of these same young men have come to believe through engagements with commercial culture that the expression of Black masculinity is necessary violent. Again, Wynter offers a way of seeing this phenomenon: 'He now begins to experience himself through the mediation of stereotyped concepts specific to a particular point of view and visual phenomenology; in other words, not as he is, but as he must be for a particular view point' (Wynter, 2001, p. 43). This paradox occurs because of liberal notions that have largely dealt with these young men in 'racial schema' (Fanon) or 'racio-ethnic' (Vontress) terms, without addressing them as Human subjects. Thus, these young men have internalized and exteriorized a violent hardness that (for example) they genuinely believe to be an authentic Black male cultural practice. So how do we fix this? Both Fanon and Vontress offer us useful ways to think about these dilemmas.

These dilemmas are exacerbated by an almost sacred belief in cultural identity as a marker of what is possible for the way some people will participate in the larger society. While it is crucial to recognized that neither Fanon nor Vontress denies the existence of racism, their project is one that seeks to move beyond its confining context to offer up a mode of practice that might allow us to break its crippling hold on us. But again, to end the crippling effects, with paradox and apprehension, both Fanon and Vontress offer us methods that come from the partial but incomplete perspective of Black subjecthood. Such a perspective is what I call, following them, diagnosis in Black.

Conclusion: Diagnosis in Black

What we get from Fanon and Vontress is a diagnosis in Black. But it is a diagnosis that seeks to question the ways in which individuals and groups have been produced within the context of modernity. The impact of modernity is a struggle that Vontress characterizes as 'culture engender[ing] frustration' (Vontress, 1985, p. 25). Two of the most traumatic ruptures of cultural frustration are the attempted genocide of Native peoples and the brutal violence of the Middle Passage and its continuing traumas. Those two modern ruptures – Native genocide and the Middle Passage – constitute the first instance of cross-cultural failure and thus of the necessary need for cross-cultural healing and recovery. The violence at the center of those traumas was the imposition of European conceptions of the human, conceptions that rendered Natives and Blacks non-human. It has been the struggle of all those rendered non-human in a post-1492 world to regain and thus resignify what it means to be Human. Cross-cultural counseling goes a long way in producing this new humanism. At the center of reclaiming a non-oppressive concept of the Human, African and Native self-determination in their totality must be approached.

Thus, both Fanon and Vontress have returned to Africa, but in ways that account for the contemporaneity of the continent. Their returns complicate history in ways that move beyond any too easy notions of loss to produce a much more dynamic interplay between the violent rupture of the Middle Passage, the ongoing colonization and genocide of Native peoples, and the birth of New peoples of the Americas. At the center of each man's return to Africa is a concern with culture. For Vontress, his engagement with Africa is in terms of making sense of how what we call traditional African healing practices can occupy an important and legitimate role in contemporary society as a practice for making the body whole within culture. This is not dissimilar from Fanon's argument that Algerian mental patients needed to be re-immersed in their cultural contexts so that healing might be possible. The central conceit of both Fanon's and Vontress's contributions to modernity is to rethink its cultural flaws as the basis for a strategic universalism (Gilroy, 2001) or from-the-bottom universalism. To do so, both Fanon and Vontress must apprehend modernity and work through it so that a philosophical and ethical project can usher in a new species of the Human.

REFERENCES

Fanon, F. (1963). *The wretched of the earth*. New York: Grove Press.

Fanon, F. (1967). *Black skin, white masks*. New York: Grove Press.

Gilroy, P. (2001). *Against race: Imagining political culture beyond the color line*. Cambridge: Harvard University Press.

Hall, S. (1996). Cultural studies and its theoretical legacies. In D. Morley and K. Chen (eds.), *Stuart Hall: Critical dialogues in cultural studies*. London: Routledge.

Jackson, M.L. (1987). Cross-cultural counseling at the crossroads: A dialogue with Clement Vontress. *Journal of Counseling and Development, 66*(1), 20–23.

Readings, B. (1997). *The university in ruins*. Cambridge: Harvard University Press.

Slack, J., and Whitt, L. (1992). In L. Grossberg, C. Nelson, & P. Treichler (Eds.), *Cultural studies*. New York: Routledge.

Vontress, C. (1985). Theories of counseling: A comparative analysis. In R. Samuda and A. Wolfgang (Eds.), *Intercultural counseling and assessment: Global perspectives*. Toronto, Canada: C.J. Hogrefe Inc.

Vontress, C. (1996). A personal retrospective on cross-cultural counseling. *Journal of Multicultural Counseling and Development, 24*(3), 156–166.

Walcott, R. (2006). Land to light on? Making reparation in a time of transnationality. In M. Margaroni and E. Yiannopoulou (Eds.), *Metaphoricity and the politics of mobility*. Amsterdam: Rodopi.

Wynter, S. (1995). 1492: A new world view. In V. Hyatt and R. Nettleford (Eds.), *Race, discourse, and the origin of the Americas*. Washington: Smithsonian Institution.

Wynter, S. (2001). Towards the sociogenic principle. In M. Dorán-Coran and A. Gómez-Moriana (Eds.), *National identities and sociopolitical changes in Latin America*. New York: Routledge.

PART TWO

Clemmont E. Vontress – An Inspiring Mentor in Cross-Cultural Counseling

4 How Clemmont Vontress Inspired and Reinforced My Cross-Cultural Passion

PATRICIA ARREDONDO

Clemmont Vontress has pioneered a complex, yet practical, approach to cross-cultural counseling. By giving counselors the skills to work within universal principles of humanity, yet respect each individual's personal and cultural worldview, his work has encouraged new standards of competence for our profession. This chapter is meant to be a reflection of the influence Clemmont has had on my professional work for the past 30–35 years. With this chronology in mind, I will discuss several themes: deliberate attention to racial and ethnic barriers in counseling, humanistic principles in cross-cultural counseling, culture-specific indigenous models of helping with clients of African heritage, and implications for cross-culturally responsive counseling.

As a counseling student in the mid- to late 1970s, I felt fortunate to find some of the early contributions of Dr Vontress. 'Cultural Barriers in the Counseling Relationship' (1969), 'Counseling Blacks' (1970), and 'Racial and Ethnic Barriers in Counseling' (1976) stood out. In the 1970s, I was in a master's and doctoral programs. I took a position as a high school counselor in 1975, working primarily with immigrant and refugee students and families. At the time, there were few articles in the counseling literature with a cross-cultural focus or attention to clients' cultural heritage and primary language. Training was very individualistic in orientation, and with our supposedly values-free, nonjudgmental approach and eclectic style, counselors-in-training learned a 'one size fits all' mindset. In two articles on cultural barriers in counseling (1969, 1973), Vontress illuminated unspoken dynamics that were later reframed as areas for multicultural competency development (Sue, Arredondo, & McDavis, 1992; Arredondo et al., 1996). I am pleased to have this opportunity to revisit and give visibility to these writings by Vontress.

Addressing Barriers in Counseling

Context is important to acknowledge. Clemmont Vontress's early contributions began in 1966, in the midst of the civil rights era. The late 1960s was a time of racial unrest in the United States, the height of the Vietnam War, the beginnings of Black pride, and assaults on the 'establishment.' Concomitantly, the passage of the Civil Rights Act of 1964 was a significant springboard for ethnic/racial minority (ERM) scholars and allies to identify issues impacting counseling with ERM individuals. Vontress was not shy about pointedly discussing various conditions and factors affecting the counseling relationship. These cultural barriers included racial attitudes, ignorance of the client's background, language differences, clients' unfamiliarity with counseling, a sex and race taboo, and 'Negro self disclosure reserve' (1969, p. 14). 'Negrophobia is so deeply ingrained in the American psyche that it crops up where least expected, even in counseling' (p. 16). He further specified: 'Perhaps the greatest blockage in the relationship is the counselor's lack of understanding of the sociopsychological background of the client' (p. 13).

As I reflect on these quotes and others from *Counseling Blacks* (Vontress, 1970), I am reminded of the direct and indirect influence Vontress had on the underpinnings of multicultural counseling competencies. The first domain addresses the counselor's awareness of values and biases, while the second focuses on the counselor's knowledge of the client's worldview. Vontress observed that the psyche of the white counselor held the master-servant paradigm, perpetuating a deficit mindset about blacks. In the multicultural counseling competencies, we point out the necessity of recognizing 'how counselors' attitudes, beliefs and values are interfering with providing the best service to clients' (Arredondo et al., 1996, p. 58) and how critical it is for counselors to 'possess specific knowledge and information about the particular group with which they are working' (pp. 63–64). Vontress urged counselors 'to leave the sheltered environment of the buildings in which they work … and go into the teeming communities where black people live' (1969, p. 16). Many counselor educators teaching a multicultural counseling course have come to value the importance of introducing our students to live cross-cultural encounters. As Vontress indicated, it was essential for training programs to help counselors relate to others of a different cultural background, 'not just in a counseling dyad but in a one-to-one human relationship' (p. 16).

Existential, Cross-cultural Lenses

I believe it was in preparation for teaching multicultural counseling at Boston University in the early 1980s that I first came across Vontress's writings discussing existential counseling from cross-cultural perspectives. Introductory courses in counselor training, not very different from today's, featured three major theories: humanistic, cognitive-behavioral, and existential. The role of culture was never discussed. More recently, multiculturalism was designated a fourth force in counseling alongside the other three theories (Pedersen, 1991), but Vontress stands alone in how he has integrated these two paradigms.

I was intrigued by how Dr Vontress threaded the existential worldview with cross-cultural perspectives. Yes, I had read about Martin Buber's I-thou construct in my undergraduate philosophy class, but I learned the theory in the abstract, definitely not in a multicultural context. I became familiar with the writings of Ludwig Binswanger and James Bugenthal, particularly *The Search for Existential Identity: Patient–Therapist Dialogues in Humanistic Psychotherapy*, which is still sitting on my bookshelf. Though very engaging writing because of the humanistic approach, I did not have the cultural 'aha.'

In reviewing the early work of Vontress, I recognized how he established common factors for existential cross-cultural counseling with a particular focus on the counseling relationship. Needless to say, counselors learn about the sanctity of the counseling relationship in training, but his fundamental premise of 'philosophical equality' between the client and therapist adds further meaning. Vontress indicates that this status of equality is essential for clients who may differ culturally from the therapist. I fully appreciate this premise because of what it implies for the training and practice of counselors in an increasingly complex world of multiple cultures and diversity.

As a proponent of multicultural perspectives in counseling (Arredondo et al., 1996; Arredondo, 1994; Arredondo, 1999), I know that the emphasis on egalitarianism in the counseling relationship is essential. Far too often, women, persons of color, persons of lower socieoeconomic status, immigrants, and other underserved and marginalized groups have not been fully valued (Arredondo, 2001). Patronizing behavior ensues and client disempowerment is the outcome. When counselors do not view clients in context and from a strengths-versus-deficit perspective, we cannot genuinely empathize with their concerns, circumstances, and pain. In this regard, Vontress relates to

Buber's third I-thou mode of opening life to one another, 'such that there can be significant human sharing' (Vontress, Johnson, & Epp, 1999, p. 44). He also states that the challenge for counselors is to have the courage to be 'caring human beings in an insensitive world' (ibid., p. xx).

The premise of valuing another's humanity is a cornerstone of Vontress's worldview and also emerges in other writings. In concluding remarks of a chapter on culture and counseling, he states: 'In cross-cultural counseling, it is best to initiate the relationship with the recognition of the common humanity that you share with clients. Differences that need to be addressed may become obvious later' (2002, p. 5).

In my own work with immigrants, I have often seen how administrative staff, clinicians, and researchers view immigrants from condescending perspectives, underestimating their life experiences just because they may not speak English well or have different formal education. How can a clinician be authentic with a person whom they view as passive, helpless, or here to take advantage of 'us' and our services? Dr Vontress would indicate that the uniqueness of all individuals is primary and that the therapist must be adaptive, creative, and responsive, truly meeting clients where they are, not where we want them to be.

Vontress on Essentials for Humanistic Diagnosis and Treatment Planning

I have always found the task of formulating a diagnosis to be problematic. On the one hand, classification of an individual based on DSM-IV criteria has become an expected practice. When the cultural syndromes were released in an earlier version of the current DSM-IV-TR, I initially considered it an advancement of the classification system. However, I found these criteria to be limiting and not considerate of cultural differences based on distinct ethnicities, country of origin, language, gender, and other individual dimensions of identity and experience (Arredondo & Glauner, 1992). Not surprisingly, I resonate with the concepts proposed by Vontress (1979) for diagnosis from existential counseling perspectives. Among these concepts are self-knowledge, courage, authenticity, becoming, meaning, and responsibility. I find it interesting that these concepts are both universal and culturally relative. Herein lies the connection to multicultural counseling. Multicultural counseling advocates such as myself know that there is more to know about and appreciate in an individual relative to their fears, frustrations, and anxieties from their cultural context.

With respect to treatment plans and interventions, Vontress is very clear:

> To be therapeutic, counselors must have four understandings. First, they need to understand the general culture in which the client was socialized ... Second, counselors need to understand the host culture in which their culturally different clients currently live. The understanding is essential because cross-cultural counselors need to comprehend the nature of multi-faceted aspects of cultural clashes impacting culturally different clients. (2002, p. 4)

In multicultural counseling we advocate for the necessity of counselor self-knowledge about cultural values and biases (Sue, Arredondo, & McDavis, 1992). Counselor self-knowledge provides a bridge to promoting and valuing client self-knowledge, experience, and, of course, respect for an egalitarian relationship. At the same time, self-knowledge is idiosyncratic, culture-bound, and contextual. This is where the appreciation for existential concepts of meaning, becoming, and courage resonate for me with respect to immigrants.

Vontress also discussed the experiences of immigrants in counseling. I share in his observation that immigrants know more about themselves, the context and culture of their country of origin, and their motivation for leaving that country. They have a cultural memory. Vontress also emphasizes the relevance of personality development in one's home or primary culture. In counseling, then, it is the therapist's responsibility to facilitate meaning-making for clients frustrated with barriers to economic advancement and other goals they hold for their lives in the new country. When therapists invite clients to tell their story, including how they have coped with adversities in their home country, they may come to validate their courage and the process of difficult life transitions they are experiencing. By so doing, it seems that therapists would be fostering increased self-respect and acceptance by clients.

Worldviews in Existential Counseling

In multicultural counseling, we use the concept of worldview to describe the influence of cultural beliefs, values, mores, and traditions on institutional and individual behaviors and emotional reactions. Existential counseling, as discussed by Vontress, is informed by the cultural worldviews of both the client and the counselor. He also reminds us that regardless of a culture's individualistic or collectivistic value orientation, the concepts of authenticity, responsibility, and courage are relevant in counseling process. The meaning of these concepts in individuals' lives can be explored for more self-understanding, empowerment, and decision-making.

One further point I would add concerns the role of language in counseling. The literature suggests that one's first language is the language of emotions (Santiago-Rivera, Arredondo, & Gallardo-Cooper, 2002). Counselors working from existential perspectives need to appreciate that meaning-making through primary-language use in counseling may facilitate the expression of blocked emotions. In counseling we learn about impasses and often attribute these to the clients' use of defense mechanisms. Although the latter cannot be dismissed, with immigrants, counselors need to be considerate about clients' language of emotions and learn how to engage with empathy and authenticity. In his writings on barriers to cross-cultural counseling relationships, Vontress made the following observation: 'Educated people, especially therapeutic personnel, communicate in abstractions and words that not only convey motivations, but that transmit, modify, and refine feelings as well. In fact, counselors hardly consider their counseling interviews successful unless their clients verbalize their feelings fluently' (1969, p. 14).

African-Centered Considerations in Counseling

As a field, multicultural counseling has highlighted the importance of inquiring about belief systems and values that shape another's worldview. As a result, there is a greater focus on religion and spirituality, as well as the role of traditional practices and their therapeutic benefits. Vontress has conducted research in different African countries to describe the bridges between healing and counseling from African-specific perspectives. He contrasts and compares African spiritual practitioners and Western-trained counselors. There are values and beliefs guiding interventions in both contexts, and neither is better than the other. However, Western-trained counselors need to be knowledgeable about their clients of African heritage in order to determine the appropriate intervention.

Based on his research, Vontress points out several considerations for cross-cultural counseling relationships with clients of African heritage. These involve the counseling relationship itself, setting, diagnostic procedures, intervention strategies, and training of counselors for cross-cultural practice (1991). I would like to address his comments on the importance of setting when counseling clients of African heritage.

Because family is the most important entity for people of African heritage, Vontress indicates that births, marriages, sicknesses, and deaths are reasons for families to come together. This practice is also very common for many of a Latino heritage, who may crowd into a hospital room when a loved one is ill (Santiago-Rivera, Arredondo, & Gallardo-Cooper, 2002). I agree with his observation on the importance of the value of collectivism and how this manifests itself as family support in particular settings. For immigrant clients from Africa, the modality for help – the counselor-client dyad in an office – may seem very ascetic and isolating. Individuals seeking assistance from a counselor may be confused by the business-like nature of the counseling encounter. Vontress suggests that 'for some clients, the display of African artifacts and the presence of African music in the background alleviate initial anxiety' (1991, p. 248). In addition, counselor knowledge of culture-specific interventions and where they may be provided needs to become common practice for counselors.

Counseling with the African American Client

Vontress has been protective of African American clients in counseling with Western-trained white counselors, analysing the deficit thinking that Whites may bring to counseling encounters, which can disadvantage the African American client seeking assistance. His concerns about counselors' and educators' deficit thinking about African Americans was hard-hitting in the 1970 article 'Counseling Blacks.' Then, he was highly critical about the terms 'culturally deprived,' 'disadvantaged,' and 'socially handicapped,' which were often used in reference to African Americans. From his perspective, white counselors could not appreciate the sociocultural and historical circumstances that prevented African Americans from having equal access to education, employment, and income. With this lack of understanding, he was not convinced counselors could be helpful. 'The counselor must know what he is doing and why; to do so he must understand his own psychodynamics and cultural conditions' (1970, p. 714). Vontress also pointed out that positive regard, as learned by counselors, is insufficient. Indeed, trying to 'do good' does not mean that a counselor will suspend judgment about the client. Multicultural counseling advocates have supported this viewpoint and also stated that all counseling is culture-bound (Sue, Arredondo, & McDavis, 1992). Thus, counseling with clients of African heritage will require counselors to first understand their prejudices in order to reduce barriers in the counseling relationship (Vontress, 1970).

Final Thought

Clemmont E. Vontress has had a distinguished career in cross-cultural and multicultural counseling, with professional contributions dating back to 1966. Here, I have been able to get another glimpse at his pioneering cross-cultural perspectives. Even when he discusses existential perspectives, Vontress grounds his ideas in the historical and sociocultural context. He is always instructing the reader that cultural differences and dynamics are present in a counseling relationship.

Weaving a person's cultural identity with his or her very unique, individual sense of self has been one of Dr Vontress's central teachings, in both a theoretical and clinical milieu. He delves into the existential balance of personal identity and the textured nature of culture. Recognizing that culture is a dynamic force that includes both the paradoxical simplicity and complexity of human nature, he explores the different 'worlds' that constitute our inner beings and the world around us. Instead of culture defining the individual, he emphasizes that culture describes individual uniqueness. Though we are all part of a larger social and cultural context, there is a universal humanness at the core of every person. I sincerely appreciate Clemmont's contributions to the literature and have been a direct beneficiary of his great thinking.

REFERENCES

Arredondo, P. (1999). Multicultural counseling competencies as tools to address racism and oppression. *Journal of Counseling and Development, 77,* 102–108.

Arredondo, P. (1994). Multicultural issues in training. *The Counseling Psychologist, 22,* 308–314.

Arredondo, P., & Glauner, T. (1992). Dimensions of personal identity. Boston, MA: Empowerment Workshops, Inc.

Arredondo, P., Toporek, R., Brown, et al. (1996). Operationalization of the multicultural counseling competencies. *Journal of Multicultural Counseling and Development, 24*, 42–78

Pedersen, P. (1990). The multicultural perspective as the fourth force in counseling. *Journal of Mental Health Counseling, 12*, 93–95.

Santiago-Rivera, A., Arredondo, P., & Gallardo-Cooper, M. (2002). *Counseling Latinos and la familia: A guide for practitioners*. Thousand Oaks, CA: Sage.

Sue, D. W., Arredondo, P., & McDavis, R. (1992). Multicultural competencies and standards: A call to the profession. *Journal of Counseling and Development, 70*, 477–486.

Vontress, C. E. (1969). Cultural barriers in the counseling relationship. *Personnel and Guidance Journal, 47*, 11–17.

Vontress, C. E. (1970). Counseling blacks. *Personnel and Guidance Journal, 48*(9),713–719.

Vontress, C. E. (1976). Racial and ethnic barriers in counseling. In P. Pederson, W. J. Lonner, & J. G. Draguns (Eds.), *Counseling across cultures* (pp. 42–64). Honolulu: University Press of Hawaii.

Vontress, C. E. (1979). Cross-cultural counseling: An existential approach. *Personnel and Guidance Journal, 58*, 117–122.

Vontress, C.E. (1991). Traditional healing in Africa: Implications for cross-cultural counseling. *Journal of Multicultural Counseling and Development, 70*(1), 242–249.

Vontress, C. E. (2002). Culture and counseling. In W. J. Lonner, D. L. Dinnel, S. A. Hayes, and D. N. Sattler (Eds.), *Oneline readings in psychology and culture* (Unit 10, 1), (http://www/wwu.edu~culture), Center for Cross-Cultural Research, Western Washington University. Bellingham, WA.

Vontress, C. E., Johnson, J. A., & Epp, L. R. (1999). *Cross-cultural counseling*. Alexandria, VA: American Counseling Association.

5 Clemmont Vontress: Reflections of a Long-Distance Mentee

FARAH A. IBRAHIM

Clemmont E. Vontress is a renowned leader in the counseling profession for introducing the term 'culture' and its ramifications into the counseling endeavor (Epp, 1998; Jackson, 1987; Lee, 1994). He is also well known in counseling circles for simplifying existential philosophy to help counselors understand the human condition and for identifying the universals that help the counselor in 'connecting' with the client (Epp, 1998). I have been honored to know him and his work for over 27 years and have seen the profound impact his thinking has had on my own research and teaching. I wish to clarify at the outset that I have never formally studied with Clemmont Vontress. However, since 1980, when I met him at an American Counseling Association convention in St Louis, Missouri, I have followed his work. I have 'adopted' him as a revered elder and a mentor, since my research interests were in the domain of cross-cultural counseling and psychotherapy, and his philosophical perspective resonated with mine. It was a natural fit.

As an immigrant scholar, I am particularly impressed by Vontress's stance on understanding the global dimension of healing and curing. The biggest limitation of counseling theories prevalent in the United States in the 1980s and earlier, pertained to a national or provincial conception of theoretical frameworks that are useful for some European Americans. I believe that Vontress broke through the boundaries of American counseling psychology by applying existential philosophy and African indigenous healing strategies. The only books that addressed the global dimension and the theories and skills of counseling that I was aware of in the 1980s were by Torrey (1986) and Marsella and White (1982). There was significant research available in transcultural psychiatry and in cross-cultural psychology; however, it was not focused on understanding how counseling techniques or theories could be modified for use with clients across cultures. It was in the late 1980s that Allen Ivey revised the microskills format to include culture and intentionality (Ivey & Ivey, 2007) and provided a bridge through microskills. Previously, Vontress's pioneering work had started to push the boundaries and opened up the issue of cultural competence in counseling and psychotherapy.

This chapter will explore dimensions of my research, highlighting Clemmont Vontress's influence on my work. The following topics will be covered: the impact of existential philosophy on cross-cultural counseling, assessment, and treatment planning; multicultural versus cross-cultural counseling; making a case for the concept of multiple identities; the debate over multicultural counseling competencies; trauma and empathy across cultures; and Vontress's spiritual perspective and its impact on cross-cultural counseling.

Cross-cultural Counseling and Existential Philosophy

What is it that impressed me 30 years ago when I met Dr Vontress? I had gone to several learning sessions at the conference; however, when I came to Dr Vontress's session on 'Cross-cultural Counseling and Existential Philosophy,' I was truly struck by his proposal to link a complex philosophical perspective to cross-cultural counseling. His presentation highlighted how human universals help establish a powerful therapeutic connection. Personally, I had seen the cultural divide not just in counseling but nationally as a matter of value differences. Hearing the presentation in 1980, I realized that a significant factor beyond values is the concept of a philosophy of life that helps us accept or reject different perspectives or worldviews (Ibrahim, 1984).

Throughout my graduate studies, I was asked to understand the client's worldview without any information on what the concept meant. In reviewing the literature, I found no clear articulation of what worldview meant, or how I would know that I had understood the client's perspectives, beliefs, values, and assumptions, beyond my 'clinical judgment.' Clinical judgment alone can create an environment for cultural malpractice and insensitivity, especially when cultural issues are involved in the counseling and psychotherapy encounter (Dana, 1998). In researching 'worldview,' I had formulated a definition that focused on the core values one held as a result of the socialization process within a specific cultural setting (Ibrahim & Kahn, 1987). I was working on developing a values-based 'scale to assess worldview' when I arrived at Dr Vontress's learning session. It then became clear to me that worldview, a value-based construct as I had defined it, was directly linked to our philosophy of life. As Vontress (1982) defines it, 'Weltanschauung or worldview refers to a person's comprehensive personal philosophy or conception of human life in the universe' (p. 361). Several pieces of the puzzle of communicating across cultures fell into place for me.

Vontress (1986) also states that 'a manifestation of social class is Weltanschauung' (p. 222), indicating that our worldview and philosophy of life is influenced by social class. Later, I found research on topological structures of reasoning that also supported Vontress's contention, and clarified my own thinking on the connection between worldview, values, and one's philosophy of life (Ibrahim, 1984, 1985, 1993, 1999, 2003). The theory that evolved for me as a result of my exposure to Vontress's work, which no longer focused just on worldview, but on worldview in the context of a philosophy of life, was called the 'Existential worldview theory' (Ibrahim, 1991, 1993, 1999).

Existentialism is a philosophy that resonates with my culture of origin, South Asia. One of the most revered poets in the Indian subcontinent is Allama Iqbal, who studied in Germany with Kierkegaard and other existentialists, and I was exposed to his work during my teens. I have also found existential themes in the works of Rumi and Omar Khayyam. In collectivistic cultural systems, where people are surrounded by other people and have no personal space, there is a strong desire to focus on the issue of human existence and the purpose of life. There is also an unsettled sense of a lack of freedom to express one's truest desires because of the social controls placed on people to create an orderly and organized society. Existential philosophy helps to integrate the crowded collectivistic world along with a constant sense of loneliness and existential anxiety amidst a crowd for people in these systems. It also helps in understanding existential angst and frustration, due to the inability to be oneself, or do what one would like to, due to cultural requirements of obedience, responsibility, and the strict guidelines for behavior in traditional collectivistic systems.

Beyond its philosophical underpinnings, Dr Vontress's work also helped me to see the impact of the intersections of social class, nondominant group membership, history, and socialization, and the influence this can have on worldview and philosophy of life, and how these variables might influence the therapeutic relationship (Vontress, 1982, 1986). In family therapy, Minuchin (1974) brought to our attention the fact that theories of family therapy were not helping families from lower socio-economic brackets; and he introduced systems theory to work with lower-social-class clients. Vontress's emphasis on these variables led to his focus on cultural empathy. This was a critical piece for my own research, as it led to incorporating cultural empathy into the therapeutic process. Further, I recognized that without understanding empathy and its expression in varied cultural contexts I could lose the client. Vontress's focus on cross-cultural counseling instead of multicultural counseling was another major influence on my research.

Cross-cultural versus Multicultural Counseling

For me, the concept of cross-cultural counseling as articulated by Vontress (1979) is much more meaningful than that of 'multicultural counseling,' because in cross-cultural counseling we are confronting the fact that we are communicating with the other, who is not of my gender, culture, age group, class, profession, sexual orientation, ability level, educational level, and so on (Ibrahim, 1984, 1985). This statement reflects my personal definition of what constitutes cross-cultural encounters. The concept of multicultural counseling somehow conveys that we are all in a culturally diverse and pluralistic world, therefore we can all understand each other's issues and dilemmas – a flattening effect that can lead to some erroneous conclusions that would be fatal to a therapeutic relationship. In addition, as with government policies, several thinkers in the 'multicultural movement' only consider African, Latino, and Native Americans as 'non-dominant' groups. This is where most of the focus in research, training, and education is most evident.

Although I agree with Vontress (1979, 1982; see also Jackson, 1987) that there are human universals, culture-specific issues are also relevant and in most cases much more salient, and these get lost in the concept of 'multicultural' counseling, since there is an assumption that we are all multicultural; ergo, we should have no trouble understanding each other. A recent example is the case of a student who announced in a group course that she really could not handle 'yet another diversity exercise.' When confronted with the fact that she is in a program committed to social justice and cultural competence, she responded that she chose this program because of this specific emphasis, being a member of a non-dominant cultural group by gender (female), and a representative of a multicultural society!

In counseling we must learn how to connect with and assist culturally different clients. We can never truly be experts in multicultural counseling because we can never understand all the various cultures, cultural contexts, languages, belief systems, and so on. In multicultural counseling there is an assumption that because I have been educated in and learned about multicultural counseling or competencies, I am now effective in all contexts and with all people. It creates a false sense of security and may even retard one's growth as a culturally effective counselor, because counselors may become too confident about their presumed skills and knowledge and decide that now they can do no harm. I believe we must commit to learning to understand, from research in cross-cultural psychology and counseling, 'what works for whom, under what conditions, in which context.'

Taking the cross-cultural counseling approach retains a level of humility that is good for us to have as we approach people very different from ourselves, and some not so different from us, so as not to become oppressive or insensitive. I often caution my students that understanding the multicultural competencies or the cultural guidelines issued by the American Psychological Association for education, practice, assessment, and consultation (APA, 2002) is not enough, and cannot make us culturally proficient in working with the other. We must not only commit to a lifelong learning process that seeks knowledge about the latest developments (research, theory, and skills) in counseling and psychotherapy, and in addition incorporate a respectful 'cultural curiosity' to constantly focus on the issue of how a specific practice would work with a person from one cultural context versus someone from another. Cultural context here pertains to all the various aspects of our identity that are formed in multiple cultural systems and that create our 'multiple identities' in our specific 'world' (Ibrahim, 2007).

The Case for the Concept of Multiple Identities

Moving forward from the perspective of cross-cultural encounters also attunes us to the fact that we are not really one 'cultural entity,' as in my case, a South Asian. I am also a woman, socialized by the nuns in a convent school. I also grew up in a secular Muslim home among followers of Mahatma Gandhi, which focused on recognizing the worth of a person based on his or her character rather than color, religion, social class, country, and so forth. In addition, my worldview is colored by my sexual orientation, which is heterosexual and puts some limits on my ability to understand other sexual orientations. My identity is influenced by my educational level and my professional orientation, along with its ethics and values. All these categories and more (life stage, ability status, social class, languages spoken, spirituality, values, and philosophy of life) create cross-cultural encounters on many levels and dimensions. Once again, it is not enough simply to recognize ethnicity alone as culture, since every one of these categories creates a cultural context and forces us to negotiate a common reality before therapeutic work can be done.

Vontress speaks about culture having five dimensions or interacting concentric circles (Jackson, 1987). He speaks of 'people as products of five concentric and intersecting cultures: (1) universal, (2) ecological, (3) national, (4) regional, and (5) racio-ethnic' (1986, p. 216). This led me to focus on identity as composed of many interacting parts derived from our gender, culture, sexual orientation, spiritual beliefs, etc., as exemplified in the Cultural Identity Check List-Revised© (Ibrahim, 2008). These interacting parts of one's identity also have cultural relevance, since socialization occurs in a cultural contexts; for instance, my perspective on my gender is mediated by my cultural and personal experiences and is not similar to that of a woman who may have been socialized in Japan or Iceland. This recognition led to reformulating my theoretical framework to reflect cultural identity along with existential worldview theory (Ibrahim, 1991, 1999, 2003). Once I started unraveling cultural identity to make it measurable, and to reflect on more aspects of a person than just ethnic identification or gender, I started to focus on the assessment of multiple aspects of identity; research literature was lacking the concept of multiple-identities assessment, and only emphasized the strength of each aspect of identity. I built these aspects into the assessment process to use the 'Cultural Identity Check List' in counseling to address multiple identities of a client (Ibrahim, 1990).

Using the existential worldview and cultural identity approach, I always start with an exploration of the Cultural Identity Check List© (Ibrahim, 1990, 1999), then I focus on understanding the worldview (values, beliefs, and assumptions) shaped by the various aspects of a client's cultural identity. The last step in this process is to develop an idea of the common ground between the counselor and the client. I call this a 'shared worldview,' or a shared reality, and consider it a bridge to the client's world, using a strength model to work from a common ground, establish a therapeutic relationship, and then move to an exploration of aspects of a person's identity (Ibrahim, 1991, 1993, 1999).

Theorists who propose using only ethnicity or familial group culture may miss a significant amount of information about the client, leading to barriers to relationship building due to constant misunderstandings between the client and the counselor. It is possible that limited cultural complexity in the way we approach clients is the reason why the literature still reports a high number of terminations in counseling for people of color and other non-dominant cultural groups in the United States (Ibrahim, 2007).

The Debate over Multicultural Counseling Competencies

I agree with Vontress and Jackson (2004) and support the concept of competence in cross-cultural encounters, yet I fear, as others have stated before, that there are several concerns that emerge from the way the multicultural competencies are articulated (Weinrach & Thomas, 2002). The concerns that are paramount in the debate can be attributed primarily to the fact that the exclusive focus on the four ethnic-cultural non-dominant groups of the United States (African, South East Asian, Hispanic, and Native American) limits the usefulness of the concept of 'multicultural competencies.' Such an exclusionary conception very much reflects the issues that led to the civil rights movement and the drive for the rights of all oppressed people, in this society and globally. In a way, from an ethical point of view, it takes us a step back from the earlier conceptions of competence in cross-cultural encounters (Ibrahim, 1985; Ibrahim & Arredondo, 1986).

Such exclusionary thinking cannot advance the counseling profession because it creates hierarchies that, interestingly, reflect the cultural conditioning of society to hierarchical structures. Further, while it acknowledges that some are hurting more than others, and need special attention, it also leads to the colonial 'divide and rule' philosophy that creates conflicts and barriers between people in a society. Human suffering abounds among all categories of people, and as Weinrach and Thomas (2002) and Vontress and Jackson (2004) contend, all must have the right to competent, empathic, and caring interventions.

Another argument that critics have made against multicultural competencies is that the manner in which these were operationalized made counselors lose focus as they started equating several personal variables to culture (Arredondo, Toporek, Brown, et al., 1996; Vontress & Jackson, 2004). The argument against the current operationalization is that the clarity of the notion that culture creates contexts having an impact on individuals within it is lost when several personal characteristics are used to define culture per se. I propose that the confusion was created *by not clearly articulating how people in the same cultural system were culturally different, since their overarching philosophy and cultural identity appears to be the same.* In my writings I have proposed that there are several concentric circles that define one's cultural identity and worldview, and these pertain to all the different socializing agents that impact a person's cultural development (Ibrahim, 2003). The resulting articulation shows several worldviews and identities that may not have equal valence. For instance, there is an overarching national/cultural identity that all people within a nation or culture share; also, there are cultural groups within a larger system that share several characteristics with a national identity, but also have subcultural characteristics that are not common to national/cultural identity (Ibrahim, 1985; Ibrahim & Kahn, 1987). Culture does mediate many aspects of our identity, and culture is experienced differently by different people based on the specific configuration of their identity. For example, people in the same culture have different experiences as men or women, heterosexual or homosexual, able-bodied or having a disability, and so on.

However we might accept or reject components of the self based on values ascribed to certain personal characteristics, none of these characteristics can be equated with the overarching culture that people in a nation or an ethnic group may have in general; for instance, all people from the United States have cultural differences among them, but when a person from another country encounters an American, they can clearly identify them as such, regardless of their cultural/ethnic identification, gender, sexual orientation, age, life stage, religion or spiritual affiliation, and so on. In using the Cultural Identity Check List-Revised© (CICL-R), I recommend that the counselor establish with the client the salience of the cultural-identity variables that have the greatest impact on the current issue he or she faces (Ibrahim, 1991, 1999, 2003). Such an approach reduces the lack of focus that may result from emphasizing personal characteristics or culture in general. Personal factors are important when working with a client, but they do not necessarily represent their cultural identity per se.

I also agree with Vontress and Jackson's (2004) contention that any model that stereotypes people by representing them only as symbols of a cultural group or a subgroup is wrong and not feasible in a socially just world, and a profession that professes a commitment to social justice must be socially just in its actions. I also agree with them that we must, instead, focus on using a cultural framework such as the one suggested by the Diagnostic and Statistical Manual of Mental Disorders (DSM-IV-TR; American Psychiatric Association, 2000) cultural formulation, or Castillo's (1997) cultural assessment model, or my worldview/ cultural identity formulation (Ibrahim, 1999) and the assessment model for a pluralistic society I have proposed with my colleagues (Ibrahim, Ohnishi, & Wilson, 1994; Lonner & Ibrahim, 2007). I further agree with Vontress & Jackson (2004) that although our profession has made significant progress in moving forward with the concept of cultural competence, we still have a long way to go. Primarily, we need to focus on how different cultural identities can get the most out of a counseling intervention. Confusing cultural socialization and personal characteristics can lead to cultural oppression and creates confusion for the client and the counselor.

Trauma and Empathy in a Cross-cultural Context

Another major influence on my research and writing was Dr Vontress's seminal work on the 'culturally wounded healer' and the impact of racism on African Americans. This line of thinking greatly affected my research on trauma and especially on how members of non-dominant cultural groups experience racism, sexism, classism, and so on (Ibrahim & Ohnishi, 2001). The inability to relate to a client's anguish that may have no relevance for the counselor can seriously limit how empathic the counselor would be in such an encounter; for instance, the long-held belief and stereotype that all women are hysterical led to minimal attention being paid to their pain and anguish in the early days of psychotherapy. Vontress (1985a) confirms this fact when he states that 'the psychotherapeutic procedure relies then, on counsellor's [*sic*] empathy (Einfuhlung) and the inner resources of the client' (p. 27).

This statement identifies the importance of empathy, several levels of which Vontress has identified as occurring naturally because of the human condition and its commonalities. I propose that we move beyond our conception of empathy within our professional orientation to a concept of 'cultural empathy.' Cultural empathy reflects back to a client an understanding of a particular issue within the client's cultural context, using language that has meaning for the client. Therefore, to be effective, and for the response to have meaning for the client, a therapist must learn to understand, and show empathy as it is expressed in the client's cultural context, for that specific issue. Empathy alone from a within-culture context will not be helpful, since it may not get communicated to the client. We must learn the skills to effectively communicate with clients, especially in cross-cultural encounters – to indicate that we have heard them in a manner that is culturally relevant and meaningful to them (Ivey, Ivey, & Zalaquett 2009).

Vontress and the Spiritual Dimension

From the beginning, I have understood Vontress's approach as very spiritual because he focuses on the search for meaning and for connection with others (Ibrahim, 2005a). James Hillman (1996), in his writing on the soul's code, addresses spirituality when he notes that when we distill all the various religions and spiritual traditions to their essence, it comes down to the universal question of 'Why am I here and what is my purpose?' Carolyn Myss (1996) also notes that the common ground in most of the world's spiritual traditions is the ultimate question of the purpose of life and connection with self, others, and ultimately the divine. She shows how this is identified in the Jewish Kabbala, Hinduism, and Christianity. It is also clearly the focus of the Sufi tradition of Islam. When we get past the 'rituals' and other trappings (pomp, glory, 'show of faith' in communal settings, etc.) of organized religions, it really comes down to the same eternal and ultimate question faced by humans. According to Buddhism, the reason for this life and connection with self and others is to ultimately achieve divinity and one-ness with the divine (Myss, 1996). Such thoughts and beliefs bring us back to the existential notion of our search for meaning (Frankl, 1978) as a universal quest.

Vontress equates the counseling relationship to a positive connection between a helper and a client based on compassion for another human being (Epp, 1998). Vontress (2002) identifies

> four levels of empathy innate to the human species. First, universal empathy is species-related. Human-beings understand the feelings of others simply because they are members of the same species. Second, ecological empathy joins people who share the same physical environment ... Third, there is national empathy ... Finally, there is racio-ethnic empathy. (p. 129)

Vontress (2002) also expresses concern regarding the Western cultural notions of 'boundaries,' and believes that too many boundaries, and worries about them, show in essence a fear of intimacy and connection with the client. He argues that an ethical, professional counselor will not fear the intimacy necessary in a counseling relationship to help the client solve his or her problem, as long as the focus is not on fulfilling the therapist's own needs but on helping the client. Vontress gives the example that Sigmund Freud 'acted like a blank slate and free associated with his clients, because that was the degree of intimacy he could tolerate. In truth the client didn't need a blank slate or a word game but a loving human being to hear his [*sic*] personal struggles' (Epp, 1998, p. 6).

Radical as Vontress's notion may sound, it resonates with the teachings of Buddha and their focus on compassion and connection. I believe that if we do have a strong sense of ethics, we will not use the psychological 'intimacy' of a counseling relationship to fulfill our own personal needs or to violate the client's trust in any way. I believe this is very close to the notion of taking the client from a crisis to resolution and balance, as it is in child rearing, where it is the parents' responsibility to take the child from infancy and complete dependence to independence without emotional, psychological, physical, or sexual abuse or violation. I am committed to personally providing the most positive and meaningful learning experience to my clients with as much psychological intimacy (vulnerability on both our parts) as necessary within our cultural restraints and the boundaries of our professional ethics. In persistently requiring this connection, Vontress humanizes the counseling profession and gives us a path on which to travel with the other.

Understanding Vontress's stance on connection and spirituality (1979; Epp, 1998) opened up another research focus for me, and that pertains to the notion of 'spiritual empathy' (Ibrahim, 2005a). I believe that I must resonate to a certain extent with the client's spiritual beliefs, values, and assumptions, and not just reflect feelings and content, to be truly empathic and to have a meaningful therapeutic relationship. Spiritual empathy pertains to letting the client see and understand how I resonate with his or her spiritual assumptions. Interestingly, in an analysis of research on worldview for over 17 years, I have found research evidence that shows the connection between religious assumptions and their influence on cultural values and beliefs; therefore, it appears that religious and cultural beliefs are connected (Ibrahim, Roysircar-Sodowky, & Ohnishi, 2001).

Challenges and Future Directions

In closing, I want to reflect on future directions for our field and the challenges that it may face. I believe Clemmont Vontress's work will continue to have an impact and enhance our ability to provide culturally competent counseling across cultures. His influence will continue to humanize the profession by not falling prey to diagnostic categories as a definition of a person and advocating for humanity and care in the use of the DSM (American Psychiatric Association, 2000; Vontress, 1985a, 1986, 2003). His work will guide the generations that follow to champion all oppressed people and respond to them with empathy and care. The challenges that our field faces are the difficulty people have with complexity and the desire for a formula or quick fix to deliver counseling. Instead, we need to focus on understanding how our socialization and cultural background can create blind spots that we may not be able to overcome without reflecting on our philosophy of life, worldview, and cultural assumptions. Another challenge is our profession's historical focus on servicing the dominant group that has affluence and power. We see the same dynamic emerging now with the focus on some groups as being 'more equal than others' and requiring special privileges, while the truly oppressed may be overlooked. This trend needs to be confronted if we do not wish for Vontress's contributions to get derailed. I look forward to his continuing contributions to our field with great enthusiasm, and hope that we who look up to him will continue to educate the generations that follow on the importance of his perspectives.

Conclusion

In closing, I want to pay tribute to a powerful scholar who broke through racism and prejudice to reach out to the counseling profession with his gifts of insight and knowledge – no small feat for a man of his generation in the United States. After having worked at Howard University and researched the challenges and oppression faced by African Americans over the last 400 years, it is clear that he has risen above so much, and continues to make significant contributions today to the counseling profession. His gentle and caring spirit is a gift to all of us. Clemmont Vontress can truly be hailed as the father of cross-cultural counseling and psychotherapy.

REFERENCES

American Psychiatric Association (APA). (2000). *Diagnostic and statistical manual of mental disorders-TR* (4th ed.). Washington, DC: Author.

American Psychological Association (APA). (2002). *Guidelines for multicultural education, training, research, practice and organizational change* (p. 102). Washington, DC.

Arredondo, P. M., Toporek, R., Brown, S. P., et al. (1996). Operationalization of the multicultural counseling competencies. *Journal of Multicultural Counseling and Development, 24*, 42–78.

Castillo, R. J. (1997). *Culture and mental illness.* Pacific Grove, CA: Brooks/Cole.

Dana, R. H. (1998). *Understanding cultural identity in intervention and assessment.* Thousand Oaks, CA: Sage.

Epp, L. R. (1998). The courage to be an existential counselor: An interview with Clemmont E. Vontress. *Journal of Mental Health Counseling, 20*, 1–12.

Frankl, V. E. (1978). *The unheard cry for meaning.* New York: Simon & Schuster.

Hillman, J. (1996). *The soul's code: In search of character and calling.* New York: Warner.

Ibrahim, F. A. (1984). Cross-cultural counseling and psychotherapy: An existential-psychological perspective. *The International Journal for the Advancement of Counseling, 7*, 159–169.

Ibrahim, F. A. (1985). Effective cross-cultural counseling and psychotherapy: A framework. *The Counseling Psychologist, 13*, 625–638.

Ibrahim, F. A (1990). *Cultural Identity Check List© (CICL).* Storrs, CT: University of Connecticut.

Ibrahim, F. A. (1991). Contribution of cultural worldview to generic counseling and development. *Journal of Counseling and Development, 70*, 13–19.

Ibrahim, F. A. (1993). Existential worldview theory: Transcultural counseling. In J. McFadden (Ed.), *Transcultural counseling: Bilateral and international perspectives* (pp. 23–58). Alexandria, VA: ACA Press.

Ibrahim, F. A. (1999). Transcultural counseling: Existential worldview theory and cultural identity: Transcultural applications. In J. McFadden (Ed.), *Trancultural counseling* (2nd ed., pp. 23–57). Alexandria, VA: ACA Press.

Ibrahim, F. A. (2003). Existential worldview counseling theory: Inception to applications. In F. D. Harper & J. McFadden (Eds.), *Culture and counseling: New approaches* (pp. 196–208). Boston: Allyn & Bacon.

Ibrahim, F. A. (2005). *Lecture: Spirituality from a culture and gender perspective.* Corvallis, OR.

Ibrahim, F. A. (2008). *Cultural Identity Check List-Revised© (CICL-R).* Denver, CO: University of Colorado Denver.

Ibrahim, F. A. (September 2007). *Accessing and assessing our multiple identities.* Workshop at the Colorado Psychological Association: Society for the Advancement of Multiculturalism and Diversity, Denver, CO.

Ibrahim, F. A., & Arredondo, P. M. (1986). Ethical standards for cross-cultural counseling: Preparation, practice, assessment and research. *Journal of Counseling and Development, 64,* 349–351.

Ibrahim, F. A., & Kahn, H. (1987). Assessment of worldviews. *Psychological Reports, 60,* 163–176.

Ibrahim, F. A., & Ohnishi, H. (2001). PTSD and the minority experience. In D. Pope-Davis & H. Coleman (Eds.), *Intersection of race, class, and gender in multicultural counseling* (pp. 89–126). Thousand Oaks, CA: Sage.

Ibrahim, F. A., Ohnishi, H., & Wilson, R. (1994). Career counseling in a pluralistic society. *Journal of Career Assessment, 2,* 276–288.

Ibrahim, F. A., Roysircar-Sodowsky, G. R., & Ohnishi, H. (2001). World view: Recent developments and future trends. In J. G. Ponterrotto, M. Casas, L. Suzuki, & C. Alexander (Eds.), *Handbook of multicultural counseling* (2nd ed., pp. 425–456).

Ivey, A. E., Ivey, M. B., & Zalaquett, C. (2009). *Intentional interviewing and counseling: Facilitating client development in a multicultural society* (7th ed.). Pacific Grove, CA: Brooks/Cole.

Jackson, M. L. (1987). Cross-cultural counseling at the crossroads: A dialogue with Clemmont E. Vontress. *Journal of Counseling and Development, 66,* 20–23.

Lee, C. C. (1994). Pioneers of multicultural counseling: A conversation with Clemmont E. Vontress. *Journal of Multicultural Counseling and Development, 22*(2), 66–78.

Lonner, J., & Ibrahim, F. A. (2007). Appraisal and assessment in cross-cultural counseling. In P. Pedersen, J. Lonner, J. Trimble, & J. Draguns (Eds.), *Counseling across cultures* (6th ed.) (pp. 37–55). Thousand Oaks, CA: Sage.

Marsella, A. J., & White, A. (Eds.) (1982). *Cultural conceptions of mental health.* Higham, MA: Reidel.

Minuchin, S. (1974). *Families and family therapy.* Cambridge, MA: Harvard University Press.

Myss, C. (1996). *Anatomy of the spirit: The seven stages of power and healing.* New York: Random House.

Myss, C. (2002). *Sacred contracts: Awakening your divine potential.* New York: Three Rivers Press.

Torrey, E. F. (1986). *Witchdoctors and psychiatrists.* New York: Harper & Row.

Vontress, C. E. (1979). Cross-cultural counseling: An existential approach. *The Personnel and Guidance Journal, 58,* 117–122.

Vontress, C. E. (1982). Social class influences on counseling. *Counseling and Human Development, 14,* 1–12.

Vontress, C. E. (1985a). Existentialism as a cross-cultural counseling modality. In P. B. Pedersen (Ed.), *Handbook of cross-cultural counseling and therapy* (pp. 207–212). Westport, CT: Greenwood Press.

Vontress, C. E. (1985b). Theories of counseling: An intercultural analysis. In R. J. Samuda & A. Wolfgang (Eds.), *Intercultural counseling and assessment: Global perspectives* (pp. 19–31). Toronto, Canada: C. J. Hogrefe, Inc.

Vontress, C. E. (1986). Existential anxiety: Implications for counseling. *Journal of Mental Health Counseling, 8,* 100–109.

Vontress, C. E. (1988). An existential approach to cross-cultural counseling. *Journal of Multicultural Counseling and Development, 16*(2), 73–78.

Vontress, C. E. (1999). Interview with a traditional African healer. *Journal of Mental Counseling, 21*(4), 326–336.

Vontress, C. E. (2002). Empathy in cross-cultural psychotherapy. In P. R. Breggin, G. Breggin, & F. Bemak (Eds.), *Dimensions of empathic therapy* (pp. 129–134). New York: Springer.

Vontress, C. E. (2003). On becoming an existential cross-cultural counselor. In F. D. Harper & J. McFadden (Eds.), *Cultural counseling* (pp. 20–30). Boston: Allyn & Bacon.

Vontress, C. E. (2005). Animism: Foundation of traditional healing in Sub-Saharan Africa. In R. Moodley & W. West (Eds.), *Integrating traditional healing practices in counseling and psychotherapy*. Thousand Oaks, CA: Sage.

Vontress, C. E., & Jackson, M. L. (2004). Reactions to the multicultural counseling competencies debate. *Journal of Mental Health Counseling, 26,* 74–80.

Weinrach, S. G., & Thomas, K. R. (2002). A critical analysis of the multicultural counseling competencies: Implications for the practice of mental health counseling. *Journal of Mental Health Counseling, 24,* 20–35.

6 My Apprenticeship to an Existentialist: Clemmont E. Vontress and His Therapeutic Philosophy

LAWRENCE R. EPP

Alfred Adler remarked that he was able to develop his psychological theory only because he stood on the shoulders of a giant. His mentor, Sigmund Freud, was the giant who propelled Adler to a new level of psychological theorizing. In a similar fashion, Clemmont Vontress has been a seminal thinker in the field of counseling for over three decades. Many prominent academics and practicing counselors have proverbially stood on Vontress's shoulders; and, in being uplifted by this great thinker, they were able to see farther than they would have without his devoted mentorship.

It is a privilege for me, as a former student of Clemmont Vontress, to describe his intellectual impact on the field of counseling. I believe that Vontress's influence on counseling as it is practiced today is profound; and, sadly, like many of his generation, his humility never allowed him to forcefully promote himself or his ideas and achieve the popular following of an Albert Ellis or a Carl Rogers. Those of us who had the good fortune of being mentored by Clemmont Vontress understood his greatness through our personal interaction with him.

In a field where there are constant battles been theoretical schools and their theoreticians, Clemmont Vontress neither enjoyed direct conflict nor promoted a cult following of zealous students to clash with those of the competing theoretical schools. He was always remarkably balanced in his approach to those who disagreed with him. Even when he was harshly challenged for his views at conferences or in meetings with fellow academics, I never saw him reflect back the animosity or one-upmanship of his challenger. I think this was because Vontress never believed that his view was the one 'true' view; instead, he strived for theoretical accommodation and integration. I think his most remarkable insight was that all the theoretical schools in counseling ultimately say the same thing, but with different emphases and terminologies (Vontress, Johnson, & Epp, 1999).

A truly macroscopic thinker, Vontress not only integrated in his mind theories that others saw as irreconcilable, he also saw counseling as part of a larger cultural phenomenon. He sensitized our field to the importance of culture in the counseling relationship (Vontress, 1979). He understood that both counselor and client bring their hidden, cultural biases to their understanding of each other. Vontress (1971a, 1971b) championed the cause of the African American client when it was unpopular to do so; and he highlighted the role of societal oppression in the psychological suffering of minorities. His concept of 'cultural depression,' which expanded mental illness beyond an individual perspective, illustrated that psychological trauma can afflict entire groups who live under similar, adverse circumstances (Vontress, Woodland, & Epp, 2007).

Clemmont Vontress was a great scholar and visionary. I certainly will not be able to summarize his contributions in these few pages, but I will attempt to offer the reader a glimpse of this thoughtful man and his rich theory of counseling. First, I will share my impressions of Vontress when I met him over ten years ago, then I will summarize the striking elements of his approach to counseling.

Clemmont Vontress as Mentor

My first encounter with Clemmont Vontress was simply the meeting of a professor and a prospective graduate student. I met Vontress in 1993 in order to learn about George Washington University's doctoral program in counseling. While I was acquainted with Vontress's reputation at the time, my meeting with him was merely a routine visit to solicit information about the program he directed. I did not consider myself an idealistic graduate student looking for a mentor to shape my career.

When I met Clemmont Vontress, I was already a veteran of academia, with two master's degrees from respected institutions. A few of my ideas had found their way into a scholarly article that was being widely cited. I had no idea that my meeting with Vontress would be a pivotal moment in my life – a moment where my career, therapeutic philosophy, and circle of colleagues and friends would find direction. In Vontress I found a masterful counselor, a true mentor, whose wise, avuncular advice was a pleasure to consider.

When I arrived at Clemmont Vontress's office, I remember him having the bearing of a philosopher. Vontress was wearing a green turtleneck sweater, with a tweed jacket hanging behind his reclining seat. Books, of both counseling and philosophy, flanked him on each side – some classic, some new, some aged with tattered bindings from repeated use. There were many books on culture, anthropology, and psychiatry. In the midst of these books sat Vontress, paging through one and carefully contemplating its content. I was struck by his misty blue eyes, which radiated both a warmth and thoughtfulness, as he looked up from his reading to greet me.

Before my conversation with Clemmont Vontress began, I remember being distracted by two photographs that hung on the wall to his left. One was of Carl Rogers, the patriarch of the counseling field, and Vontress. The other was of Vontress standing beside a tribal healer from a primitive village in West Africa. The latter picture looked as if it were lifted from the field notes of a turn-of-the-century anthropologist. The juxtaposition of these two photographs, I inferred, was some kind of subtle intellectual commentary. I surmised that Vontress was lampooning the cultural relativity of great healers.

When Clemmont Vontress and I began discussing the doctoral program, I realized that I was in the presence of a gifted scholar. His ideas were novel and unlike those I had heard before. Vontress was unafraid to question the status quo of the counseling profession. Instead, he seemed to enjoy challenging the field to think critically. I wanted to understand who this unusual professor was as a person. While superficially Vontress looked as though he were an American of African heritage, that would be a very incomplete description of the worldly and multilingual professor I sensed him to be.

I slowly learned that Clemmont Vontress was a polyglot, a student of the world's well-known and exotic cultures, and an international traveler. Within each of his ideas, I could perceive a global perspective on human behavior. I sensed that he had made himself in the image of his existential philosophy – he sought to be a 'citizen of the world,' and not restricted to his ethnicity, nationality, or even the traditional confines of his profession.

From my first meeting, I was immediately drawn to Clemmont Vontress as a mentor. I do not remember the details of our conversation, only that it sparked the intellectual curiosity that had lain dormant in me for many years. Whatever we talked about, I remember feeling that if I 'apprenticed' myself to this unique professor and learned the philosophy of counseling and life that guided his therapeutic approach, I would come away enriched. Vontress seemed very wise to me; and I aspired to possess the same wisdom. What is more, he had an equanimity that I found admirable and comforting to be near. I would like to describe the tenets of Vontress's therapeutic philosophy from my unique vantage point as his student, graduate assistant, and 'apprentice.'

Clemmont Vontress and His Therapeutic Philosophy

When one works closely with Clemmont Vontress, either by osmosis or the power of his ideas, one becomes a convert to his existential perspective on counseling and the human experience. Vontress wins you over to the depth of this viewpoint and the sobering truths it espouses. Sadly, many counselors are unfamiliar with the existential approach and are unwilling to digest the dense prose that often describes its central tenets. Vontress was a willing simplifier and translator, who made existentialism more accessible and applicable to the concerns of the practicing counselor. In fact, he revealed in his scholarship that many of the humanistic schools of counseling draw heavily from existentialism, if unknowingly:

> [I] believe that other counselors already follow existentialism either unknowingly or through practicing counseling theories, such as Gestalt, Adlerian, or Reality Therapy, whose tenets were grounded in existentialism but whose names do not reflect this foundation. In fact, it is my contention that existentialism … [is] embedded in every culture and philosophical system. (Vontress, Johnson, & Epp, 1999, p. 33)

Clemmont Vontress's therapeutic philosophy was not simply a dry thesis he composed. Vontress lived and breathed what he preached. He formed close relationships with all of his doctoral students that became life-long friendships. In his mentorship of doctoral students, he modeled the core element of his therapeutic philosophy – that the depth and quality of a relationship with another human being is paramount. When one talked with Vontress, either formally or informally, one spoke with a very present and attentive listener who reflected back an inspiring mix of caring and wisdom that made one feel supported and truly understood.

If I were asked to simplify Clemmont Vontress's therapeutic philosophy, I would say its first tenet (Vontress 1979, 1996) is that individuals live within four dynamic 'worlds.' There is the 'private world' of the human personality where our secret thoughts and feelings about ourselves and others reside. It is the part where our desires, fears, and imagination intermingle to produce our unique reactions to the world that others may see as the 'irrational part of us.'

Second, there is an 'interpersonal world,' a part of us that is influenced by others, most prominently our parents, closest relatives, and friends. In fact, Vontress might say that each of us is the composite of our many contacts with valued others. In this respect, those who most influence us in life live within us – perhaps gaining an immortality as they live on as parts of our personality, both good and bad (Vontress & Epp, 2001).

Third, Clemmont Vontress believed that we are influenced by the 'natural world.' While many theorists took the physical environment for granted as a behavioral influence, Vontress felt that the conditions of our physical environment were critical to our daily happiness. Men and women who live in ghettos among squalor and filth have a different psychology than those who live in the pleasant surroundings of manicured suburbs (Vontress & Epp, 2001). Vontress felt that people cannot simply filter out the unpleasantness of their environment with cognitive tricks. They are inevitably influenced by their physical environment, which shapes their mood, personality, and ways of relating to others. His well-known concept of 'historical hostility' reflected his belief that multi-generational oppression, discrimination, and poverty shape the personality to be highly defensive and hostile (Vontress & Epp, 1997).

What is more, Clemmont Vontress believed that how we interact with our environment is a powerful determinant of our mental health. Our interaction includes our patterns of eating, exercise, and sleeping. These three activities are as important to our mental well-being as the content of our thoughts. Vontress decried the reductionism of many counseling theorists who argued that simply changing our thinking or family interactions would yield positive mental health. All aspects of the human experience are important. Thus, for Vontress, counselors must be holistic thinkers to be effective healers (Vontress & Epp, 2001).

Fourth, Clemmont Vontress believed that human beings require a 'spiritual world' for their mental health. They require the love and affection of a higher power, or invisible force, who gives the universe an ultimate purpose. They need to believe that departed loved ones reside in a spiritual world; and that, from time to time, these 'spirits' are able to intervene in the living world for the good. The spirit world provides a positive destination for all living things. Without it, life would seem tragically short and meaningless. The spiritual realm also includes intangible and transcendent feelings, such as love, empathy, universality, and altruism that bind the human community together in an interconnected web (Vontress & Epp, 2001).

Clemmont Vontress was not a religious man. I do not recall him worshiping a particular deity or espousing a faith, but he did believe that we each must formulate a spiritual understanding of life. Whether this understanding is a byproduct of organized religion or personal imagination, it is an important psychological defense mechanism that maintains our sanity in the face of life's tragedies and uncertainty. While Vontress believed counselors must use their client's spirituality as a healing tool, I believe that he himself lived within a scientific worldview. I never asked Vontress pointedly whether he believed in god, for I predicted that he would reply that human beings must have faith in an entity that gives their life meaning. Whether this entity is god, a higher power, science, or one's own self is immaterial, it is the act of believing blindly that ironically maintains our sanity. In a world where so much is opaque to our understanding, we must cope by creating meaning within the darkness that science cannot decipher (Frank, 1961). In other words, we must create our own pillar of firmness in the quicksand of real life.

Clemmont Vontress promoted the concept of holism – the notion that a counselor must evaluate all the 'worlds' of a client's existence. He was averse to any sort of therapeutic reductionism that posits an easy answer to happiness that may lie in positive thinking, renewed family dynamics, or the like. He believed the lines of therapeutic attack should consider all of the client's life activities (Vontress & Epp, 2001). He loved to quote Van Deurzen-Smith (1994) who eloquently summarized this idea: 'It is not possible to work exclusively in one [of the client's existential] spheres and neglect all the other aspects. Though clients frequently emphasize their struggle in one particular dimension, it is usually essential to ensure that difficulties in living get worked through on all dimensions' (p. 88).

Clemmont Vontress saw life as an intricate balancing act. The physical, interpersonal, private, and spiritual worlds each require attending to, or else their neglect will form a hungry vacuum that cries out for nourishment (Vontress & Epp, 2001). Each person needs to harmonize successfully the various existential worlds to form a consistently satisfying life – an integrated 'Gestalt' of living. However, Vontress realized that certain individuals will find this task more challenging than others, as there are great variations in the intellectual, emotional, and material endowments with which each person enters the world with (ibid.).

Although Clemmont Vontress believed in the sanctity of each human life, he saw that each life is unequal in its ability to derive the maximum benefits from living (Vontress & Epp, 2001). He posited that each human life begins at a different starting point, and fate deals each person a different life span in which to unfold their existential possibilities. Some will experience long and harmonious lives; others will face brief and nasty struggles ending in an unfair death (ibid.). Vontress believed that the goal of the counselor is to help clients face whatever existence fate bequeaths them with courage, hope, and a striving to find meaning amid life's suffering (Bingswanger, 1962; Boss, 1963; Frankl, 1962).

Clemmont Vontress was always mindful of our collective mortality. However unequal our existences in the four worlds, he reminded graduate students and clients not to lose their humility, as each of us inevitably moves toward death, in which all humans find their ultimate equality (Vontress & Epp, 2001). Human beings cannot stop time: the sifting of the hourglass's grains is the most rigid and unmerciful aspect of living (May, 1967a). Yet, this irrevocable movement enriches life and reminds us of the short chronological boundaries to our existence (Vontress & Epp, 2001). The striving to transcend death is among the creative forces behind our monuments, inventions, books, artistic creations, and products of sexual reproduction – all of which are in part conceived to gain individual immortality through the realms of descendents, ideas, or physical creations (Yalom, 1980). Vontress saw the prospect of death as liberating to the human spirit: 'It would appear that people who accept their eventual death are more courageous than those who deny it. They are decisive, can make choices, and are more likely to implement them, for they realize that their days are numbered ... They do not want their lives to be consumed by trivia' (Vontress, Johnson, & Epp, 1999, p. 51).

Clemmont Vontress believed that some persons become stuck in the past to distract themselves from their movement toward death (Vontress & Epp, 2001). The sad result is that this retrospective existence hampers their creativity and enjoyment of the present. It is easy to blame the past for life's unhappiness; it is harder to find the courage to move forward and make the best use of the time remaining (ibid.).

The Simplifier of Cross-Cultural Counseling

Clemmont Vontress's greatest gift to his students as a mentor was that he simplified the complex relational dynamics in cross-cultural counseling and made this counseling specialty engaging to the profession. When Vontress lectured, he often mesmerized the students in his audience with his bold concepts and their implications for the practice of cross-cultural counseling. He was able to build concepts that drew not only from psychology but the allied social sciences, such as anthropology and sociology. The most provocative of these concepts are briefly surveyed here (see also Vontress & Epp, 2001).

Vontress saw the tension between individualism and collectivism as the most important difference between American society and other cultures that impacts cross-cultural counseling. In America, individualism is a powerful cultural influence that shapes every aspect of behavior. It is a worldview that elevates the importance of individual achievement over group, clan, or family achievement. However, in many parts of the world, Vontress felt the competitive, individualistic nature of American society is not admired, but rather is seen as detrimental to family and group unity (Vontress, Johnson, & Epp, 1999).

Vontress often commented that many non-Western cultures despise America because its emphasis on individualism unintentionally threatens their collectivistic worldview. America's powerful television and print media are alluring to the young of other cultures, creating generational tensions between parents and their children, the latter becoming seduced by the American media and its values. In collectivistic parts of the world, individual pleasure and expression are strictly controlled in the interest of cultural homogeneity. The American media offers a competing worldview that contradicts many cultures' traditional values.

America is the cultural antithesis of collectivistic societies, where authority figures carry tremendous social influence. In these cultures, the head of the family assumes a powerful and respected role. Disrespect of parents, teachers, and other authority figures is rare, and when it occurs, is harshly sanctioned. The American media, in contrast, turns authority on its head; and although authority figures are presumed to be respected, the media seems to glamorize rebelliousness, disrespectful language, and disregard of one's parents and teachers.

Clemmont Vontress recommended that counselors need to ascertain the extent to which clients are the products of individualistic versus collectivistic socialization. He felt it was good practice to ask clients if there was someone at home or elsewhere who should be consulted regarding the presenting problem and its solution. To enter into counseling without respecting the head of the family, he contended, might impact negatively the outcome of counseling. The recommendations decided on in counseling might be rejected by family authority figures unless they are consulted early in the counseling process (Vontress, Johnson, & Epp, 1999).

Clemmont Vontress saw other elements of our culture that would go unnoticed by American counselors but alienate their culturally different clients. He believed that the American therapeutic style would likely offend many culturally different clients, since American counselors are often direct and confrontational, particularly those with a cognitive-behavioral orientation; and he felt that this is a reflection of the impatient and assertive American culture, and not the communication style of non-Westernized cultures. In other parts of the world, indirectness and subtlety are the vehicles through which sensitive, personal information is conveyed. A counselor must be aware of the type of communication style a culturally different client is accustomed to, since direct communication styles may be offensive in some cultures.

Not only is American culture too confrontational for some culturally different clients, Vontress argued that we may be overzealous about our privacy. In some cultures, privacy is not as cherished a value as it is in industrialized, urban societies. Individuals are less apt to be split into two personas – one private and the other public (Vontress, Johnson, & Epp, 1999). Vontress felt that the therapeutic concept of 'counselor anonymity,' whereby counselors refuse to share anything of their own life with the client, would be perceived as non-reciprocal and impersonal. Instead, he believed that personal questions asked by the client might be signs of respect that should not be discouraged. Culturally different clients often want to indicate that, through their personal inquiries, they value counselors as human beings (ibid.).

While members of other cultures may prefer a reciprocal relationship with their counselor, Vontress recognized that this does not mean that they have a psychological perspective on life that they can share. In many cultures, it may be considered improper or unhealthy to focus on one's own needs and aspirations as distinct from those of the family or community. The person is subsumed by the whole (Vontress & Epp, 2001). However, some clients do not assume a psychological perspective for other reasons. Clients who have had histories of oppression or exposure to violence may resist the psychological process of introspection because what they discover about themselves may be so painful that they do not want to share it with anyone (Vontress, Johnson, & Epp, 1999).

Many African American clients avoid psychological reflection for this very reason. Vontress argued that because of historical oppression and discriminatory practices, many African Americans harbor unrecognized negative feelings toward white Americans (Vontress & Epp, 1997). This phenomenon, which he called historical hostility, is a form of transference wherein a minority client's negative experience with a culture is projected onto a non-minority counselor. Vontress was expanding the Freudian idea of transference beyond its familial origins. In essence, human beings live in cultures as well as families that affect their unconscious reactions to others.

Clemmont Vontress decried American counselors' attraction to simple, reductionistic analyses of client problems. He felt that American counselors have made themselves into narrow specialists whose theories exclude important aspects of their clients' lives and who often pigeonhole their clients' problems into one of four groups: physical, psychological, social, and spiritual. Vontress felt that American counselors only address the psychological dimension of existence, and delegate to other specialists complaints in other areas – often considering it unprofessional to address issues that do not neatly fall within their carefully defined psychological bailiwick (Vontress & Epp, 2001).

In many societies, human beings and their problems in living are understood holistically. Persons from other cultures may seek out a Western-trained counselor for practical concerns that have no psychological dimension, and may not understand why the counselor must be restricted to his or her office when providing help. They may not understand why a counselor discourages them from talking about health problems or immigration issues as something they cannot help with. American counselors who focus exclusively on the psychological dimension of their clients' lives must recognize that, in many cultures, the psychological, social, physical, and spiritual dimensions of a person's life are not neatly separated (Vontress & Epp, 2001). Therefore, it is unfortunate that counselors often dismiss clients' concerns that would seem the province of other types of helpers, since this would be perceived as both confusing and alienating by some culturally different clients (Vontress, Johnson, & Epp, 1999).

Challenges of the Cross-Cultural Relationship

Clemmont Vontress's most genuine act of mentorship was reflected in his passionate distaste for stereotypes, which he instilled in his graduate students. He saw stereotypes, and the discrimination they engender, as the greatest challenge to the field of counseling and to American society. He always gently corrected his students' generalizations about clients that were based on race, religion, or gender. He was never impolite or patronizing, but he made it clear that he thought it was harmful to approach a client with a stereotype or cultural profile.

Vontress felt that differences in socioeconomic status, religious beliefs, and educational attainment confound one's ability to make any generalization about a group member (Vontress & Epp, 2001). In fact, he questioned the reality and purity of ethnic groups, asserting that everyone is ultimately 'multicultural.' He believed that we are all composed of multiple cultural influences and not culturally monolithic. He declared boldly at the outset of his last book, 'Approaching cross-cultural clients with a stereotype can cause as much misunderstanding as approaching them with stark ignorance of the cultural values they hold' (Vontress, Johnson, & Epp, 1999, p. 14).

Vontress saw stereotyping as a universal coping mechanism to manage the diversity of people we encounter. Because he saw stereotyping as a natural, human process that did not necessarily have a malicious intent, he urged all counselors, even the most tolerant and open minded, to be mindful of how stereotyping could enter the three important dimensions of counseling: the relationship, the diagnosis, and the intervention (Vontress & Epp, 2001).

Vontress was not absolute in his denial of stereotypes. He felt it was useful to recognize that in all cultural groups some clients respond to counseling similarly because of their socialization (Vontress & Epp, 2001). For many, the idea of introspection and self-disclosure is cause for anxiety. For others, historical hostility or prejudice toward the counselor's cultural or racial group may impede the establishment of effective rapport. Other clients may expect a friendly, relaxed, and personal relationship with their helpers, an expectation which may be threatening to counselors who perceive helping as a scientific enterprise demanding a prescribed social distance (Vontress, Johnson & Epp, 1999).

Vontress recognized that potential clients present too many perceptions and expectations of helpers for counselors to be aware of each possible therapeutic pitfall. Instead of relying blindly on therapeutic relationship prescriptions, counselors should realize that this relationship, as modeled in Western counseling textbooks, is imbued with cultural assumptions that may need to be altered creatively to serve the culturally different client (Vontress, Johnson, & Epp, 1999).

What is more, Vontress felt that clients from 'lower status' racial, ethnic, socio-economic, and national backgrounds are unaccustomed to relating to their 'higher status' counselors as equals. They often feel uncomfortable in a cross-cultural counseling relationship, because they feel they are being judged by someone who is affluent, more educated, and perhaps unfamiliar with the moral compromises and complexities of a less privileged existence (Vontress, Johnson, & Epp, 1999). In a few instances, culturally different clients may desire an unequal relationship with their counselor, owing to their culture's belief that professionals are wiser and able to provide accurate advice. While professionals do possess a wellspring of useful information, and clients may accord them the deference of a respected elder or guru, Vontress believed that it is important for the counselor to maintain a posture of equality with clients, so to empower them as agents of change, rather than foster dependency on the counselor (Epp, 1998; Buber, 1964).

Clemmont Vontress felt the counseling relationship should strive to approach a deep fellowship stressing honest sharing and mutual regard. It would not be an overstatement to characterize this relationship as one that generates a platonic exchange of loving feelings (Vontress & Epp, 2001). While underemphasized in other counseling theories, Vontress saw sharing and generation of platonic love as a powerful therapeutic force, essential to all significant relationships, not simply the therapeutic one (Rogers, 1995; Breggin, 1997).

In contrast to psychodynamic theorists, Vontress denied that the counselor is a blank slate awaiting transference. In fact, he felt the counselor's interpretation of transference is peripheral to the counseling relationship, since he assumed that seeking parental relationships or friendships with a counselor is a natural striving, disguising the very human desire for connection, bonding, and love (Vontress & Epp, 2001). To be effective facilitators of such authentic relationships, Vontress felt counselors must be truly willing to help others as a 'calling' and be at peace with themselves as imperfect and mortal human beings who can draw on their own negative experiences and frailties and share these with their clients (Epp, 1998).

Vontress felt that the counseling relationship should be spontaneous, unselfish, and respectful, and show reverence for the client's uniqueness. He felt counselors must love their clients as they love themselves. They must be personalistic in the counseling relationship. The person is more important than anything else in life – more than role, status, class, money, or attractiveness (Vontress & Epp, 2001). While ironic in a profession that prides itself on its caring, Vontress noted how radical the notion of a caring therapeutic relationship is to the professional counseling community. As he said,

> Over the years, my colleagues have come to see me as an iconoclast because I reject the notions of therapeutic objectivity and professional distance and declare them to be anti-therapeutic ... I believe that we must genuinely care about our clients as fellow human beings. I have come to despise the professional games and bureaucracy that we dispense as our means of helping others. No wonder clients often come to hate counseling centers; these organizations often reflect the insensitivity of the client's world instead of offering a place of refuge and healing. (Epp, 1998, p. 12)

Within the counseling relationship, diagnosis is the greatest challenge, since it requires the counselor to be judgmental within a relationship that is advised to be non-judgmental. Because diagnosing is actually a process of assigning a psychological 'stereotype' to a person, Vontress worried that counselors' cultural stereotypes – many of which are unconscious – would confound their ability to render accurate diagnoses. His intuition was proven correct by later research, which showed that minority clients are often over-diagnosed, and majority culture clients under-diagnosed, by American counselors in the severity of their presenting problem (Vontress & Epp, 1997).

Even if a counselor could free him- or herself of stereotypes, Vontress disliked the simplicity of DSM-IV diagnoses. He believed the human personality is by its very nature contradictory and not easily reducible to a single diagnosis (Lowen, 1980). For Vontress, human beings are both rational and irrational, good and evil, aggressive and compassionate, depressed and content, and so on (Vontress & Epp, 2001). Due to life circumstances, upbringing, and, perhaps, genetics, some have learned to keep these polarities tilted in the positive direction, but it is naive to think that most people live without pathology or evil--all live managing their negative polarities, so that they do not hurt themselves or others (Epp, 1998). Vontress saw psychological suffering as an inevitable part of what makes us human and what allows us to grow: 'Suffering is not sheer pain without meaning. It is often the most precious teacher in admonishing us not to revisit the past actions that brought the suffering upon us. In essence, without suffering, there would be no growth' (Epp, 1998, p. 8).

As easy and convenient as it might be for practicing counselors, Vontress felt they should resist the temptation to select a DSM-IV diagnosis and use this as the sole intellectual framework through which to understand their clients. He urged counselors to consider that our diagnostic system is culturally bound. Thus, a diagnosis of, for instance, depression, is not universal in its symptomatic expression, as some culturally different clients experience depression as more somatic and consider it a physical ailment.

Since Vontress disliked the oversimplicity of modern diagnosis, he worried that this same reductionism would seep into the counseling interventions themselves. While he respected the insights of the cognitive-behavioral approach that has emerged as the pre-eminent orientation, he worried that its reliance on 'cookbook' style therapeutic protocols would undermine the artistic and creative elements of counseling that are essential, since no two people, or the diagnosis they manifest, are the same. Vontress rejected the notion that psychotherapy is a science embodying facts, principles, and methods which must be memorized and applied in a standardized way to all clients (May, 1991). In fact, he believed that counselors who emphasize techniques too much run the risk of becoming technicians, not therapists; and their clients become objects to be manipulated in accordance with prescribed techniques (Ungersma, 1961). In a sense, a scientific approach to psychotherapy can often be unwittingly anti-therapeutic (Vontress, Johnson, & Epp, 1999).

Clemmont Vontress believed that not all counselors are equipped for the rigors of the therapeutic relationship. Being an intimate friend, in a therapeutic sense, is emotionally draining for the counselor, however healing for the client. He believed that counseling techniques are not for the client's benefit but for the counselor's, as they are a structure for the therapeutic interview as well as the filler or white noise to use when the counselor is unsure of what to do (Epp, 1998). Vontress argued that culturally different clients often do not 'see' the science or understand the techniques of counseling. They see and understand only the helper who is there with them – the other human being – who cannot substitute technique for true caring, because phoniness, superficiality, and indifference are recognized by members of every human culture (Vontress & Epp, 2001). Vontress expressed the universal need of all clients in a single powerful sentence that became the dedication of his last book: 'We are one human culture whose basic language is love' (Vontress, Johnson, & Epp, 1999, p. iii).

Conclusion

Just as Clemmont Vontress transcended the racial stereotypes that misrepresented him as a scholar and human being, he was passionate in his belief that stereotypes are a faulty lens through which to understand anyone. He saw human groups as always changing and possessing great diversity among their members. Although cultural differences can be sources of cross-cultural misunderstanding, when one scratches off the patina of culture from a human being, one finds at core a humanness that is universal. Clemmont Vontress believed that counselors should approach every culturally different client as a unique human being. Yet he felt they should not ignore the power of culture in the client's life. He felt clients should be understood through cultural concepts that exist over a continuum rather than in terms of popular stereotypes. He was very critical of theorists who stereotype ethnic groups, because he felt the degree of diversity within groups is not reducible to a profile or list of common characteristics.

Clemmont Vontress was an ardent existentialist. He felt that this approach was the most useful in helping clients of all cultures find contentment in their lives. He liked to correct existentialism's detractors: 'Existential counseling is not a process of morbid rumination nor a philosophy of resignation, as it is often misconstrued. Rather, it ultimately seeks to develop and enhance our relationship with ourselves' (Vontress, Johnson & Epp, 1999, p. 32). He believed that his approach to counseling offers a holistic view of life. He saw the interconnections between mind and body, culture and mental health where others saw only disparities. He saw the similarities between counseling theories and the futility of advocating one over the other when ultimately it is the caring and investment of the counselor in the client that is the ultimate curative factor. Vontress called his existential viewpoint an 'umbrella approach,' because it could encompass other psychological theories and be enriched, rather than rivaled, by them. At heart, Vontress wanted counselors to concertedly explore with clients all of life, not simply the random issues that emerge in a session, whose transient importance may only fade into the background of a larger scheme of life that has gone unexplored (Epp, 1998).

REFERENCES

Binswanger, L. (1962). *Existential analysis and psychotherapy*. New York: Dutton.

Boss, M. (1963). *Psychoanalysis and daseinsanalysis*. New York: Basic Books.

Breggin, P. (1997). *The heart of being helpful: Emapthy and the creation of a healing presence.* New York: Springer.

Buber, M. (1964). *I and Thou* (W. Kaufmann, Trans.). New York: Scribner.

Bugental, J.F.T. (1976). *The search for existential identity: Patient–therapist dialogues in humanistic psychotherapy*. San Francisco: Jossey Bass.

Epp, L. (1998). The courage to be an existential counselor: An interview of Clemmont Vontress. *Journal of Mental Health Counseling*, 20(1), 1–12.

Frank, J.D. (1961). *Persuasion and healing*. Baltimore: Johns Hopkins University Press.

Frankl, V.E. (1962). *Man's search for meaning*. Boston: Beacon Press.

Lowen, A. (1969). *The betrayal of the body*. Toronto: Macmillan.

Lowen, A. (1980). *Fear of life*. New York: Macmillan.

May, R. (1967a). *Psychology and the human dilemma.* Princeton, NJ: D. Van Nostrand.

May, R. (1967b). *Existential psychotherapy*. Toronto: CBC Publications.

May, R. (1975). *The courage to create*. New York: W. W. Norton.

May, R. (1991). Existence: A new dimension in psychiatry and psychology. In J. Ehrenwald (Ed.), *The history of psychotherapy* (pp. 388–393). Northvale, NJ: Jason Aronson.

Rogers, C.R. (1995). *A way of being*. New York: Houghton Mifflin.

Turner, V. M. (1986). Body, brain and culture. *Cross Currents, 36*, 156–178.

Ungersma, A. J. (1961). *The search for meaning: A new approach in psychotherapy and pastoral psychology*. Philadelphia: The Westminster Press.

Van Deurzen-Smith, A. (1994). *Existential counseling in practice*. Thousand Oaks, CA: Sage.

Vontress, C.E. (1971a). The black male personality. *The Black Scholar, 2*, 10–16

Vontress, C.E. (1971b). *Counseling Negroes.* Boston: Houghton Mifflin.

Vontress, C. E. (1979). Cross-cultural counseling: An existential approach. *Personnel and Guidance Journal, 58*, 117–122.

Vontress, C. E. (1986). Social and cultural foundations. In M. D. Lewis, P. Hayes & J. A. Lewis (Eds.), *An introduction to the counseling profession* (pp. 215–250). Itasca, IL: Peacock.

Vontress, C. E. (1991). Traditional healing in Africa: Implications for cross-cultural counseling. *Journal of Counseling and Development, 70*(1), 242–249.

Vontress, C. E. (1996). A personal retrospective on cross-cultural counseling. *Journal of Multicultural Counseling and Development, 24*(3), 156–166.

Vontress, C. E., Johnson, J. A., & Epp, L. R. (1999). *Cross-cultural counseling: A casebook.* Alexandria, VA: ACA Press.

Vontress, C. E., & Epp, L. R. (1997). Historical hostility in the African American client: Implications for counseling. *Journal of Multicultural Counseling and Development, 25*(3), 170–184.

Vontress, C.E., & Epp, L.R. (2001). Existential cross-cultural counseling: When hearts and cultures share. In K. J. Schneider, J. F. T. Bugental, & J. F. Pierson (Eds.), *The handbook of humanistic psychology* (pp. 371–388). Thousand Oaks, CA: Sage.

Vontress, C.E., Woodland, C., & Epp, L.R. (2007). Cultural dysthymia: An unrecognized disorder among African-Americans. *Journal of Multicultural Counseling and Development, 35*(3), 130–141.

Yalom, I. (1980). *Existential psychotherapy.* New York: Basic Books.

7 Counseling across Cultures: The Work of Clemmont E. Vontress from 1976 to 2007

PAUL PEDERSEN

Clemmont Vontress is one of a very small number of leaders in the field of counseling and psychotherapy who have continuously advocated the centrality of culture. He discovered the generic importance of culture early in his career. Since all behavior is learned and/or displayed in a cultural context, accurate assessment, meaningful knowledge, and appropriate intervention require that all counseling be provided in the client's cultural context (Pedersen, 2000a). The consequences of these assumptions are that all counseling is multicultural.

This chapter will review the ideas presented by Clemmont Vontress as an author over the six editions of the book *Counseling across Cultures* since the first edition was published in 1976. The ideas of Clemmont Vontress 'have legs' and stand the test of time quite well. They have provided a foundation through six editions of *Counseling across Cultures*, the first two editions as a chapter author and the last two as author of the foreword. This chapter will discuss the framework of Vontress's chapters in the 1976 and 1981 editions of the book and in the foreword in the 2002 and 2007 editions.

Vontress defines culture as a 'way of life' including the totality of an individual's 'artifacts, behaviors and mental concepts, including the visible and invisible, cognitive and affective, conscious and unconscious, internal and external, rational and irrational and coercive and permissive at the same time' (Vontress, 2002, p.ix). People do not always think about culture and take it for granted, failing to recognize how culturally learned assumptions shape our decisions. Our personality becomes the internalized culturally learned attitudes. Imagine a thousand 'culture teachers' surrounding you as a counselor and another thousand surrounding the client, collected over a lifetime from friends, enemies, family, fantasies, mentors, and mentees. This provides a image of counseling across cultures (Pedersen, 2000b).

The United States is characterized by cultural diversity, first described as a 'melting pot' that assumed ultimate assimilation, it later displayed a cultural pluralism that assumed a degree of tolerance, cooperation, and democratic variety. 'The term implied cooperation between majority and minority; it suggested mutual respect, appreciation, and acceptance of cultural differences; and it inferred that minorities would not have to fear repression or obliteration of their heritages' (Vontress, 1976, pp. 43–44). The ideals of cultural pluralism were tested by the civil rights movement in the 1950s and 1960s, when Americans of African descent demanded equal rights. This in turn led to other racial, ethnic, and social groups declaring their equal rights. The dominant culture reacted sometimes with humanitarian concern and sometimes with overt anger or hostility and exclusion. 'Because of the dominant group's intense reactions to real and imagined differences, primary variables, singly or interactively, eventuate into numerous potent secondary exclusionary forces, such as differences in language, values, education, income, housing, general culture and lifestyle' (p. 44). These differences became the rationale for excluding minorities while blaming the victims at the same time for being excluded.

Counseling across Cultures was published just as the civil rights movement was gaining momentum.

> In retrospect, it was a courageous publishing venture, because the dust had hardly settled from the social earthquake caused by the civil rights movement. However the timely book became a beacon for counselors, psychologists, and other psychotherapeutic professionals who were trying to find their way through the maze of problems they encountered in working from cultural backgrounds that were new to them. As the social and cultural landscape changed, the subsequent editions of the book continued to stay abreast with the psychosocial demands of the time. (Vontress, 2002, p. x)

The climate was changing from an ideocentric model of individualism toward an allocentric model emphasizing relationships (Pedersen, Crethar, & Carlson, 2008).

The book's sections included 'The Relationship between the Counselor and Client,' 'Psychosocial Barriers and Recurring Issues in Therapy,' 'The Problem with Diagnosis,' 'Conversation with Clemmont Vontress,' and 'Challenges and Future Directions.' This thirty-year-old framework by Clemmont Vontress provides a relevant point of departure for looking at contemporary counseling across cultures. In some ways we have not progressed far in these thirty years in finding answers to the problems we face. In other ways, however, our understanding of the problems themselves has become much more accurate and informed.

Almost all the ideas in this chapter belong to Clemmont Vontress, although I also share his perspective and have tried to represent his ideas faithfully. Think of this chapter as an interview, or perhaps a conversation, with Clemmont Vontress that takes place over a 30-year time period.

The Relationship between the Counselor and Client

The one necessary but not sufficient characteristic of competent counseling that appears in the research is a 'good relationship' between the counselor and the client. This factor is particularly important in multicultural counseling, where cultural bias frequently inhibits the formation of a good relationship. Vontress (1976) pointed out how cultural bias destroys counseling relationships when he says:

> The cultural bias implicit in counseling services available to racial and ethnic minorities combines with the client's cultural resistance to encumber his or her ability to communicate. Because many diagnostic skills are invalidated, attempts to identify preventive and remediative measures are often destroyed, and the benefits of counselor intervention are nullified. Differences in racial and ethnic background and socioeconomic status together with language difficulties and other factors interact to create problems in establishing rapport. More than usual attention should be paid to structuring the relationship, especially when the special population is typically suspicious of outsiders and when socialization patterns in that group encourage structured solutions. (p. 42)

Vontress (1976) goes on to specify some of the problems facing a cross-cultural counseling relationship then, as they do now. First of all, there is the problem of transference or countertranference, which may be conscious or unconscious. The client and counselor's previous experiences are likely to influence the relationships along with a multitude of other content and process factors. Second, there is the problem of diagnosis, given that the measures and indicators suggest that counselors are, to a greater or lesser extent, culturally biased. The solution is not to throw out all diagnostic measures, but to compensate for cultural bias in using those measures with culturally different clients. There has been some improvement in compensating for cultural bias in diagnosis, although it continues to be a problem. Third, counseling across cultures is a complex process, and to the extent that the cultural differences are more numerous or greater, that complexity is magnified. The counselor must attend to the client as a total person in all of his or her needs as defined by the client's cultural context (Pedersen, Crethar, & Carlson, 2008).

The counseling relationship is especially vulnerable to the dynamics of cultural bias in the various aspects of therapy. First, there is an issue of establishing rapport. Rapport describes a comfortable and unconstrained mutual trust and confidence between people. Vontress describes rapport as an emotional bridge in therapy. To the extent that the content of the interview is controversial, the bridge of positive relationship is more important in the construction of empathy. To the extent that cultural differences are greater, the construction of empathy will be more difficult. Sometimes the cultural differences are so oblique that the client may not be able to articulate them, but he or she can 'feel' their influence on the counseling relationship.

Second there is an issue of structure. The counselor will want to clarify his or her role to the client, especially if the minority client has had few positive experiences with other counselors.

> Therefore, the counselor working within such a context should structure or define his role to clients; that is, he should indicate what, how, and why he intends to do what he will do. It is also important to communicate to the client and sometimes to the client's loved ones what is expected of everyone involved in the relationship. Failure to structure early and adequately in counseling can result in unfortunate and unnecessary misunderstanding, simply because the counselor's interest and concern are unclear to the client, the client's parents, or significant others. (ibid., p. 43)

Third, there is an issue of resistance. Resistance occurs when the client opposes the goals of counseling as he or she understands them, and may manifest itself in a variety of ways, such as self-devaluation, intellectualization, or overt hostility. In some cases, the resistance may present itself like a game played by the minority client who is playing along' with the counselor. 'It is somewhat similar to a sandlot basketball game in which the ball is being passed to all players but one, the isolate. In this case, the counselor is the outsider' (p. 48).

Fourth, there is the factor of transference. Transference occurs when the person's reaction is similar to his or her reactions toward other similar persons in the past. The potentially negative consequences of transference are particularly difficult in the relationships between members of minority and majority cultures. The counselor needs to have both awareness and knowledge about how other past relationships might be influenced by and repeated in the interview.

Fifth, there is the issue of countertransference, wherein a majority counselor's reaction to a minority client may be influenced by previous experiences with other minority clients in the past. A counselor might quickly identify issues of transference but not recognize the presence of countertransference as well.

> Their professional training has tended to inculcate in them the notion that they should be imbued with empathy, with congruence and with a positive regard that is unconditional. Therefore they fail to admit that they are also mothers and fathers, voters, property owners, tax payers, Northerners and Southerners, and Republicans and Democrats – in a word, that they are human beings with a variety of attitudes, beliefs and values, conscious and unconscious, that invariably affect the counseling relationships that they have established with minority-group people. (p. 50)

Sixth, there is the issue of language. If the counselor does not understand the client's language, he or she will probably not understand the client's culture as well. Language, of course, includes gestures, postures, inflections, and knowledge about the client's institutions, values, and lifestyle. What is not said may be as important or more important than the explicit verbal message. Even the same words might have a completely different meaning in the client's cultural context. 'Paraphrasing, reflection and interpretation presuppose understanding the client's language. In order to reflect accurately what the client is experiencing and feeling, the counselor must be able to interpret nonverbal behavior. He must not allow skin color or accent to blind him to cues which would be otherwise obvious if he were counseling a majority-group client' (p. 53).

Establishing a good counseling relationship between the client and counselor is a necessary but not sufficient condition for 'good' counseling throughout the research literature. However, the means for establishing that relationship are not always clear. From the beginning Vontress focused on the necessary steps for growing a meaningful counseling relationship, and the central point was always to begin with the client's cultural context and not by imposing the counselor's own cultural context on the client. I have found experiential simulations useful in teaching counseling across cultures (Pedersen, 2004) and staying true to the perspective Vontress developed to provide classroom experiences for multicultural learning.

Psychosocial Barriers and Recurring Issues in Therapy

As a result of the civil rights movement of the 1960s, African Americans attacked labels such as 'disadvantaged,' 'culturally deprived,' and 'culturally disadvantaged' (Sue & Sue, 2003). Culture became a source of pride and a badge of dignity representing for each minority their distinct way of life. Removing the construct of culture from the ivory tower and the popularization of its definition had many implications for counselors and therapists. 'Previous to this rather significant event, "Counseling was counseling." But if there was not just one culture, but many equally viable ones, what did the new view mean to the work of counselors?' (Vontress 2002, pp. ix–x). Problems' designated healers, and their methods of treatment were now culturally defined and mediated.

There are many psychosocial barriers to effective counseling. Self-disclosure implies trust, and trust is frequently lacking in minority/majority relationships. Self-hatred by minority members of ostracized excluded or oppressed groups may include hatred of the oppressor as well as of the person him- or herself. Machismo may become an issue of honor, respect, and dignity for the minority client that is not easily understood by a majority counselor. Personalized rebellion against authority might become an issue among clients who perceive the counselor as an agent of authority. As racial and ethnic groups became more prominent, the idea of 'cultural pluralism' gained attention for its commitment to democratic ideals and its degree of tolerance.

> Cultural pluralism was put to a severe test during the great push for civil rights in the 1950s and 1960s when the largest and most severely excluded minority in the United States, Americans of black African descent, stood forth as never before with great pride in their racial heritage. Similarly,

> other racial and ethnic groups – American Indians, Spanish heritage people, American Jews, to name a few – reaffirmed their identities as they decribed the inequalities inflicted upon them by dominant group Americans. (Vontress, 1981, p. 87)

Counseling has been influenced by the lack of understanding and goodwill between minority and majority culture peoples. 'Indeed, citizens in the American society are separate and unequal – a fact evident throughout the social order. Whenever and wherever majority group members meet and greet members of minority groups, the likelihood of misunderstanding and ill will is great' (ibid., p. 88). The reluctance of minority clients to disclose is one effect of perceived inequality. 'In fact, many black clients fear being understood, for it implies engulfment, loss of autonomy, being found out, and that is the same as being destroyed in a society which is perceived as racist' (p. 97). The fear of being understood has serious implications for counseling, to the point that some black clients consider counselors dangerous if they understand too much.

These examples do not mean that counselors refrain from making recommendations, but rather show how most therapeutic recommendations are influenced by mainstream cultural values. Therefore, the biased recommendations might be antithetical to the values of a minority client's culture.

> Therefore the counselor must help clients to make a series of intermediate adjustments prerequisite to becoming comfortable with the demands and expectations of the dominant culture. Often the problems are related to guilt feelings associated with having left behind people who still suffer as they have suffered. There is also fear of achievement which is pervasive among disadvantaged minorities. This phenomenon upon closer inspection is essentially fear of the envy of one's racial and ethnic fellows. (ibid., p. 104)

The more counseling changes, the more it remains the same. Vontress (2002) identifies three realities that present barriers to cross-cultural counselors at present. The first of these is the American Psychiatric Association's *Diagnostic and Statistical Manual of Mental Disorders*, which dictates diagnostic labels and procedures for all clients. The examples of cultural bias in the DSM are widely reported in the literature. The second is found in biological psychiatry, where psychological problems are linked to brain chemistry. The medical model often presumes to be culture-free in defining standards of competence. The third barrier is the prevalence of managed care, wherein psychotherapeutic methods are mandated that reflect the status quo in counseling.

There are at least three recurrent problems encountered by minorities: economic deprivation, educational deficiency, and a negative self-concept. The unemployment rate for minorities far exceeds that for majority groups.

> On countless reservations and in many ghettos and barrios, more able-bodied people are unemployed than are employed. Economic deprivation, resulting from unemployment and low-paying jobs, in turn leads to a complex of psychosocial problems. For example, inadequate and high density housing fast gives rise not only to family dissension but to increased morbidity as well. Life becomes so difficult that short-run hedonism necessarily becomes one's goal. (Vontress, 1981, p. 102)

Each minority-group counselee should be perceived and counseled as an individual, and stereotypes of both minority and majority people should be avoided. At the same time, similar common problems are evident among minorities in the United States. The impact of these problems depends on many factors, such as geographic location and level of assimilation and deprivation. People who experience the status of victims over an extended period of time will soon come to view themselves in negative terms as well.

The problems of counseling across cultures are products of cross-cultural barriers that result in miscommunication, distortion of perceptions, and cultural contact under unfavorable conditions. The latter is likely to result in disharmony, increased conflict, and negative consequences. The task of a cross-cultural counselor is to construct favorable consequences for cross-cultural contact so that positive consequences will result.

Paradoxically, the more minority groups have proclaimed and manifested differentness from the majority, the more those same people came to resemble the majority.

> Their demands for acceptance and equality gradually resulted in the commencement of an imperceptible assimilation. Although declarations of differences are still heard throughout society there is simultaneously evidence of cultural similarities. These similarities have been ushered in primarily

> by our educational institutions, which have served as a cultural mixing bowl. (Vontress, 2002, p. x)

The Problems Associated with Diagnosis

Even though the minority client comes from a racially and ethnically different cultural background than the majority-culture client, the counselor typically depends on measures and procedures standardized for counseling majority-group clients. This puts the counselor – as well as the client – in a difficult position. As Vontress (1976) says:

> There are several problems inherent in using these instruments with minorities. The first one can be described as situational. For disadvantaged minority-group individuals, lengthy structured situations demanding assiduity are physically and psychologically annoying. Unusual surroundings, formal procedures, and unfamiliar people so characteristic of large-group testing environments, individually or combined, aggravate their annoyance and often account for anxiety sufficient to depress scores of reluctant examinees. (p. 17)

The testing environment can be changed, but language provides a second, more difficult problem. 'In general, language constitutes a handicap for minorities taking standardized tests, not necessarily because it serves as a people's vehicle for communication, but because of its role in the transmission of culture from one generation to another. As a major aspect of culture, it is also a barometer which reflects changes in cultural demands and expectations, however subtle' (p. 52). Language differences are indicative of larger global and significant cultural perspectives. The counselor needs to compensate for differences in the interpretation of assessment measures.

Part of diagnosis involves therapeutic recommendations about what should be done. 'In counseling disadvantaged minorities, the counselor must make recommendations that reflect explicitly or implicitly, directly or indirectly, an immediate or long range attempt to help the client move from his racial or ethnic cultural influences to mainstream status or living style' (p. 60). When the community itself is indifferent to the needs and problems of minority group clients the problems of therapeutic intervention are magnified.

Clemmont Vontress is very personable and easy to talk with. Therefore, it is hard to capture his charisma in a chapter 'talking about'

Clemmont Vontress. The real 'mensch' does not come through the sentences and paragraphs. To personalize the reader's contact with Vontress a conversational interview is included here. Imagine yourself sitting down with Clemmont Vontress and enjoying a conversation about his work and ideas.

In Conversation with Clemmont Vontress

Paul Pedersen (PP): How would you describe your most meaningful contribution to the field of counseling and psychotherapy?
Clemmont Vontress (CV): I think that it would be my development of an existential approach to cross-cultural counseling. It is a global perspective as opposed to a culture-specific or race-specific model. However, my contribution is what others say it is. An idea, good or bad, is only as good as it is useful to others.
PP: Who were your culture teachers and mentors?
CV: My culture teachers were my sociology professors at Indiana University. In the Fifties and Sixties, some of the best sociologists in the country were housed at that university. Yet, many of them lectured about the culturally deprived, socially disadvantaged, and the like, when they really wanted to say black people. As a student in their classes, I was confused. How could someone exist without a culture? Since I was the only black student in most of my sociology classes, I kept quiet. However, I knew deep down inside that they were wrong. Culture is a human necessity. My professors, although learned scholars, influenced me in a negative way. I was determined to look into the matter more deeply. Unfortunately, some of my counseling professors also echoed the views of the sociologists.
PP: What were the most challenging difficulties you faced in your professional life?
CV: Perhaps the most difficult thing in my professional life was remaining true to my own beliefs. Along the way, many of my close colleagues begged me to modify my views about various things. I remember when I was director of counseling in a predominantly black high school in the Indianapolis Public Schools, I wrote an article in a national publication. In it, I criticized slum schools in the United States. Some of my black friends came to me and told me that I should 'keep it down.' They were afraid that I would get in trouble or lose my job. When the superintendent of the school system read the article, he told me that he agreed with my views. When I was in the Senate of the American Personnel and

Guidance Association (now ACA), black colleagues petitioned the governing body to establish a separate division for minorities. I refused to go along with their petition, because I felt that the entire association should commit itself to counseling all citizens equally. I was afraid that a separate division would take the association 'off the hook,' that they would be able to dismiss minorities without feelings of guilt or shame.
PP: Have you ever had to choose between what your conscience said was 'right' and the professional guidelines for counselors?
CV: I feel that people should always go with their gut feelings. It is not easy to do this. We live in a democratic society, in which decisions are made by the group. We all want to be a part of the group. People often play along to get along. However, we as counselors are trained in interpersonal skills. We need to recognize the realities of living with others. This means that we should always try to understand where the other person 'is coming from.' That is, each person needs to empathize with the other, without compromising his or her authenticity. It is a delicate balance.
PP: What have been the most important changes in counseling and psychotherapy over the last 30 years?
CV: The most important changes in counseling and psychotherapy over the last 30 years are the almost imperceptible shift of what used to be called counseling and guidance to counseling and psychotherapy. Although some writers maintain that counselors espouse the wellness model and that psychologists adhere to the medical model, the differences hardly exist anymore. The main reason for the merger is external forces over which professionals have little control. First, we all use the same diagnostic tools, especially the DSM. Secondly, third-party payers look to economize. They search for the cheapest provider. Often that provider is a licensed counselor. Thirdly, counselors, psychologists, social workers, and psychiatrists often work in the same counseling center. There is a cross-fertilization of these co-workers in terms of theories, practices, tools, and procedures.
PP: What are the most important ideas in counseling and psychotherapy that have remained the same over time?
CV: Perhaps the most important thing that remains the same over the years is the recognition and appreciation of individual differences. A course titled 'Individual Differences' or 'Differential Psychology' used to be a mainstay in counselor education. Although the focus is no longer as obvious as it used to be, it is still very much a part of each counselor's training. Counselors also continue to emphasize the

importance of the relationship. The emphasis probably is an offshoot of the Rogerian theory, which considered the relationship to be the most significant aspect of counseling.

PP: What do you predict for the future of multicultural counseling and psychotherapy?

CV: I predict that multicultural counseling and psychotherapy as we know it today will no longer exist. Already, culture is being infused into the general curriculum. Already, professors who heretofore were not considered experts in culture are teaching multicultural and cross-cultural counseling courses. Culture has become re-defined to include the physically and mentally challenged, gays, elders, women, and others who used to be excluded under the definition. This means that professors may teach a course labeled cross-cultural counseling without including racial or cultural minorities as we used to define them.

PP: What advice do you have for graduate students in counseling and psychotherapy?

CV: I would advise graduate students to take care of their own preparation for entry into the counseling profession. They need to research the requirements for licensure in the context where they want to practice and make sure that the courses they are taking will enable them to get licensed as a counselor or psychologist. In traditional Africa, counselors are considered wise men, because they have lived long and embody the wisdom of the group. In the United States, counselors are their counterparts. Their wisdom comes from books, instruction, and other sources of knowledge. That means that counselors must be people who are broadly educated. They must know as much about human existence as they can possibly learn. This suggests that they read widely. They should not restrict their knowledge to what they learn in their university courses.

Therapeutic Recommendations and Interventions

In counseling minorities there is a tendency to reflect the values of the dominant majority culture, either directly and explicitly or indirectly and implicitly, as the preferred means to help a minority client. The counselor needs to anticipate accurately the short-term and long-term consequences of those recommendations and interventions from the client's point of view. 'For example, an Anglo counselor new to the black ghetto may recommend that a child be removed from his or her home which the counselor considers deplorable without realizing that by local community standards the home is quite good' (Vontress, 1981, p. 103). The counselor might need to make cross-cultural recommendations, but it is important to understand the extent that these recommendations have been shaped by the counselor's own culture.

What should be done? Counselors often ask for special techniques to use with minority clients. Others want to know if minority clients should be matched with minority counselors.

> Few counselors ever ask what they can do to change themselves; few want to know how they can become better human beings who, through the accident of birth, are racially and ethnically different. The failure of counselors to ask these questions indicates essentially why counseling minorities continues to be a problem in this country. Counselors are products of a culture which has been characterized as racist. In spite of having had a few graduate courses in counseling and psychology, they are shaped by that culture. (p. 62)

There is not just one culture to which people adjust. All of us are guided by 'culture teachers' from at least five interactive cultures (Vontress, 2007). First, there is a universal culture based on our physical and biological needs. Each of us has many of the same needs and wants for our survival as a species. Second, we share the same ecological context with countless other life forms. We live in what Vontress calls an 'existential relationship with our environment.' Third, we each belong to a national culture based on our political loyalties to a particular country and the peoples living there. Our national culture represents an allegiance to a way of life that we each value and protect. When new arrivals, such as refugees or immigrants, move to 'our' nation they accept aspects of our national culture which might be quite different from their 'back home' culture in exchange for the benefits of being citizens in that nation. Fourth, we are unique from the people around us according to demographic variables such as age, gender, socioeconomic status, and region of residence. Each region or special interest group defines within-group differences of our personal cultural orientation. Fifth, we depend on learning from and about the racial or ethnic group into which we and our families were born and socialized. These racial and ethnic groups are typically divided into minority groups and a dominant majority cultural group. Separatism is likely to occur to the extent that minorities are denied equal opportunity or feel rejected by their dominant group fellow country-persons. We are taught who we are by culture teachers from each of the thousand or more cultures to which we belong and this has a profound effect on counseling.

> It is no longer just a way of life impressed on the individual by biological, ecological, national, regional, and racio-ethnic forces that are passed on to future generations. It now also includes the way of life of any group that deviates from a perceived cultural norm. Many clients deviating from social standards in terms of sexual orientation, psychophysical challenges, gender, and age declare themselves to be culturally different and demand that they be viewed as such by counselors. Their demands are now reflected in current psychotherapeutic literature. (Vontress, 2007, p. 4)

Until the middle of the 20th century the topic of culture was defined in academic categories of anthropology or sociology. The political and economic forces of the ivil rights movement in the United States redefined and popularized the concept of 'culture' and multiculturalism into a cause for social justice. In this new definition of political activism the push for social, political, and economic equality – or at least equal opportunity – caused minorities to reject their identity as 'outsiders' in their own country. This tension between majority and minority cultures continues to shape our society and particularly helping services such as counseling by minority group members who rejected the many cultural norms and racist attitudes of the dominant majority culture. The dominant majority culture fought back and continue to oppose the ideals of pluralism in which minority- and majority-culture people have truly equal opportunities.

Conclusion

> In the first decade of the 21st century, most counselors attempted to achieve their goal by stereotyping minorities. That is, in general, professors lecture about the general characteristics of racial and ethnic groups and discuss their implications for counseling. The same is often the case in cross-cultural counseling research. Usually, researchers design research in which they compare racio-ethnic groups. For example, they compare most often groups which they designate as Hispanic, Asian, European, or African American. Little or no attention is given to the country of origin of the subjects, degree of acculturation, or the social class of the participants. Such omissions tend to call into question the value of much of the research.

> Indeed, cross-cultural counseling seems to be at the crossroads of an important and innovative movement. (Vontress, 2007, p. 5)

This book celebrates the insights and contributions of Clemmont Vontress as one leader in the fields of counseling and psychotherapy who has contributed toward our increased awareness, knowledge, and skill. Vontress has challenged the assumptions of both minority and majority group members, never avoiding controversy from either group, and following the ideals of a plural society with more accurately defined assumptions. Vontress has contributed a great deal to the meaningful knowledge and comprehension of cultural identity and the implications of that identity for the fields of counseling, both in the domestic and international context. He has defined appropriate intervention skills for counselors and psychotherapists sensitive to the demands of both minority and majority interests. Clemmont Vontress emerges as a preeminent culture teacher for all of us who attempt to contribute to counseling and psychotherapy.

REFERENCES

Pedersen, P. (2004). *110 experiences for multicultural learning*. Washington, DC: American Psychological Association Press.

Pedersen, P. (2000a). *A handbook for developing multicultural awareness*. Alexandria, VA: American Counseling Association Press.

Pedersen, P. (2000b). *Hidden messages in culture-centered counseling: The triad training model,* Thousand Oaks, CA: Sage.

Pedersen, P., Crethar, H., & Carlson, J. (2008). *Inclusive cultural empathy: Making relationships central to counseling and psychotherapy*. Washington, DC: American Psychological Association Press.

Sue, D. W., & Sue, D. (2003). *Counseling the culturally diverse: Theory and practice.* New York: Wiley.

Vontress, C. (1976). Racial and ethnic barriers in counseling. In P. Pedersen, W. J. Lonner, & J. G. Draguns (Eds.), *Counseling across cultures* (pp. 42–64). Honolulu, HI: University Press of Hawaii.

Vontress, C. (1981). Racial and ethnic barriers in counseling. In P. Pedersen, J. G. Draguns, W. J. Lonner, & J. E.Trimble (Eds.), *Counseling across cultures: Revised and expanded edition* (pp. 61–86). Honolulu, HI: An East West Center Book from the East-West Culture Learning Institute, Published for the East-West Center by the University of Hawaii Press.

Vontress, C. (2002). Foreword. In P. B. Pedersen, J. G. Draguns, W. J. Lonner & J. E.Trimble (Eds.), *Counseling across cultures* (5th ed., pp. ix–xi). Thousand Oaks, CA: Sage.

Vontress, C. (2007). Foreword. In P. B. Pedersen, J. G. Draguns, W. J. Lonner & J. E. Trimble (Eds.), *Counseling across cultures* (6th ed.). Thousand Oaks, CA: Sage.

PART THREE

Clemmont E. Vontress – Challenging the Traditions of Transnational Counseling Contexts

8 Clemmont E. Vontress and His Work within the Sociopolitical Context of the United States, 1950–2000

COURTLAND C. LEE AND JESSICA M. DIAZ

The purpose of this chapter is to highlight the seminal work of Clemmont Vontress within the context of United States history in the last half of the 20th century. The chapter explores the historical and social context of the United States from the 1950s to the beginning of the 21st century. This provides a backdrop for understanding the rise of multiculturalism as a discipline within counseling. The chapter next focuses on how the work of Clemmont Vontress impacted multicultural theory and practice within this period. An exploration of how historical events shaped Vontress's thinking and writing in each decade from the 1960s to the 1990s is conducted. Beginning in the 1950s, the chapter explores how racial segregation influenced Vontress's thinking as a student and beginning counseling professional. Continuing against the backdrop of the social ferment of the civil rights movement of the 1960s, the chapter discusses how Vontress found his voice as a major theorist on the impact of culture in counseling. This continues with the ferment of the 1970s, as the chapter discusses Vontress's leadership in the cross-cultural counseling discipline with his seminal writings. The chapter then explores the social conservatism of the 1980s and how Vontress's broadly based ideas about culture led him to an existential viewpoint with respect to counseling. Finally, Vontress's experiences in Africa in the 1990s, which led to his important work on traditional healing, are considered. A selected review of some of his major writings in each of these decades will highlight Vontress's significant impact on the rise of cross-cultural counseling.

Clemmont Vontress has been a major intellectual force in the counseling profession for more than 40 years. His early thoughts and writings about human diversity helped to shape the development of multicultural counseling as a major discipline within the profession. His work continues to play a significant role in advancing the important issues of culture in mental health intervention. Many of his writings throughout the years have become classic works, citied extensively in the counseling literature.

Insightful and provocative, Vontress has served as an important role model for scores of practicing counselors and scholars seeking to address the mental health needs of culturally diverse client groups. He has also been a powerful voice of cultural consciousness and reason within the American Counseling Association (ACA) and its divisions.

In order to appreciate Vontress's work, it is important to understand it within a historical and social context. His work has been profoundly influenced by events in the United States immediately following the Second World War and continuing through the last half of the 20th century. This can be characterized as a period of great change in American society that was spurred by a fundamental questioning of the nature of social exclusion for many groups of people. Groups that had been historically marginalized and oppressed began to demand, as never before, social, economic, and political inclusion within the mainstream of American life. These demands manifested themselves in large-scale social and political movements that ultimately forced significant changes to the country's landscape. At the vanguard of these movements was the struggle for racial/ethnic equality that served as a major catalyst for the efforts of other traditionally excluded groups to demand access, equity, and social justice.

1950s: The Rise of the Challenge to Social Exclusion

The civil rights movement in the United States effectively began with significant events in the 1950s. First among these was the landmark Supreme Court decision handed down in the case of *Brown v. Board of Education of Topeka* in May 1954. In this case the Supreme Court decided that segregated education for Black children was unconstitutional, denying the legal basis for school segregation. This case altered the traditional nature of American education and began a process of institutional change throughout society.

In 1955, Rosa Parks, a seamstress in Montgomery, Alabama, refused to give up her seat on a city bus to a white passenger, as was mandated by both tradition and law. For her defiant action, she was arrested and put on trial, which sparked a boycott of Montgomery buses by Black riders. The ultimate result of Parks's action and the subsequent bus boycott was a Supreme Court ruling in 1956 that segregation on transportation is unconstitutional. Her courageous act brought the Civil Rights Movement to full national prominence.

With respect to counseling scholarship, a pervasive theme of the 1950s was the minimal discussion of issues related to cultural diversity. As the counseling profession began to define its identity during this era, the theoretical and practical focus was almost exclusively on European-American cultural realities. An in-depth review of the *Personnel and Guidance Journal*, the flagship periodical of the American Personnel and Guidance Association (APGA), for example, reveals that little consideration was given to communities of color during this decade.

Clemmont Vontress finished his undergraduate and graduate work during this period and began his career as a counseling professional. Starting in 1958 he served as director of counseling at Crispus Attucks High School (an all-Black school) in Indianapolis, Indiana. While at Attucks High School, during this period of social change in the country, Vontress became a keen observer of the problems that Black students were having in school. It was from these observations that he first became interested in the concept of counseling across cultures. A major aspect of these observations became the basis of one of the recurring themes that he was later to explore in his scholarly work, namely, racial self-hatred. Vontress was on the verge of significant scholarly work as perhaps the most turbulent decade of the 20th century began.

1960s: The Civil Rights Movement – A Period of Major Social Transformation

The definitive decade in this crucial era of United States history is the 1960s, a decade of great social ferment and significant social reconstruction. It can be characterized as the height of the challenge to social exclusion. During the 1960s the civil rights movement reached its apogee, providing the context for new opportunities for Blacks and other Americans of color. Also, spurred on by the momentum of the civil rights movement, other groups which had experienced discrimination and exclusion became empowered and began to challenge the nature of their marginalization and oppression.

The 1960s are remembered for significant racial unrest and civil rights demonstrations, particularly in the South. Black people and their committed white allies actively challenged the status quo of racial segregation. The stage for the social action of the 1960s was effectively set in 1963 when more than 200,000 people, taking part in the March on Washington for Jobs and Freedom, gathered at the Lincoln Memorial. The march focused on the gap between American democratic principles and the status of Black Americans. It was during this march that the Reverend Dr Martin Luther King, Jr, delivered his famous "I Have a Dream" speech.

The momentum from the march on Washington led to the passage of two significant pieces of legislation by the US Congress that altered the restrictive structure of American society. The first was the Civil Rights Act of 1964, which made racial discrimination in public places illegal. The second was the Voting Rights Act of 1965, which outlawed literacy tests and poll taxes as a way of assessing whether anyone was fit or unfit to vote. The act struck down barriers to Black enfranchisement and was the capstone to more than a decade of major civil rights legislation.

By this time, Black Americans who questioned the effectiveness of nonviolent protest had gained a greater voice. More militant Black leaders, such as Malcolm X of the Nation of Islam and Eldridge Cleaver of the Black Panther Party, called for Blacks to defend themselves, using violence, if necessary. From the mid-1960s, the Black Power movement urged Black Americans to look to Africa for inspiration and emphasized Black solidarity, rather than integration.

While progress was being made in the halls of Congress, there was also significant action on the streets of American cities that called into question the nature of access and equity in the country. Riots in urban centers such as Watts in Los Angeles in 1965, Chicago in 1966, and Detroit and Newark, New Jersey, in 1967, underscored the nature of poverty and racism inherent in American society.

During this crucial decade, as Black Americans pushed for civil rights, so too did Mexican Americans. In 1968, for example, the Mexican-American Legal Defense and Educational Fund (MALDEF) was founded and became the most prominent civil rights organization in the Mexican American community. Significantly, the Chicano movement blossomed in the 1960s. This movement had roots in the civil rights struggles that had preceded it, adding to them the cultural politics of the era. It focused on the most immediate issues confronting Mexican-Americans: unequal educational and employment opportunities, political disenfranchisement, and police brutality.

Against this backdrop of significant social change, the counseling profession saw some major events which marked the beginning of an intense focus on issues of multiculturalism and diversity. During this decade there was an attempt to begin to develop specific theoretical and applied notions about the impact of culture, in particular race and ethnicity, on counseling.

Clemmont Vontress became a significant voice in this developmental movement. Spurred by his experiences as a school counselor with Black students, he began to publish a series of articles in the *Journal of Negro Education* dealing with 'negro issues.' In articles such as 'Patterns of Segregation and Discrimination: Contributing Factors to Crime among Negroes' (Vontress, 1962), 'The Negro against Himself' (Vontress, 1963), and 'The Negro Personality Reconsidered' (Vontress, 1966), Vontress explored issues of racial injustice toward Black people and how racial discrimination negatively impacted the Black psyche, ultimately contributing to racial self-hatred. He writes during this period: 'In effect, a large segment of today's Negro population may be thought of as "les enfants terribles," reckless *déracinés* who have been denied by the dominant group a place in the American stream of life' (Vontress, 1963, p. 237).

Significantly, his first counseling-related article, entitled 'Counseling Negro Students for College' (Vontress, 1967b), appeared in *The Journal of Negro Education*. In this article, Vontress details the problems that Black students face in applying for and attending college and the challenges inherent in conducting college counseling with this group. Vontress implores counselors to 'engage in aggressive counseling with the Negro student' (Vontress, 1969a, p. 14). In this type of counseling a counselor must aggressively counsel both Black parents and students about the need for college and that goal can be achieved.

Upon completing his doctorate in counseling in 1965, Vontress joined the faculty in counseling at Howard University. He went on to join the faculty in counseling at George Washington University in 1969. This was a period of significant scholarly activity related to issues of counseling Black clients. In 1967, his article 'Counseling Negro Adolescents' (Vontress, 1967a) appeared in *The School Counselor*. He stated there that considering race as an important determinant in counseling outcomes seemed important in view of the push toward integration in American society at that time. In this article Vontress provides a context for the issues which, given the rise of Black nationalistic sympathies in the

1960s, confronted Black youth in urban areas. He provides white counselors with specific directions for effective counseling with Black urban youth.

This was followed by three significant journal articles in 1969, including 'Counseling the Culturally Different in our Society' (Vontress, 1969a), 'Cultural Barriers in the Counseling Relationship' (Vontress, 1969b), and 'Cultural Differences: Implications for Counseling' (Vontress, 1969c). In these articles Vontress highlights the cultural realities, not only of Black Americans, but American Indians, Hispanics, and Appalachian whites as well. He attempts to redefine the terms *culturally deprived, disadvantaged,* and *underprivileged.* He discusses relationship building challenges with Black clients due to the distinct cultural differences between counselor and client. These differences are seen as distinct barriers to the counseling process and include racial attitudes, ignorance of the client's background on the part of white counselors, language barriers, Black client's unfamiliarity with counseling, the reluctance of Black people to self-disclose, and a taboo with respect to sex and race, particularly in a white female–Black male dyad. Vontress delineates specific awareness, knowledge, and skills that he deems crucial for white counselors to possess if they are to effectively address these barriers to the counseling process. Vontress (1966, 1967a,b, 1969a,b,c) placed an emphasis on recognizing the importance of cultural differences and adjusting Euro-centric counseling approaches when working with racial/ethnic minority clients.

During this decade, progressive ideas began to develop on how counseling professionals should work specifically with racially/ethnically diverse populations. Vontress (1969c) suggested that if cultural minorities are considered underprivileged it is because society excluded them. According to him, 'A more desirable approach in relation to cultural minorities would be to recognize and appreciate their differences' (Vontress, 1969c, p. 12). This thinking on Vontress's part was crucial to what followed in the 1970s, when multiculturalism took on wider dimensions as other groups pushed for access and equity.

1970s: The Expansion of Civil Rights Initiatives

After the dynamic social activism of the 1960s, the decade of the 1970s saw continued movement by groups that had been historically marginalized and oppressed. For example, feminism began to take flight starting in 1970, with the fiftieth anniversary of the passage of the Nineteenth Amendment to the United States Constitution, which legalized female suffrage.

Likewise, the Gay Liberation Movement saw tremendous gains over the course of the decade. As an example, the American Psychiatric Association removed homosexuality from its list of psychiatric disorders in 1973. Also, gay-rights ordinances were passed by several cities and a few openly gay people were elected to political office. Significantly, in 1979, approximately 100,000 people marched on Washington in the largest pro-gay-rights demonstration up to that time.

In 1972, the American Indian Movement (AIM), seized the Bureau of Indian Affairs headquarters in Washington. In 1973 AIM was involved in a standoff with federal officials at Wounded Knee, South Dakota, on the Pine Ridge Indian Reservation. AIM led protests advocating indigenous American interests, inspired cultural renewal, opposed the use of indigenous caricatures as mascots for sports teams, monitored police activities, and coordinated employment programs in cities and in rural reservation communities across the United States.

Within the counseling profession, the 1970s saw the beginning of a prolific scholarly progression with respect to multiculturalism and diversity. Clemmont Vontress was a leader of this progression with his seminal works. For example, in 1970 he published a classic article entitled 'Counseling Blacks' in the *Personnel and Guidance Journal*. In this article Vontress stresses that Black people are a sub-cultural group in US society. In this position Black people have developed unique environmental perceptions, values, and attitudes that are a reaction to racism. He goes on to state that such perceptions, values, and attitudes can impact the counseling relationship and make it difficult for a counselor to establish and maintain positive rapport with Black clients. Using Carol Rogers's ideas as a basis, Vontress offers direction for the in-service training of counselors that will help them to be more effective with Black clients.

This article was followed by the publication of Vontress's classic book *Counseling Negroes* in 1971, in which Vontress synthesizes much of his thinking about the culture of Black people and its importance to the counseling process. He attempts to introduce counselors to racial and cultural barriers they may encounter in counseling Blacks from adolescence through adulthood. Using his experiences as a counselor in a Black inner-city school, Vontress explores the issues of Black adolescence and adults that are necessary to understand in counseling with

Black clients. These issues included the unique culture of Black people, the challenges of self-concept to Black adolescents, issues to consider in preparing Black students for college, and Black male–female relationships. He also explores the nature of cultural bias with respect to testing Black individuals. It is interesting to note that Vontress titled the book *Counseling Negroes* as opposed to *Counseling Blacks*. In spite of the Black consciousness movement of the late 1960s and early 1970s, Vontress resisted using the term 'Black' in the title of the book. 'Implied in the racial designation *Black* is the idea that the person so named is proud of his racial heritage, that he no longer hates himself, either because of skin color or other physiological features' (Vontress, 1971, p. 2).

In 1972, against the backdrop of the Black Power movement in the United States, Vontress published an article entitled 'The Black Militant as a Counselor,' in which he discusses counseling relationship in which the counselor is a Black militant and his/her client is either white, a Black militant, or a Black person who prescribes to a more peaceful solution to racial injustices. He concludes that a Black militant counselor is probably more effective counseling whites than he or she would be counseling a Black client. He urges counselor educators to help angry young Blacks in training to accept both their humanity and their Blackness to be effective with all clients.

In 1976, Vontress was invited by Paul Pederson, Walter Lonner, and Juris Draguns to contribute a chapter to their edited book *Counseling across Cultures*. His chapter, entitled 'Racial and Ethnic Barriers in Counseling,' poses the fundamental question 'Should a counselor from one culture work with a client from another?' In answering this question, Vontress examines how racial-ethnic differences can trap both the counselor and the client between the world as it is and as it should be. He goes on to provide specific guidelines for counseling across cultures, the highlight of which is the important theme of attending to the client as a total person in all of his or her needs within a cultural context. A major emphasis of this chapter is that it is important that the client's cultural values define the counseling process rather than the cultural values of the counselor. This chapter is important because it brought the perspective of a Black counseling scholar to an important work on cross-cultural counseling.

The social ferment of the 1960s and 1970s can be seen coalescing in the ideas that Vontress expressed in his writings about counselors of one racial-ethnic group counseling clients from another racial-ethnic group. In particular, Vontress's writings of this period provide important caveats and suggestions for white counselors working with clients of color. Three particular works, 'Racial Differences: Impediments to Rapport' (Vontress, 1971), 'Racial and Ethnic Barriers in Counseling' (Vontress, 1973), and 'Barriers in Cross-cultural Counseling' (Vontress, 1974), underscore Vontress's entreaty to white counselors to be aware of cultural differences when working with clients of color. Vontress and other scholars focusing on issues of culture and counseling would be challenged as they moved from the 1970s to the 1980s. Sociopolitical events marked an end to many aspects of activism that had characterized the previous two decades.

1980s: A Period of Social Conservatism

With the election of Ronald Reagan in 1981, a period of social conservatism was ushered in that severely threatened the social, economic, and political gains that marginalized and oppressed groups had made over the past two decades. Despite the conservative climate in the country, however, significant strides were still made with respect to social and economic inclusion. For example, the decade saw the election of the first African American governor, L. Douglas Wilder of Virginia, in 1989.

Despite Reagan and conservatism, within the counseling profession, theoretical and applied concepts related to multiculturalism and diversity reached their apex. Leading this rush of theoretical and applied work was the writing of Clemmont Vontress. In his writings of the late 1970s and 1980s, Vontress called upon his early experiences with existential philosophy. Having spent time in France in the 1950s, Vontress was exposed to and became enamored with the salient ideas of existentialism being espoused by the philosophers Jean-Paul Sartre, Simone de Beauvoir, and Albert Camus.

In 1979, Vontress published his first article in which he attempted to place his ideas on cross-cultural counseling into an existential framework. Despite the conservative political and social tenor of the decade, Vontress was able to break important new ground in cross-cultural counseling theory and practice. As an example, his article 'Cross-cultural Counseling: An Existential Approach' (Vontress, 1979), which appeared in the *Personnel and Guidance Journal* in October of that year, was an early attempt to explore issues of culture in counseling from an approach that focused on the commonalities that human beings share rather than their differences. This important article viewed cross-cultural counseling from an approach that called for understanding cultural differences while simultaneously focusing on human similarity. Vontress states: 'I make no attempt to interpret existentialism as posited by various writers or to advance a set of techniques to guide counselors. Rather, I describe a philosophical vantage point constructed to help counselors bridge cultural differences' (p. 117). Significantly, a review of his writings during the decade of the 1980s reflects his ongoing interest in and advocacy of an existential approach to cross-cultural counseling.

1990s: From Multiculturalism to Diversity

The last decade of the 20th century saw an even greater appreciation and consolidation of issues of inclusion and diversity within the United States. In July of 1990, for example, the Americans with Disabilities Act was signed into law. In addition, the 1990s saw an increase in gay visibility in the mainstream media. With the growing appreciation of the importance of inclusion in this decade also came an explosion in technological advances. The computer and access to the Internet, for example, underscored the global aspects of multiculturalism and diversity.

The counseling profession during the 1990s experienced remarkable theoretical expansion that more fully embraced these global concepts of multiculturalism and diversity. With his reputation as one of the leading thinkers in the discipline of cross-cultural counseling firmly established, Vontress's work began to reflect this growing sense of global interconnectedness that was pervasive in society.

During the decade, Vontress began to travel to Africa to investigate traditional healing practices. In his travels, he had the opportunity to meet with a number of traditional African healers. Through his interviews with them he discovered some important links between their healing practices and contemporary counseling in the United States. In an important article in the *Journal of Counseling and Development* (Vontress, 1991), 'Traditional Healing in Africa: Implications for Cross-cultural Counseling,' Vontress explores the nature of indigenous healing, the role of the African family in health maintenance, the nature of the healing relationship, diagnostic techniques used by healers, specific healing techniques, and the selection and training of healers. He then considers the important implications of these aspects of traditional healing for cross-cultural counseling.

Significantly, by the 1990s Vontress had over 40 years' experience as a counselor and as an observer of the civil rights movement and its aftermath. In both roles he experienced the trials and tribulations that people of color (in particular, African Americans) had in dealing with racism and oppression. His experiences, both personal and professional, led him to attempt to explain a visceral reaction that people of color often exhibited in their response to racism. His 1997 landmark article (with Epp) in the *Journal of Multicultural Counseling and Development*, 'Historical Hostility in the African American Client: Implications for Counseling,' was an attempt to operationally define a pattern of responses that many African Americans exhibit that may stem from their prolonged subjection to racism and oppression in American society. He labeled these responses *historical hostility*. According to Vontress, 'The expression of historical hostility in African Americans can be as mundane as a daily defensiveness against non-Black and other African Americans, which may be misinterpreted as a hardness or unkindliness. But it can also escalate into a rage or lashing out in protest, unrest, or excessive violence at some real or perceived indignity dealt by the majority culture' (Vontress, 1997, p. 170). He offered counselors strategies for addressing this phenomenon with African American clients.

Future Directions

As the 21st century continues to unfold, Clemmont Vontress's work has some important implications for future directions in cross-cultural counseling, theory, and practice. In particular, Vontress has laid important groundwork in the areas of cultural differences, historical hostility, existential counseling, and traditional healing practices. His writings implore counselors to continue to consider cultural differences between counselor and client in the helping relationships. However, his writings on existential issues in counseling suggest that counselors in cross-cultural counseling encounters must also look beyond cultural differences to common human realities.

Vontress's stimulating notions on historical hostility among African Americans appear to have broad implications for any group of people who find themselves in long-standing oppressive or exploitative relationships with others. He provides counselors with a contemporary context for understanding strong negative emotions which impact inter–group relationships anywhere in the world.

Finally, Vontress's recent work on traditional healing practices in Africa provides important direction for expanding the concept of counseling. His work sheds new light on concepts of both illness and wellness and provides counselors with new perspectives on the interrelatedness between physical, mental, and spiritual health. As the counseling profession moves forward, these perspectives will produce interventions that encompass both Western and non-Western helping practices.

Conclusion

This chapter has chronicled the evolution of the scholarly work of Clemmont Vontress within the context of the major sociopolitical changes which took place in the United States in the last half of the 20th century. As societal barriers to full participation began to erode for many groups of marginalized and oppressed people, a series of transformations occurred within the counseling profession. These transformations have been characterized by the advent of new ideas pertaining to the process of promoting human development that underlies counseling as a helping profession.

Clemmont Vontress has been a scholarly leader, contributing significantly to these new ideas about counseling with his writings. A keen observer of the social and political upheavals of the last half of the 20th century, his writings generally reflect aspects of that era. In reflecting on his own work, Vontress identified five themes that he explored with respect to counseling across cultures: self-hatred, cultural differences, historical hostility, existential counseling, and traditional healing (Vontress, 1996). Each of these themes can be seen as a reflection of important social and historical events of late-20th-century US culture. In considering Vontress's work within a sociopolitical context in the United States, it is obvious that his writings are a major influence on the discipline of cross-cultural counseling. Significantly, this influence has transcended the borders of the United States to reflect the growth of counseling throughout the world.

REFERENCES

Vontress, C. E. (1962). Patterns of segregation and discrimination: Contributing factors to crime among Negroes. *Journal of Negro Education, 31*, 108–116.

Vontress, C. E. (1963). The negro against himself. *Journal of Negro Education, 32*, 237–252.

Vontress, C. E. (1966). The negro personality reconsidered. *Journal of Negro Education, 35,* 210-217.

Vontress, C. E. (1967a). Counseling negro adolescents. *The School Counselor, 15,* 86–91.

Vontress, C. E. (1967b). Counseling negro students for college. *Journal of Negro Education, 16,* 22–28.

Vontress, C. E. (1969a). Counseling the culturally different in our society. *Journal of Employment Counseling, 6,* 9–16.

Vontress, C. E. (1969b). Cultural barriers in the counseling relationship. *Personnel and Guidance Journal, 48,* 11–17.

Vontress, C. E. (1969c). Cultural difference: Implications for counseling. *Journal of the Negro Education, 38,* 266–275.

Vontress, C. E. (1970). Counseling blacks. *Personnel and Guidance Journal, 48,* 713–719.

Vontress, C. E. (1971a). *Counseling negroes.* Boston: Houghton Mifflin.

Vontress, C. E. (1971b). Racial differences: Impediments to rapport. *Journal of Counseling Psychology, 18,* 7–13.

Vontress, C. E. (1972). The black militant as a counselor. *Personnel and Guidance Journal, 50,* 574-80.

Vontress, C. E. (1973). Racial and ethnic barriers in counseling. In P. Pedersen, W. Lonner, & J. Draguns (Eds.), *Counseling across cultures.* Honolulu: University of Hawaii Press.

Vontress, C. E. (1974). Barriers in cross-cultural counseling. *Counseling and Values, 18,* 160–165.

Vontress, C. E. (1979). Cross-cultural counseling: An existential approach. *The Personnel and Guidance Journal, 58,* 117–122.

Vontress, C. E. (1991). Traditional healing in Africa: Implications for cross-cultural counseling. *Journal of Counseling and Development, 70,* 242–249.

Vontress, C. E. (1996). A personal retrospective on cross-cultural counseling. *Journal of Multicultural Counseling and Development, 24,* 156–166.

Vontress, C. E., & Epp, L. R. (1997). Historical hostility in the African American client: Implications for counseling. *Journal of Multicultural Counseling and Development, 25,* 170–184.

9 Clemmont E. Vontress and Multicultural Counseling in Canada

NANCY ARTHUR AND SANDRA COLLINS

When discussing multicultural counseling in the 21st century, it is important to consider what we have learned from the past, how it influences where we are today, and what we might want to take forward for future learning and debate. As one of the founders of cross-cultural counseling in the United States, Dr Clemmont Vontress proposed many core ideas over a career spanning more than 30 years that have informed our journey and helped to chart our future. In the current decade, academics and practitioners are questioning what is unique about the cultural context of their nations and communities, and what can be transferred and applied from others. The purpose of this chapter is to highlight selected contributions from Vontress's writings (1982, 1985, 1986, 1996, 2001, 2002, 2004) and to consider the cultural validity of his ideas for multicultural counseling in the Canadian context.

The Canadian Context

Canada is a nation founded on cultural plurality, and the country's population growth and economic future depends upon increasing rates of immigration. Immigration patterns during the past 30 years have resulted in greater heterogeneity, as source countries shifted from Europe to include southeastern Asia, Latin America, Africa, and the Middle East (Esses & Gardner, 1996). There are growing numbers of Canadians with multiple ethnic origins due to intermarriage between people whose families have lived in Canada for several generations. The number of Canadians who identify themselves as members of visible minority groups has also increased dramatically. Within the next 10 years, Canadians who identify as visible minorities are expected to reach 20% of the adult population and 25% of Canadian children (Statistics Canada, 2004).

Canada's national identity is defined by the ideal of welcoming people of all cultural backgrounds and encouraging them to participate actively in society while openly maintaining their distinctiveness. Although Canada's multiculturalism policy is often praised by people from other countries, it has been criticized for ignoring the many groups and individuals living in Canada who continue to face cultural oppression and discrimination on a regular basis. Similarly to other industrialized nations, we have a long history of systemic racial and ethnic oppression with Aboriginal people and immigrant populations. Many Aboriginal communities continue to struggle against the adverse effects of the residential school system, which has been equated to cultural genocide (Arthur & Collins, 2005). The current mental health issues of many Aboriginal people need to be considered in light of systemic racism and assimilation practices. At the same time, counselors need to be educated about the strengths and core values of Aboriginal worldviews while respecting the diversity within this population (Blue & Darou, 2005). The extent to which multiculturalism stands as a viable model for guiding the practice of counseling and psychotherapy has been debated (Moodley, 2007). Multicultural policies break down in practice where a covert hierarchy of preferred cultures exists, and political and systemic inequities continue to determine who is considered 'more' Canadian.

As Canadian psychologists and counselor educators, we have found that an additional challenge emerges as we attempted to draw from a predominantly American literature. On one hand, there is no doubt that American scholars have paved the way with a body of conceptual work on multicultural counseling that has informed professional education and practice in many other countries (e.g., Pedersen, 1991; Sue & Sue, 1990; Arredondo et al., 1996). At the same time, we need to be mindful of the cultural differences between Canada and the United States in terms of our history, cultural demographics, attitudes and values, and political and systemic norms that impact quality of life. Our views of cultural diversity, as well as views of professional roles and responsibilities are strongly influenced by our personal socialization and our experiences of professional education in different nations.

Culture-Infused Counseling

Culture is a fundamental concept in the lives of all individuals and in the interactions between counselors and their clients. Counselors need to examine their views of culture and of clients they define as 'culturally diverse.' Vontress stated that 'everybody has a culture, nobody is deprived of it' (Jackson, 1987, p. 21). However, he cautioned against placing too much emphasis on group affiliation and reminded us that 'humans are more alike than they are different. Therefore, counselors are advised to acknowledge the sameness of humanity and focus on similarities instead of cultural differences' (Vontress, 1979; 1986, p. 241). However, there continue to be controversies about 'who counts' in the focus on multicultural counseling.

We agree that all clients need to be understood in light of cultural influences on their unique worldview. Although it is critical that counselors be informed about historical contexts that have adversely impacted members of particular cultural groups as well as continued experiences of racism and other forms of oppression (Helms, 1994; Sue & Sue, 1990), we argue that counselors must be concerned about culture in the counseling process with all clients. The appeal of the universalistic perspective is that an individual's experience is not tied to one cultural identity by virtue of group membership. Rather, it opens up the possibility of exploring multiple cultural identities that are fluid and adaptable across relationships and responsive to multiple contextual influences (Collins, 2007; Stead, 2004).

Accordingly, counselors are charged with understanding both themselves and their clients from their unique cultural perspectives and contexts. This approach challenges diversity training that focuses solely on general group information. Although it is important to gain general knowledge about group differences, such training falls short in facilitating multicultural counseling competence. As noted by Vontress (1996), 'Cross-cultural counseling, in short, does not intend to teach specific interventions for each culture, but to infuse the counselor with a cultural sensitivity and tolerant philosophical outlook that will befit all cultures' (p. 164).

This balance between emic and etic approaches was highly influential in the conceptualization of our own model of multicultural counseling, developed to contribute to the general multicultural counseling literature and to focus on what it means to be a multicultural counselor in Canada. We named our model 'culture-infused counseling' (Arthur

& Collins, 2005; Collins & Arthur, 2007, in press a, in press b), to reflect our position that culture needs to be located centrally in the principles and practices of counseling with all clients. 'Culture-infused counseling ... is the *conscious and purposeful infusion of cultural awareness and sensitivity into all aspects of the counseling process and all other roles assumed by the counselor*' (Arthur & Collins, 2005, p. 16). Our model of culture-infused counseling is represented by three competency domains:

- Domain I: Cultural awareness of self – active awareness of personal assumptions, values, and biases;
- Domain II: Cultural awareness of others – understanding the world-view of the client; and
- Domain III: Culturally sensitive working alliance.

We advocate expanding the focus on ethnicity and race to a fuller range of cultural identity factors such as gender, sexual orientation, ability, age, and religion along with their intersections in the identity construction of clients (Arthur & Collins, 2005; Collins, 2007). However, it is not group membership per se that imbues understanding; the meanings and interpretations of culture derived by individuals are emphasized.

Culture-infused counseling emphasizes exploring multiple cultural identities that interact and shift in salience across relationships and contexts (Collins, 2007). Culture-infused counseling is a model that applies to all clients and all counselors in all domains of practice, including applied practice, counselor education, supervision, consultation, research, and advocacy for social justice (Arthur & Collins, 2005).

Multicultural Counseling Competencies

Since the 1980s there has been a focus in the professional literature on articulating core competencies for multicultural counseling. Readers are encouraged to review fuller accounts referenced in Collins and Arthur (2005, in press a). The American Psychological Association (APA, 2002) endorsed the *Guidelines on Multicultural Education, Training, Research, Practice and Organizational Change for Psychologists*, which proposes six core principles. The first two principles reflect the earlier competency frameworks as foundational guidelines for all practitioners: (a) awareness of one's cultural self and (b) knowledge of the cultures of others. Four additional guidelines focus on specific practice contexts: education, research, applied practice, and organizational development.

It is now widely recognized that culture is not something that applies only to non-dominant populations. Rather, each of us carries with us our personal cultural identities that impact the way in which we interact with our clients (Ho, 1995; James, 1996). Counselor self-awareness is consistently identified as the starting point for development of cultural competence (APA, 2002; Arredondo et al., 1996; Sue et al., 1992). Lack of self-awareness may result in personal and professional ethnocentrism that can directly or inadvertently harm clients (Pedersen, 1995). The consequence, as noted by Vontress (1982), is that 'the counselor finds fault with the client, not self' (p. 355). Further research and writing is required about the processes that foster self-examination and reflective practice (Collins, Arthur, & Wong-Wiley, in press).

The multicultural counseling competencies proposed by Sue and colleagues (1982, 1992, 1998) and Arredondo and colleagues (1996) have had a tremendously positive impact in shaping the direction of counselor education. However, the competencies have also been critiqued on a number of conceptual and content grounds (e.g., Collins & Arthur, in press a; D'Andrea et al., 2003; Patterson, 2004; Weinrach & Thomas, 2002; Reynolds & Pope, 2003). As Vontress and Jackson (2004) remind readers, 'disagreement is conducive to enlightenment' (p. 74).

A key criticism emphasized by Vontress is the exclusive focus of earlier multicultural counseling competency frameworks on the four main national minority groups in the United States: African, Asian, Hispanic, and Native American. Vontress (2001) comments on the increasingly pluralistic nature of our world and the difficulties of applying group-specific approaches.

> It is untenable to suggest that the same insights beneficial in counseling national minorities in Europe, Canada, or the US are also efficacious in counseling immigrants. The group approach that is generally used in the US is unrealistic, since immigrants come from too many countries, ethnic groups, and socioeconomic levels for counselors to acquire enough information about any single group that is useful in consultation. (p. 13)

Vontress (2004) takes a strong stand in arguing that the multicultural counseling competencies are potentially anti-therapeutic if the uniqueness of the individual's perspective, experiences, and presenting concerns are lost in an overemphasis on race and ethnicity. The group-specific focus also presents challenges in applying the competency frameworks in other countries, such as Canada, where demographics and group experiences differ. Vigilance in actively opposing culture oppression is essential; however, it must be balanced with recognizing the complexity of individual cultural identities (Collins, 2007).

Our view of multicultural counseling supports the expansion of multicultural counseling competency frameworks to be more inclusive. Although demographical information and group affiliation might provide some general knowledge, this information is severely limited in understanding individual client's needs (Arthur & Collins, in press b; Pedersen, 2001b). Vontress reminds us to consider the multicultural counseling competencies in light of how well they guide counselors to address clients' presenting concerns: 'The focus of counseling should always be on clients, not on a group with which they may or may not identify' (Vontress & Jackson, 2004, p. 78).

The multicultural counseling competencies (Arredondo et al., 1996) were intended as a starting place for reflection and further development. We have recently proposed an updated competency framework to support culture-infused counseling (Collins & Arthur, in press b) that offers an expanded definition of culture identities and links competencies to expanded professional practice roles and domains of practice. Our framework is conceptually based to address concerns raised about the integration of other areas of conceptual development relevant to multicultural counseling competence (Mollen et al., 2003; Ridley & Kleiner, 2003). Specific attitudes, knowledge, and skills are identified to promote effective practice from the moment of initial encounter to termination (Arthur & Collins, 2005; Collins & Arthur, in press a).

Strengthening the Working Alliance in Multicultural Counseling

In our model of culture-infused counseling, we propose that the construct of the working alliance replace the earlier, narrow focus on appropriate intervention strategies and techniques as the third core competency domain (Arthur & Collins, 2005; in press a, in press b). The working alliance is a pantheoretical and superordinate construct that provides the conceptual link between cultural awareness (of self and of client) and the counseling process. Intervention strategies and techniques may then be assessed in terms of their contribution to the purposeful and collaborative work that characterizes a culturally sensitive working alliance.

We were struck by the attention to the therapeutic alliance that pervades Vontress's writing. Three areas are selected for discussion in this chapter. First, his writing alerts us to the challenges of establishing a trusting relationship in light of historical oppression. Trust may be impeded in a current therapeutic relationship due to legitimate hostility on part of the client about broader dominant and non-dominant group dynamics (Vontress, 1996).

We appreciated the vivid descriptions of the potential influences of historical oppression on the therapeutic alliance, which were later expanded upon by writers such as Pedersen (1995) and Ridley (1995) in talking about unintentional racism and, in our more recent work, cultural oppression (Arthur & Collins, 2005). This is perhaps one of the most difficult journeys to invite counseling students and practicing professionals to take. We must all examine not only who we are as cultural beings, but how our own cultural group affiliations position us relative to both current and historical events at the local, national, and international levels. There is a fine line between facilitating self-examination and ownership of responsibility for overcoming historical oppression and fostering defensive reactions, expressed in statements such as 'It's not my fault, that happened a long time ago,' 'I feel so guilty, I feel frozen when confronted with blame by my clients,' or ' I avoid these issues unless the client brings it up.' More examples are needed of teaching and learning methodologies that encourage deep reflection and strengthening of the working alliance.

Second, Vontress's writing has provided provocative and direct challenges related to interpersonal judgment (Vontress, 1982). For example, he claims that 'the client and counselor continuously take stock of each other' (p. 360). This infers that counselors must be skilled at recognizing the value bases that form their judgments and at uncovering and working with the judgments made by their clients. Vontress's (1986) writing about cultural transference and countertransference illuminates how our prior experiences are like suitcases that must be opened and examined so that our limited worldviews do not lead us to blame clients for their problems.

Professional judgment is also required to match therapeutic approaches with client expectations, as determined from their cultural norms. At a minimum, clients need to be educated about counseling and respective counselor-client roles so that their culturally derived judgments do not impede their success. However, insisting that clients fit into Western notions of helping may lead many clients to believe that they have received little help at all. Vontress notes that many people from traditional societies 'are disappointed with authority figures who force them to solve their own problems' (1986, p. 225). He reminds us that preference for help-givers and help-giving is culturally determined.

Third, Vontress suggests a wonderful metaphor related to the working alliance: 'Counseling is most productive when clients psychologically surrender themselves to the process' (Vontress, 1982, p. 347). We interpret the metaphor of *therapeutic surrender* to mean that full engagement in the counsellor-client therapeutic alliance in multicultural counseling requires a deep level of interpersonal trust, respect, and empathy on the part of both the client and the counselor. What would it mean for counselors to surrender themselves to the process of cross-cultural engagement? Are we prepared to model what we ask of clients? Vontress characterizes counselors as 'smugglers of middle-class values' (1986, p. 226), who are tuned out by their clients and often lack capacity to tune into their clients' worldviews. He reminds us, 'Although it is usually described in benevolent terms, counseling is in fact a power relationship' (p. 231). Counselors need to actively address their capacity for experiencing cultural empathy and for communicating empathy to clients (Vontress, 2002). Vontress challenges counselors to consider how far they will go to join with their clients.

Social Class and Multicultural Counseling

In spite of the expanded definition of culture, socioeconomic status has been marginalized in both feminist and multicultural dialogues (Collins, 2007). Vontress made a major contribution by heightening awareness of the significant influences of social class on mental health and human behavior. Counselors need to be informed about economic disparities within society and their influence on personal identity, client issues, and available resources. Vontress (1982, 1986) expanded on the relationship of social class to worldview and provided practical examples and considerations for counseling across social class. His contributions on the influences of social class challenge counselors to deepen their understanding of others and, more critically, to examine the impact of class on their own worldview. Social class may significantly alter the very meaning of other cultural factors, such as gender or ethnicity (Collins, 2007).

In 2000, the APA adopted the 'Resolution on Poverty and Socioeconomic Status,' recognizing poverty as detrimental to psychological health and urging psychologists to 'treat and address the needs of low-income individuals and families' (p. 4). The resolution included 17 recommendations to address poverty, classism, public policy, and practitioner competence and training. The Canadian Code of Ethics for Psychologists (Canadian Psychological Association [CPA], 2000) states that the psychologist's 'greatest responsibility is to protect the welfare of those in the most vulnerable position' (p. 20). The code of ethics of both the CPA (2000) and the Canadian Counseling and Psychotherapy Association (CCPA, 2007 identify socioeconomic status as a key variable in defining client diversity.

There is a notable absence of dialogue about socioeconomic status and the influence of social class on client concerns in the Canadian psychology and counseling literature (Pope & Arthur, 2009). More than 15% of Canadians may be classified as low-income (Statistics Canada, 2006), with much higher rates among unattached seniors, families led by single mothers, members of visible minorities, and people with disabilities (National Council of Welfare, 2006). When compared with other economically developed nations, Canada exhibits a demographic profile that is characterized not only by relatively high poverty rates but also by poverty persistence (Valetta, 2006). The lack of economic and social mobility among low-income Canadians is a major determinant of poor physical and mental health (Canadian Institute for Health Information, 2004). Counsellors need to understand the adverse impacts of poverty for mental health and take greater responsibility in advocating for individuals and families (Pope & Arthur, 2009). Following Vontress's lead, we need to incorporate social class into multicultural counseling curriculum related to privilege, power, language, and counseling processes.

Challenges and Future Directions: The Call for Social Justice

Although some critics argue that multicultural counseling competency frameworks already go too far in pushing a social justice political agenda (Weinrach & Thomas, 2002), we join those who support this agenda (Arredondo & Toporek, 2004). We can no longer ignore the direct link between culture and contextual factors that influence client problems. As noted by Vontress (1982), 'Problems in living usually are rooted in social context' (p. 361). The surge in attention to social justice issues in multicultural counseling challenges counselors to consider their roles and responsibilities for addressing social structures that adversely impact clients' health and wellbeing (Vera & Shin, 2006). We have adopted the axiom *the professional is political* in our writing as the basis of linking culture and social justice issues in professional practice (Arthur & Collins, 2005).

Vontress (1982) was clearly passionate about exposing the adverse impacts of social class, including intersections with race and ethnicity, on mental health. He believed that counseling had a fundamental role in addressing the social conditions that influenced client concerns. This is evident when he described the purpose of counseling:

> The goal of counseling is to assist the recipients directly or indirectly in adjusting to or otherwise negotiating environments that influence their own or someone else's psychological well-being. To accomplish this, counselors must relate and communicate with their clients; determine their state of adjustment to one or more environments; decide alone or with them the course of action needed to improve their current or future situation, while simultaneously anticipating the outcome of therapeutic recommendations; and intervene at some level of competency to assist the clients. (p. 346)

He reminded us that we are all influenced by our social environments and that our actions are inextricably linked to social structures. Counselors are challenged to expand their repertoire of counselling interventions to include systemic change. Although Vontress (1986) targets systemic change in counseling, he is also realistic about the barriers and personal costs to counselors who act as social change agents.

> Trying to adjust to the new culture by changing it to a more comfortable fit is usually not possible. That is not to say that cross-cultural counselors should not be change agents in their attempts to improve conditions that have a negative impact on culturally different clients. It is imperative, however, to recognize what is immediately changeable and what is not. Counselors who attack 'the system' in blind frustration on behalf of their clients run the risk of endangering their own mental health. (p. 242)

There is clearly a balance between accepting responsibility for actively addressing social injustices, and doing so in a way that optimizes the chance of success in promoting systemic change.

In their critique of the multicultural counseling competencies (Sue et al., 1982; Arredondo et al., 1996), Vontress and Jackson (2004) encourage mental health professions to embrace a social activist political agenda through the democratic process. However, they caution that 'mental health counselors should not turn counseling sessions into encounters in which they impose their activist agendas on their clients (see Vontress, 1972)' (p. 76). Counselors should be mindful of his strong commitment to making sure that client needs are driving the direction of counseling interventions as we move forward to define the professional processes related to social justice.

The discussion about social justice counseling as a 'fifth force' (Ratts, D'Andrea, & Arredondo, 2004) needs to be matched with explicit competencies and examples of best practices for multicultural counseling. The *Advocacy Competencies* (Lewis, Arnold, House, & Torporek, 2002), endorsed by the American Counseling Association in 2003, provide practice guidelines. We have incorporated conceptually based social justice competencies within our framework of culture-infused counseling (Collins & Arthur, in press b) and are currently engaged in research to refine a framework of social justice competencies for career development practitioners, based on practitioner's experiences working with clients. We are committed to a future direction in multicultural counseling that helps counselors define scope of practice and levels of intervention related to social justice.

Conclusion

Many scholars have contributed to contemporary views of multicultural counseling. In reviewing selected publications, we were left with admiration about how clearly Clemmont Vontress led the way with his discussion of culture and counseling. His writing from the previous century helped us to revisit some basic concepts that have complex implications for multicultural counseling. Some of his key contributions include (a) defining and emphasizing the ever-present influences of culture for counseling, (b) moving beyond race and ethnicity in the discussion of cultural influences, (c) delineating concepts that can be used to strengthen the working alliance, and (d) targeting social structures in the amelioration of mental health concerns. More than 20 years ago, Vontress (1986) alerted us to the work that needed to be done and to the advantages of infusing culture into all counseling. Today, we simultaneously celebrate growth in the multicultural counseling field and acknowledge a sense of uneasiness that we have not moved far enough in theoretical development, models for practice, curriculum design, and practical strategies to support work with clients who are culturally diverse. We agree with writers who position culture as the concern of all counselors (e.g., Pedersen, 2001a; Paterson, 2007); however, the research to support models of practice and related counselling methods requires additional attention.

The multicultural counseling movement in psychology and counseling challenges us to consider what it means to practice within international, national, and local contexts. The burgeoning literature suggests new directions, theoretical innovations, ethical imperatives, and a host of recommendations directed at improving multicultural counseling competence. Students and counseling practitioners may wonder how to make sense of it all and how to translate the conceptual literature into practices with a diverse clientele.

Perhaps the greatest contribution that Clemmont Vontress offered us is a philosophy of life that inspires us to keep trying to make a difference through multicultural counseling. Through an existential lens, he continues to emphasize the similarities that unite humankind.

> There are no shortcuts in life. There is no easy way to live out our existence. One thing seems clear, however, whoever or wherever we may be, our existence is more fulfilling when we realize how much we all need to understand and support one another. It is also especially important for therapists to realize the empathic bonds which allow them to reach out to culturally different clients and help them through their life's journey. (2002, p. 134)

Vontress's wisdom helps us to examine our past, to understand the importance of what we do now, and to continually reflect about our future journey in multicultural counseling within and across nations.

REFERENCES

American Psychological Association. (2000). *Resolution on poverty and economic status*. Retrieved 14 February 2006, from http://www.apa.org/pi/urban/povres.html.

American Psychological Association. (2002). *Guidelines on multicultural education, training, research, practice, and organizational change for psychologists*. Retrieved 15 September 2003, from http://www.apa.org/pi/multiculturalguidelines.pdf.

Arredondo, P., & Toporek, R. (2004), Multicultural competencies = ethical practice. *Journal of Mental Health Counseling, 26*(1), 44–55.

Arredondo, P., Toporek, R., Brown, S. P., et al. (1996). Operationalization of the multicultural counseling competencies. *Journal of Multicultural Counseling & Development, 24*, 42–78.

Arthur, N., & Collins, S. (Eds.). (2005). *Culture-infused counseling: Celebrating the Canadian mosaic*. Calgary, AB: Counseling Concepts.

Blue, A., & Darou, W. (2005). Counselling First Nations Peoples. In N. Arthur & S. Collins (Eds.), *Culture-infused counseling: Celebrating the Canadian mosaic* (pp. 303–330). Calgary, AB: Counseling Concepts.

Canadian Counseling and Psychotherapy Association. (2007). *Code of ethics*. Retrieved 18 March 2010, from http://www.ccacc.ca/en/resources/codeofethics/.

Canadian Institute for Health Information (2004). *Improving the health of Canadians*. Ottawa: Canadian Institute for Health Information. Retrieved 28 October 2006, from http://secure.cihi.ca/cihiweb/products/IHC2004_ch6_e.pdf.

Canadian Psychological Association (2000). *Canadian code of ethics for psychologists* (3rd ed.). Retrieved 14 February 2006 from http://www.cpa.ca/cpasite/userfiles/Documents/Canadian%20Code%20of%20Ethics%20for%20Psycho.pdf.

Collins, S. (2007). Women on the margins: Honouring multiple and intersecting cultural identities. Manuscript submitted for publication.

Collins, S., & Arthur, N. (2005). Multicultural counselling competencies: A framework for professional development. In N. Arthur & S. Collins (Eds.), *Culture-infused counselling: Celebrating the Canadian mosaic* (pp. 41–102). Calgary, AB: Counselling Concepts.

Collins, S., & Arthur, N. (2007). A framework for enhancing multicultural counseling competence. *Canadian Journal of Counseling, 41*(1), 31–49.

Collins, S., & Arthur, N. (in press a). Culture-infused counseling: A fresh look at a classic framework of multicultural counseling competencies. *Counseling Psychology Quarterly.*

Collins, S., & Arthur, N. (in press b). Culture-infused counseling: A model for developing cultural competence. *Counseling Psychology Quarterly.*

Collins, S., Arthur, N., & Wong-Wiley, G. (in press). Enhancing reflective practice in multicultural counseling through cultural auditing. *Journal of Counseling & Development.*

D'Andrea, M., Daniels, J., & Noonan, M. J. (2003). New developments in the assessment of multicultural competencies. In D.B. Pope-Daviset al. (Eds.),

Handbook of multicultural competencies in counseling and psychology (pp. 154–167). Thousand Oaks, CA: Sage.

Esses, V. M., & Gardner, R. C. (1996). Multiculturalism in Canada: Context and current status. *Canadian Journal of Behavioural Science, 28*(3), 145.

Helms, J. E. (1994). How multiculturalism obscures racial factors in the therapy process: Comment on Ridley et al. (1994), Sodowsky et al. (1994), Ottavi et al. (1994), and Thompson et al. (1994). *Journal of Counseling Psychology, 41,* 162–165.

Ho, D. Y. F. (1995). Internalized culture, culturocentrism, and transference. *The Counseling Psychologist, 23*(1), 4–24.

Jackson, M. L. (1987). Cross-cultural counseling at the crossroads: A dialogue with Clemmont E. Vontress, *Journal of Counseling and Development, 66,* 20–23.

James, C. E. (1996). Race, culture and identity. In C. E. James (Ed.), *Perspectives on racism and the human services sector: A case for change* (pp. 5–35). Toronto: University of Toronto Press.

Lewis, J., Arnold, M. S., House, R., & Toporek, R. L. (2002). ACA Advocacy Competencies. Advocacy Task Force, American Counseling Association. Retrieved 1 October 2007, from http://www.counseling.org/Resources.

Minister of Public Works and Government Services Canada. Retrieved 28 October 2006, from http://www.ncwcnbes.net/htmdocument/reportPoverty-Profile20022003/PP20022003Eng.pdf.

Mollen, D., Ridley, C. R., & Hill, C. L. (2003). Models of multicultural counseling competence. In D. B. Pope-Davis et al. (Eds.), *Handbook of multicultural competencies in counseling and psychology* (pp. 21–37). Thousand Oaks, CA: Sage.

Moodley, R. (2007). (Re)placing multiculturalism in counselling and psychotherapy. *British Journal of Guidance & Counselling, 35*(1), 1–22.

National Council of Welfare. (2006). *Poverty profile 2002 and 2003.* Ottawa: author.

Paterson, J. (2007). Multicultural counseling: Not just for specialists anymore. *Counseling Today, April,* 1, 46–47.

Patterson, C. H. (2004). Do we need multicultural counseling competencies? *Journal of Mental Health Counseling, 26*(1), 67–73.

Pedersen, P. (1995). The culture-bound counselor as an unintentional racist. *Canadian Journal of Counseling, 29,* 197–205.

Pedersen, P. (2001a). Multiculturalism as a generic approach to counseling. *Journal of Counseling & Development, 70,* 6–12.

Pedersen, P. (2001b). Multiculturalism and the paradigm shift in counseling: Controversies and alternative futures. *Canadian Journal of Counseling, 35*(1), 15–25.

Pope, J., & Arthur, N. (2009). Socioeconomic status and class: A challenge for multicultural psychology in Canada. *Canadian Psychology, 50*, 55–65.

Ratts, M., D'Andrea, M., & Arredondo, P. (2004). Social justice counseling: Fifth force in field. *Counseling Today*, 28–30.

Reynolds, A. L., & Pope, R. L. (2003). Multicultural competence in counseling centers. In D. B. Pope-Davis et al. (Eds.), *Handbook of multicultural competencies in counseling and psychology* (pp. 365–382). Thousand Oaks, CA: Sage.

Ridley, C. R. (1995). *Overcoming unintentional racism in counseling and therapy: A practitioner's guide to intentional intervention.* Thousand Oaks, CA: Sage.

Ridley, C. R., & Kleiner, A. J. (2003). Multicultural counselling competencies: History, themes, and issues. In D. B. Pope-Davis et al. (Eds.), *Handbook of multicultural competencies in counseling and psychology* (pp. 3–20). Thousand Oaks, CA: Sage.

Statistics Canada. (2004). *Visible minority populations*, 2001 Census Canada. Retrieved 24 March 2004, from http://www.cic.gc.ca.

Statistics Canada. (2006). *Persons in low income before tax by prevalence in percent (2000–2004)* (Statistics Canada catalogue no. 75-202-X). Ottawa: Statistics Canada. Retrieved 28 October 2006, from http://www40.statcan.ca/l01/cst01/famil41a.htm.

Stead, B. G. (2004). Culture and career psychology: A social constructionist perspective. *Journal of Vocational Behavior, 64*, 389–406.

Sue, D. W., Arredondo, P., & McDavis, R. J. (1992). Multicultural counseling competencies and standards: A call to the profession. *Journal of Counseling and Development, 70*, 477–483.

Sue, D. W., Bernier, J. B., Durran, M., et al. (1982). Position paper: Cross-cultural counseling competencies. *Counseling Psychologist, 10*, 45–52.

Sue, D. W., Carter, R. T., Casas, J. M., et al. (1998). *Multicultural counseling competencies: Individual and organizational development*. Thousand Oaks, CA: Sage.

Sue, D.W., & Sue, D. (1990). *Counseling the culturally different : Theory and practice.* New York: Wiley.

Valetta, R. (2006). The ins and outs of poverty in advanced economies: Poverty dynamics in Canada, Germany, Great Britain, and the United States. *Review of Income and Wealth, 52*, 261–284.

Vera, E. M., & Shin, R. Q. (2006). Promoting strengths in a socially toxic world: Supporting resiliency with systemic interventions. *The Counseling Psychologist, 34*, 80–89.

Vontress, C. E. (1972). The black militant as a counselor. *Personnel and Guidance Journal, 50*, 574–580.

Vontress, C. E. (1979). Cross-cultural counseling: An existential approach. *Personnel and Guidance Journal, 58,* 117–122.

Vontress, C. E. (1982). Social class influences on counseling. *Counseling and Human Development, 14,* 1–12.

Vontress, C. E. (1985). Theories of counseling: A comparative analysis. In R. J. Samuda & A. Wolgang (Eds.), *Intercultural counseling and assessment: Global perspectives* (pp. 19–31). Toronto: C.J. Hogrefe.

Vontress, C. E. (1986). Social and cultural foundations. In M. D. Lewis, R. Hayes, & J. Lewis (Eds.), *Introduction to the counseling profession* (pp. 215–250). Itasca, IL: Peacock Publishers.

Vontress, C. E. (1996). A personal retrospective on cross-cultural counseling. *Journal of Multicultural Counseling and Development, 24*(3), 156–166.

Vontress, C. E. (2001) Cross-cultural counseling in the 21st century. *International Journal for the Advancement of Counseling, 23*(2), 83–97.

Vontress, C. E. (2002). Empathy in cross-cultural psycholtherapy. In P. R. Breggin, G. Breggin, & F. Bemak (Eds.), *Dimensions of empathic therapy* (pp. 129–134). New York: Springer, 2002.

Vontress, C. E. (2004). Reactions to the multicultural counseling competency debate. *Journal of Mental Health Counseling, 26*(1), 74–80.

Vontress, C. E., & Jackson, M. L. (2004). Reactions to the multicultural counseling competencies debate. *Journal of Mental Health Counseling, 26*(1), 74–80.

Weinrach, S. G., & Thomas, K. R. (2002). A critical analysis of the multicultural counseling competencies: Implications for the practice of mental health counseling. *Journal of Mental Health Counseling, 24,* 20–35.

10 Clemmont E. Vontress and British Multicultural Counseling

VALERIE WATSON

The study of culture[1] is central to Clemmont Vontress's work. In fact. he argues that counselors are 'obliged' to be students of culture (1986b, p. 216). His publications testify to his diligence. He states: 'Counselors and clients share something in common, the universal culture. They also share the same destiny, death, which places the relationship on a very high plane. There is not time for petty pursuits' (Vontress, 1988, p. 76). His declaration espouses two major principles of existential counseling practice: the need to continually confront mortality and to recognize the universality of human experience (1982, p. 362). Cultural difference, existential counseling, historical hostility, traditional healing, and self-hatred are identified as the five main themes in his work (Vontress, 1996, p. 157). This chapter considers the relevance of these themes in the context of counseling and psychotherapy[2] in Britain. Beginning with references to the terminologies and debates associated with multiculturalism, race, and race relations there follows a review of the development and limitations of multicultural counseling and the place of traditional healing within therapeutic relationships. Next, there is a discussion about existential counseling as practiced and understood by Vontress, briefly examining what the approach offers to client and therapist. An exploration of the impact of internalized oppression, class, and demographic change in the counseling relationship is considered in the light of Vontress's contributions on effective practice. The chapter concludes with a brief evaluation of Clemmont Vontress's influence on counseling theory and practice in Britain, outlining elements of the challenge agenda for the future direction of counseling with regard to issues of race and culture.

In their summary of the chronology and substance of the continuing debates on the use and definitions of the terminologies of 'race,'[3] racism, anti-racism, multiculturalism, ethnicity, and 'black,'[4] Moodley and Palmer (2006) argue for clarity and flexibility in our understanding of these terms in relation to the health care of ethnic minorities subject to the detrimental effects of rigid thinking and unhelpful stereotyping (p. 12). In Britain, these terms are criticized and their relevance successively questioned by theorists and social commentators, who have tended to reject them as ineffective and divisive social constructs.

Parallels can be drawn between the development and practice of counseling and psychotherapy in Britain from the late 1940s and the rise of multiculturalism as a national policy since the 1970s. Dryden, Mearns, and Thorne (2000) propose that the history of counseling in Britain 'tells the story of a collaborative response ... by widely different people from different sectors of the community to human suffering' (p. 471).

Multiculturalism has a similar narrative, initiated at local, then national levels to counteract the observable effects of inequality and social unrest apparent in education and other spheres. Through legislation and government organizations such as the Commission for Racial Equality (subsumed into the Commission for Equality and Human Rights since 2007), multiculturalism was seen as a way of uniting the nation while respecting and celebrating the cultural differences and practices of diverse community groups. Since then, politicians and social commentators use the term multicultural(ism) euphemistically to raise provocative issues about 'race' immigration and race relations in Britain, often to criticize the perceived privileging of ethnic minority groups.

Counseling, psychotherapy, and multiculturalism began with a tacit acceptance of pluralism. Recently, multiculturalism has been declared redundant by political and social commentators, with a shift toward integration, downplaying difference in favor of highlighting similarity, and governmental encouragement to declare allegiance to shared values of Britishness through formalized citizenship ceremonies. Although resisted in some quarters, counseling and psychotherapy have been urged to amalgamate. This will be underwritten by statutory regulation promoting cohesion, safety, and accountability. Plans for the professionalization and regulation of counseling and psychotherapy practitioners will be complete by 2010, including defining competencies and qualifying criteria and devising monitoring procedures of the practice for those registered. Among the competencies will be a stipulation that practitioners have proof of understanding about the issues of cultural diversity or multicultural competence.

Identification of the therapeutic interventions that seem to help people most rather than adherence to a specific counseling approach is a priority. This is evident within the restructured National Health Service, where the focus for funding is to be based on the outcomes of evidence-based and practice-based research (Paley and Lawton, 2001). Government support exists through financial grants for training and increased access to psychological therapies (IAPT) for all sectors of the community. Indicators suggest a preference for cognitive behavioral therapy because it has supportive research evidence of effectiveness. While Vontress (2001, p. 386) might applaud the expansion of counseling provision in Britain, he might be critical of the bias toward the cognitive behavioral approach, arguing that its scientific bias and reliance on specified techniques is inappropriate for clients in general and particularly for those more responsive to traditional healing approaches.

Multicultural Counseling Reviewed

Ivey, Ivey, Simek-Morgan et al. (1997), Pedersen (1995), and Sue, Carter, Casas, et al. (1998) claimed the development and practice of the multicultural approach to be the predominant (fourth) force in counseling and psychotherapy. The multicultural approach challenges the three theoretical 'forces,' insisting that counselors recognize and address cultural differences and contexts in the therapeutic encounter. Use of a multicultural approach implies the counselor is aware of the societal structures that can affect and oppress the individual and uses this knowledge alongside a theoretical understanding for effective therapy. Exploration of the client's worldview and his/her in-the-world experiences is an essential part of the work. This focus is akin to the existential approach described by Vontress (1988), which emphasizes the cooperative and 'symbiotic' alliance between counselor and client as they examine the ways in which the sociopolitical circumstances of the client contributes to their feelings of distress.

West and McLeod (2003) note that 'issues of cultural identity and difference, and how they are negotiated in relationships, appear to have become a major theme within counseling and psychotherapy in Britain' (p. 84). McLeod (2003) is optimistic about the potential for 'extending and renewing the practice and profession,' noting evidence of an increase in the literature available on this subject and attempts to raise awareness about cultural difference in the therapeutic relationship.

Among others in Britain, Fernando (1991), Lago and Thompson (1996, 2002), Littlewood and Lipsedge (1989), and Moodley and Dhingra (1998) have raised the central issues relating to 'race' culture, cultural identity, and cultural awareness in mental health and therapeutic practice. They consider the impact of miscommunication and power differentials in cross-cultural counseling relationships. These authors also question assumptions about the perceptions and worldviews of black clients and the appropriateness of dominant Eurocentrist notions of counseling theory and practice. In their attempt to advance the debate and improve counseling practice, Lago and Thompson (1996, 2002) devised a model for the culturally skilled counselor influenced by the work of North American theorists, including Sue, Arredondo, and McDavis (1992) on multicultural competence and Helms (1995) on racial identity development.

Other influential concepts from North American theorists such as the use of appropriate language, and the impact of internalized oppression on counselor–client relations, now appear regularly in British counseling literature. Moodley (2003) has explored the complexity of individual ownership of multiple identities and allegiances relating to gender, sexual orientation, ethnicity, and sociopolitical status. This work challenges simplistic views of identity based on singular or visible difference alone. Alleyne (2004), writing on workplace oppression among black clients, focuses on the legacy of internalized oppression. McKenzie-Mavinga (2003), Lawrence (2003), and Watson (2004) have investigated the historical and current perspectives of race, and cultural issues emerging in training and practice. Emerging themes of 'race,' culture, and identity have been variously explored by Moodley (1998), white identity by Tuckwell (2002), and from an Asian perspective by Laungani (1999). d'Ardenne and Mahtani (1989) and Eleftheriadou (1994) have considered the process and tasks faced by the counselor and client in their communications.

With the exception of a few volumes, such as the work of Palmer and Laungani (1999), Palmer (2002), Lago (2004), and Tuckwell (2002), much has been reported but little research done or ideas formulated which considers anew the British context of the multicultural approach to counseling and highlights ways of approaching issues of race and culture in the therapeutic relationship. In emphasizing the cross-cultural nature of all counseling relationships, Vontress (2004; Vontress & Epp

2001) argues that continuing debates about race with a focus on cultural signifiers are an unhelpful distraction. As Moodley and Palmer (2006) suggest, the majority of ethnic minority people are more concerned with their social and economic position and the realities of the impact of power relations than with semantics (p. 17). The point is echoed by Chantler (2005), a person-centered counselor, who contends that the focus on culture, cultural sensitivity, and diversity rather than inequalities obscures real problems inherent in the 'race' debate in Britain.

The British Context of Multicultural Counseling

Broad acceptance of multiculturalism has been blamed for condoning 'unacceptable' cultural practices such as female circumcision, enforced marriage, homophobia, and oppression as well as preventing integration through the disproportionate support of multilingualism (at the expense of learning English) and the establishment of separate religious schools. Through its promoted tolerance of cultural diversity, multiculturalism is held responsible for the incubation of terrorist conspiracy. Critics of multiculturalism show evidence of its failure in the reported rise in Islamophobia, hostility toward asylum seekers and refugees, and the persistence of impenetrable institutional racism at all levels of British society.

In advance of these events, Solomos and Back (1996) predicted that globalization and advances in international communication would, paradoxically, increase national tension and conflicts (p. 121). In their view, ethnic identities are created in response to 'an unequal conversation between dominant and minority groupings' (p. 126). This analysis is a likelier explanation for the rise in discord among differing cultural groups than the ineffectiveness of multiculturalism. Multiculturalism is about the acceptance of difference and the harmonious coexistence of communities. Terrorist or separatist activity attempts to reinstate and reify difference as a virtue, attempting to decouple a group or groups from mainstream Westernism, which is often identified as corrupt.

Moodley and Palmer suggest that 'individuals are often torn between the need to experience themselves existentially in the "here and now" and the desire to be historically or psychically connected to a specific, but not too distant, past. This may be constructed in ethnic cultural and racial terms (2006, p. 19).

The contested terms of race and race relations are worthy of continued attention because they are created and used by those with power to define and control black people. Engaging in this debate is a way for black people in Britain to continuously reclaim and redefine their identity(ies) in the way that, historically, other political movements have always done, challenging the status quo and reflecting demographic and political change.

Limitations of Multiculturalism as It Relates to Counseling Training and Practice

A complaint against multicultural competence (or diversity) training is that the oft evoked feelings of guilt and shame among white participants, in particular, lead to its focus being deflected toward dealing with 'white guilt' rather than examining ways of combating the effects of racism. Research into the effectiveness of training counselors in multicultural competence (or diversity training) is contradictory and inconclusive. Glockshuber (2005, p. 301) presents evidence which indicates that such training does not necessarily make counselors more effective on a practical level. This is in contrast to Wade and Bernstein's research, cited by McLeod (2003), which found that counselors trained to be culturally competent were rated more positively by clients regardless of their ethnicity.

While Vontress (1979) and others might be sceptical about the need for and efficacy of training in multicultural competence, evidence of the current political climate of fragile tolerance toward all racial and social minority groups points to its necessity. Though flawed holistically and presenting cultural difference as problematic, diversity training provides an opportunity to explore the potentials of inclusion. As Vontress suggests and others agree, at its best this training encourages counselors to identify and make use of their own cultural identity(ies), while exploring notions of sameness, difference, and inequality.

However, acknowledgment of cultural difference and in-depth knowledge of specific cultures does not guarantee sensitivity toward the needs of minority clients. Despite years of multiculturalism and diversity training in Britain, reports from numerous sources (such as EMPIRIC, 2002) show that the rate of referral for talking therapy is low and the diagnosis for schizophrenia and psychosis is disproportionately higher among ethnic minority people, as is the prescription of high doses of psychotropic medication and hospitalization. This phenomenon has been attributed to the frequency of last-minute crisis referrals for ethnic minority clients who, it is claimed, tend to avoid mental health services out of resistance or fear of incarceration in a mental hospital. Braid (1999) reports that significant numbers of minority clients in Britain prefer to consult spiritual or traditional healers when experiencing mental distress. For the client, this increases the chance of ethnic matching and assumed cultural understanding, which may not be accessible through statutory services.

Vontress (1982, 1986b), notes that counselors are more likely to be able to empathize with clients who share their culture, language, race, values, and ethnicity. Elsewhere, he questions the empathic ability of counselors who do not share the same 'conscious and unconscious loadings as their clients' (1985a), implying that ethnic matching in some instances could be important, while also insisting that cultural difference is more perceived than real (1987, p. 22) and that the focus should be on the 'etic' rather than the 'emic' experience. The ethnic-matching debate has been discussed by Alladin (1993), Laungani (1999), and Moodley (2001) and others, who identify the advantages and impracticalities of ethnic matching purely on the basis of visible racial similarity. Research by Farsimadan, Draghi-Lorenz, and Ellis (2007) and practice evidence in the work of Shoaib and Peel (2003) highlight the effectiveness of ethnic matching wherein a preference was stated, especially the importance of a shared language. Provision of culturally sensitive mental health services for minority ethnic groups has proved beneficial, enabling ethnic matching and opportunities for traditional healing approaches and spiritual perspectives to be used. An example of this is My Time (Lilley, 2007), an independent practice in the West Midlands United Kingdom (with 70% black minority ethnic population) that claims to cater for the varying therapeutic social, spiritual, education training, and employment needs of all clients under one roof.

Traditional Healing

Patel and Fatimilehin (1999) contend that 'the overwhelming bias towards the use of traditional, Western models of psychological health and psychological and psychiatric practice is a testimony to one of the most blatant, yet often covert, forms of racism in the mental health system' (p. 63). A similar opinion is shared by Lago and Thompson (1996), Fernando (1991), Moodley (2000), and a growing number of counseling theorists. They argue that this policy perpetuates racism because it makes incorrect assumptions about the behavior and needs of ethnic minority clients, implying as it does white superiority and minority deficiency. Vontress advocates 'bringing the world into the therapy room.' This involves consideration of local, national, and world issues as well as a willingness to incorporate traditional healing methods where possible and appropriate to the needs of clients. Reporting on his work with clients, Vontress (1996) appears comfortable with a high level of self-disclosure, directing and advising his clients about courses of action, diet, social contacts, and exercise. This approach coincides with most traditional healing methods, which are holistic in their diagnoses and practice using the five layers of culture (Jackson, 1987) identified by Vontress. Attention is paid to the uniqueness of the individual, his/her spiritual concerns, and community or family connections. Although they are heavily criticized for their lack of scientific proof, the growing interest in alternative therapies in Britain is partly in response to the appeal of their holistic approach. On a small scale, some British practitioners are making use of alternative therapies, a range of spiritual perspectives, traditional healing practices, and various environmental resources such as equine therapy. Therapeutic training courses are available in music, arts, and dance therapy and drumming. Like Dryden, Mearns and Thorne (2000), and McLeod (2003), Vontress advocates that counselor training should include the study of life sciences, philosophy, and anthropology, thus going beyond the psychological and being supportive of interdisciplinarity in both training and practice, an emphasis that could be instrumental in discouraging the Eurocentric hegemony of current counselor training and practice.

Vontress and Existentialism

Vontress describes existential philosophy as a 'philosophy of humankind,' asserting that evidence of existentialist concepts are present in African and Asian philosophy pre-dating the growth of existentialist philosophy in Europe (Epp, 1998, p. 7). Using the phenomenological concepts of *Umwelt*, *Mitwelt*, and *Eigenwelt* developed by Binswanger with his addition of the spiritual dimension *Überwelt*, Vontress (1996) developed a schema of concentric circles to describe five interconnected cultural influences: the universal, ecological, national, racio-ethnic, and regional, which intersect continuously in relationship. The first four influences also describe levels of empathy and culture. Vontress argued that clients should be viewed holistically and diagnoses should refer to the five layers of cultural influence, with an increased focus on the spiritual, cultural, and environmental aspects, rendering a focus on ethnic matching or the use of specific techniques unnecessary.

Vontress describes existential counseling as a 'philosophical discussion,' a talk about life, love, death, suffering, and searching for answers (Epp, 1998, p. 3), stating: 'The goal of existential therapy is a relationship that allows clients to discover their individual uniqueness and to give it full expression. Existential counselors must concern themselves with the human condition in general before addressing the specifics of the client's culture because people are more alike than they are dissimilar' (Vontress, 1985b, p. 28). In his view, the universal applicability of existential counseling means that it 'transcends cultural and national boundaries' (1985a, p. 207); existential counselors as 'world citizens' are best able to 'bridge' cultural difference. According to Vontress, existential counselors should be seen as 'close, concerned, but non-possessive friends and guides' (p. 210), a perspective echoed by van Deurzen (2001), who describes the therapist as 'tutor' to the client. Spinelli (2001) says that the existential therapist is 'one who walks beside you and through being with you illuminates not just your world but all worlds' (p. 20). Spinelli (2001) and Vontress (2004) agree that the quality of the relationship and the effectiveness of the therapy is more important than 'rituals of the enterprise' (p. 77). It is not assumed that the client has the answers to their problems within themselves; these may emerge through Socratic dialogue (Jackson, 1987, p. 23), joint problem solving, and meaning making with the therapist. Emphasis is placed on the continual recognition of personal choice and freedom to act within limits, with acknowledgment of the possible consequences of actions (Vontress, 1985b, p. 28). Eleftheriadou (1994) queries the appropriateness of existential counseling with unacculturated clients for whom talking in an egalitarian relationship about their emotional life may be an alien concept. This has been noticed by counselors working with ethnic minority clients more familiar with the directions given within traditional healing approaches.

Existentialist counseling practice and its philosophy values stoicism and mental toughness, active engagement rather than victimhood. These characteristics are extolled by Vontress especially in relation to the predicament of ethnic minority and working-class clients, and are values that he believes should be instilled in black clients within counseling relationships. Arguing that personal experience, rather than the perceptions of others, determines how people feel about themselves (2004, p. 76), he continually explores the effects of black self-hatred (also defined as internalized oppression) and historical hostility (1979, 1982, 1986b, 1996) on the counseling relationship, concluding that the existential approach offers the best opportunity for all clients to optimize their potential. This extends to his personal rejection of racial oppression and his resistance to the 'cultural wounding' he endured when accused of betrayal by black colleagues (2003, p. 23) for challenging the formation of a professional black caucus. Fanon's description of how he liberated himself from the label of Negro and its negative connotations seems to capture the essence of Vontress's own journey toward existential philosophy:

> There are two ways out of this conflict. Either I ask others to pay no attention to my skin, or else I want them to be aware of it. I try then to find value for what is bad – since I have unthinkingly conceded that the black man is the color of evil. In order to terminate this neurotic situation, in which I am compelled to choose an unhealthy, conflictual solution, fed on fantasies, hostile, inhuman in short, I have only one solution: to rise above this absurd drama that others have staged round me, to reject the two terms that are equally unacceptable, and, through one human being, to reach out for the universal. (Fanon, 1967, p. 197)

Although he initially identified himself as an existential therapist, Vontress has questioned the term's relevance as a descriptor of his practice, an indication of his unwillingness to be defined or confined by labels (1996, p. 161).

Describing existential counseling as a 'therapy of bleakness,' Mick Cooper (2003) distinguishes the European existentialist movement from its North American counterpart, which he claims is more optimistic and upbeat in its worldview. While both hold similar views about impermanence and the importance of considering the inevitability of death, Cooper asserts that their theoretical and practice perspectives diverged as a result of their differing post–Second World War experiences. He suggests that North American existentialism is expansionist and individualistic in its ethos, drawing on a humanistic theory and practice prevalent in North America (p. 64). He describes European existentialism as being more uncertain in its stance opposing the notion of a trouble-free world. This latter European view seems consistent with Vontress's worldview and is in accord with the black American experience challenging the optimism of the American dream. Throughout his work Vontress insists that blacks, no matter how rich they become, cannot escape racism. He reserves some of his harshest criticism for black Americans who, he implies, are supine and have surrendered their position, probably through the effects of internalized oppression or historical hostility. Vontress (1979) has questioned the continued relative underachievement of black Americans, contrasting them with the position of black émigrés from the Caribbean and elsewhere. Similar questions are asked in Britain of African Caribbeans, who, overall, fare less well in all spheres than more recently arrived ethnic minority groups. Vontress claims that what existentialist philosophy offers to black clients and therapists is the chance to continuously reject an assigned position of inferiority.

Challenges for Counselors in Britain

Internalised Oppression

Lennox Thomas (1997) suggests that 'questions of being and meaning are the most difficult for therapists to deal with. Often they are still on the path of finding their own answers or finding ways of reconstructing the question. In gender terms, women are many steps ahead of men in this regard' (p. 24). Ontological questions about being and meaning are further complicated for the black therapist by the corrosive effects of internalized oppression, transference, and counter-transference. Vontress (1986b, p. 219) notes that blacks are bound to internalize racism and in turn become oppressors, as racism is the prevailing ethos of the society they inhabit. The impact of internalized oppression has been explored by counseling theorists (Lago and Thompson 1996, 2002; Alleyne 2004) in Britain through the permutations of the black-white therapeutic dyad. Lennox Thomas (1997), a black psychoanalyst, has been concerned about the pervasive negative image of black men in British society and their persistent relative underachievement. While conducting a black male therapy group, Thomas noted evidence of collective 'combat fatigue' among the participants, manifested in forms of internalized oppression, frustration, impatience, pessimism, and weariness. Most in the group questioned whether they could ever be seen as 'just men' or would always have to be black men. This is reminiscent of Fanon's (1967) questioning of his existence and desire to be free of the dehumanizing effect of racism. 'Emancipate yourselves from mental slavery. None but ourselves can free our minds.' These lines from Bob Marley's 'Redemption song,' using words from a speech by Marcus

Garvey, captures the spirit of Vontress's existential argument and is a rallying cry for all those enslaved by their history to take personal action to achieve freedom. Arguably, counselors' use of Vontress's interpretation of existential counseling would enable client-counselor exploration of all the cultural influences of the black client rather than focus on his/her racio-ethnic identity.

Vontress (2001, p. 379) describes 'historical hostility' as the way in which ethnic minority clients tend to respond in the moment to the known misdeeds and conflicts of a previous generation answering to a trans-generational imperative. In her analysis of the same observed phenomenon, Alleyne (2004), a British theorist and practitioner, describes this response as the effect of the 'internal oppressor,' 'an aspect of the self of black peoples' resulting in negative responses to the 'real or perceived' historical experiences of oppression. Alleyne suggests that the internal oppressor is capable of damaging black people to an even greater extent than the experience of racism and could adversely affect the black-black therapeutic dyad. From the client's perspective, this might be seen in their envy and mistrust of the counselor, the denigration of minority groups, denial of internalised racism, and their focus on the effects of racism at the expense of specific and personal concerns (see Vontress, 1986b). It is therefore important for black counselors to be alert to the presence of internalized oppression in the therapeutic relationship.

The prevalence of diagnosed depression, stress, and anxiety and the escalating social welfare costs of mental ill health in Britain has led to the promotion of a 'happiness agenda' spearheaded by politicians and leading economists as a way of enhancing a general sense of well-being in the populace, thereby increasing productivity and economic growth. Schools are being encouraged to include 'happiness' and emotional intelligence as part of their curriculum. From an existentialist position, the focus on happiness, thus minimizing social welfare costs, misses the point, denying that the roots of unhappiness and anxiety lie in an unwillingness to deal with the inevitability of death. In agreement with Spinelli (2001) and McLeod (2003), Vontress has argued in favor of giving more attention to the spiritual concerns of clients in counseling, looking beyond the individual's presumption of a return to happiness, and giving more care to an appreciation of collective community obligations.

In his observation that black and white counselors operate differently, Vontress (Jackson 1987, p. 23) declares that white counselors seem to concentrate on methods, 'tricks of the trade,' while black counselors focus on changing themselves in order to help their clients. Moodley and Dhingra (1998) and Watson (2004) found that black counselors reported engaging in post-qualifying additional study in their efforts to meet the needs of their black clients. Uwahemu (2004), a black psychotherapist, writes of developing a 'proxy self' in which she ignores or hides her cultural heritage as a way of dealing with oppression, a learnt survival strategy that her parents had adopted in order to be accepted in Britain. However, Vontress asserts, 'for Blacks what you are speaks so loudly that no amount of programmed behavior will conceal the true self' (Jackson, 1987, p. 23). One reading of this statement is Vontress's expectation that black counselors bring the distillation of their historical and current experiences and are equipped to deal with the major themes of therapy because of who and what they are.

Social Class

Vontress (1986b) claims that 'structuring' by the counselor is needed when there is a social and cultural gap between counselor and client. By receiving instruction about the rules of engagement, 'structure,' language, and social mores of the counseling process, naive clients will be in a better position to access what counseling has to offer. This is of importance in relation to existential counseling, which Vontress refers to as a philosophical venture rather than a curative process (1985b, p. 210). It is about living with ambiguity. Class, as a factor of cultural difference in the counseling relationship, may have more of an impact in Britain than elsewhere. British social and political history is steeped in a class system dating back to the early eighteenth century of which many remnants remain. This is evident in the access to counseling and counseling training. Until recently, psychotherapy and counseling training was mostly available only to the middle classes. Over the past decade the position has changed; an increase in counseling and counseling training provision through independent, voluntary, and statutory services has led to improved access in all sectors of society. As counseling has become more accessible it has evolved in its delivery, with some counselors taking a more deliberate political stance, speaking out against social injustice as a group rather than maintaining an objective clinical distance. The establishment of the group Psychotherapists and Counsellors for Social Responsibility (PCSR) in 1995 is a case in point. There have also been changes in the modes of delivery, with greater flexibility of approach. Some counselors also elect to work directly in the community, adopting a similar role to the traditional healer by being flexible in their approach as well as working with family or community groups in a systemic way. These developments are in accord with Vontress's views (2004) about the need for counselors to take an active role in the community and, in particular, to encourage working clients to seize opportunities available to them for self-improvement.

Multiple or Mixed-Heritage Issues

The United Kingdom census data for 2001 (National statistics online, 2007) records a total population of 58.8 million people, 7.9% of whom constituted the ethnic minority population. Among these are a growing number of refugees, economic migrants, and asylum seekers. Of the minority ethnic population, 45% lives in London, while 14.6% identified themselves in as being of mixed race or multiple heritage. This group includes those who claim a multiple heritage not based on skin color. The mixed-race or multiple heritage population is the fastest growing sector of the ethnic minority population, accounting for 4% of the total United Kingdom population under five years of age. This demographic change challenges the notion of 'race,' the essentialism of distinct races, and a fixed 'black identity.' Hall (1996) argues that black identity is in flux, constructed and learned from historical and contemporary experiences of oppression (p. 166). In addressing the socialization of mixed-race children, Vontress (1979) anticipates some of the emerging themes of concern in Britain, where children are often 'socialized in contradistinction to their appearance and that of one parent[;] many are hostile toward one or both racial groups that their parents represent' (p. 118). Vontress (1986a) presents the common scenario, wherein blacks and whites can become estranged from their own racio-ethnic community because of their elevated social class caused by education, occupation, or wealth.

It seems that those who identify themselves as being of mixed race or multiple heritage can and do make choices about their racio-ethnic identity, though they are often racially assigned as 'black' by the ethnic majority. When multiple heritage status is visible on the basis of skin color, there is a tendency for it to be regarded negatively or as problematic. For the individuals concerned, the sense of having multiple identities and allegiances may connect with dilemmas and conflicts about owning their cultural heritage. The impact of historical and transgenerational woundings, not being seen as 'black' or 'white' enough, being on the receiving end of hostility from black and white people, the shock of being labeled as 'black' and feelings of estrangement and alienation are some issues that are reported as some of the themes of exploration in counseling relationships with mixed-race/multiple-heritage clients. It is anticipated that issues relating to mixed race and multiple heritage will form part of a growing area for exploration in British counseling relationships. Research conducted by Watson (2004) shows how one mixed-race counselor assumed a fluidity of identity in their work: 'I feel white when with a white client and I feel like I'm a black counsellor when I'm with black people' (p. 233). Another British therapist, Chung (2007), views her mixed heritage as an asset. Aware of the initial distrust from her clients, she attempts to dispel her own inherited internal oppressor and is willing to adapt her counseling methods to meet the needs of her clients. Similarly, Khalid (2007) uses her knowledge of Islamic perspectives to inform her work with Muslim clients.

Conclusion

This chapter has considered Clemmont Vontress's contribution to counseling theory and practice in Britain by reflecting on his work. Research (Watson, 2004) and personal testimony available shows that, like Vontress, black counselors in Britain may have journeyed towards becoming a counselor with the experience of being 'culturally wounded' and having a sense of mission, a desire to influence. Vigilance with respect to the presence and effects of internalized oppression is particularly important for black counselors. And as Vontress states, existentialist philosophy and practice offers freedom from the constraints of historical hostility and mental slavery. Vontress emphasizes that 'the client's culture is the healing instrument' and the therapeutic personality of the counselor is 'the healing agent' who relates to the client as a fellow traveler on the same route to death (1996, p. 161). The equalizing inevitability of death is another essential feature of Vontress's work that carries a sense of urgency in its insistence on taking clients' whole cultural experience into account by examining the problems presented through the lens of the five cultural layers and clients' ability to claim a multiplicity of identities. Vontress points out that wealthier people have more time for introspection; this applies to much of the Western populace and in part explains both the rise in interest in counseling and the increased levels of dissatisfaction, often experienced as depression and anxiety. While accepting that 'race is more socially cohesive than education, money or occupation' (1982, p. 362), Vontress asserts that attention to counseling techniques and a focus on 'race' are 'petty pursuits' occupying valuable time and space which could be devoted to what unites rather than divides us as humans. Many of Vontress's observations, although not necessarily publicized or popularized in Britain, have echoed the ideas of contemporary counseling and social theorists. He could be described as having the influence of a subtle and persistent pioneer.

NOTES

1 Vontress, C.E. (1999 October), Interview with a traditional African healer, *Journal of Mental Health Counseling, 21*(4), 326–336. Vontress defines culture as 'perceptible, and imperceptible; cognitive and affective; material and immaterial; secular and spiritual; and even more. We see it, hear it and feel it. It is our envelope of life' (p. 335). This definition will be adopted throughout the chapter.

2 The terms counseling and psychotherapy will be used interchangeably throughout this chapter as there remains inconclusive evidence that there is a significant difference between the two in terms of practice, although efforts are being made through statutory regulation to create some qualifying criteria.

3 'Race' is a social and social scientific construct used to identify color and difference both by those theorists who deny it, and yet continue to use it in their writing, and by those that accept it as a useful term. Solomos and Back (1996).

4 The term 'black' is used in this chapter to describe a politically defined group who do not identify as being white and have a shared history and experience of colonialism, imperialism, and racism. This refers to those of African and South Asian descent who could be identified as black based on their skin colour.

REFERENCES

Alladin, W. J. (1993). Ethnic matching in counselling: How important is it to ethnically match clients and counsellors? In W. Dryden (Ed.), *Questions and answers on counselling in action* (pp. 50–56). London: Sage.

Alleyne, A. (2004a). Black identity and workplace oppression. *Counselling and Psychotherapy Reasearch, 4*(1), 4–8.

Alleyne, A. (2004b). The internal oppressor and black identity wounding. *Counselling and Psychotherapy Journal, 15*(10), 48–50.

Braid, M. (1999). Voodoo versus the NHS. *The Independent*, 12 February 1999, p. 8.

Chantler, K. (2005). From disconnection to connection: 'Race,' gender and the politics of therapy. *British Journal of Guidance and Counselling, 33*(2), 239–256.

Chung, A. (2007). Daring to be different. *Therapy today, 18*(2), 31–34.

Cooper, M. (2003). *Existential therapies*. London: Sage.

d'Ardenne, P., & Mahtani, A. (1989). *Transcultural counselling in action*. London: Sage.

Dryden, W., Mearns, D., & Thorne, B. (2000). Counselling in the United Kingdom: Past, present and future. *British Journal of Guidance and Counselling, 28*(4), 467–483.

Eleftheriadou, Z. (1994). Transcultural counselling. London: Central Book Publishing.

Epp, L. R. (1998). The courage to be an existential counselor: An interview of Clemmont E. Vontress. *Journal of Mental Health Counseling, 20*(1), 1–12.

Ethnic Minority Psychiatric Illness Rates in the Community (EMPIRIC). (2002). A survey carried out on behalf of the Department of Health, K. Sproston & J. Nazroo (Eds.). Accessed 14 October 2007, at http://www.official-documents.co.uk/document/deps/doh/empiric/empiric.htm.

Fanon, F. (1967). *Black skin, white masks*. New York: Grove Press Inc.

Farsimadan, F., Draghi-Lorenz, R., & Ellis, J. (2007). Process and outcome of therapy in ethnically similar and dissimilar therapeutic dyads. *Psychotherapy Research, 17*(5), 567–575.

Fernando, S. (1991). *Mental health, race and culture*. London: Macmillan.

Glockshuber, E. (2005). Counsellors' self-perceived multicultural competencies model. *European Journal of Psychotherapy, Counselling and Health, 7*(4), 291–308.

Hall, S. (1996). New ethnicities. In H. A. Baker, Jr, M. Diawara, & R. H. Lindeborg (Eds.), *Black British cultural studies* (pp. 163–172). Chicago: University of Chicago Press.

Helms, J., (1995). An update of Helms' White and People of Color Racial Identity models. In J. G. Ponterotto, J. M. Casas, et al. (Eds.), *Handbook of multicultural counseling* (pp. 181–198).Thousand Oaks, CA: Sage.

Ivey, A. E., Ivey, M. B., Simek-Morgan, L., et al. (1997). *Counseling and psychotherapy: A multicultural perspective* (4th ed.). Boston: Allyn & Bacon.

Jackson, M. L. (1987). Cross-cultural counseling at the crossroads: A dialogue with Clemmont E. Vontress. *Journal of Counseling and Development, 66*(1), 20–23.

Khalid, S. (2007). Counselling from an Islamic perspective. *Therapy Today, 18*(2), 34–37.

Lago, C., & Thompson, J. (1996). *Race, culture and counselling*. Buckingham: Open University Press.

Lago, C., & Thompson, J. (2002). Counselling and race. In S. Palmer (Ed.), *Multicultural Counselling* (pp. 3–20). London: Sage.

Laungani, P. (1999) Culture and identity: Implications for counselling. In S. Palmer and P. Laungani (Eds.), *Counselling in a multicultural society* (pp. 35–70). London: Sage.

Lawrence, D. (2003). Racial and cultural issues in counselling training. In A. Dupont-Joshua, (Ed.), *Working inter-culturally in counselling settings* (pp. 120–141) Hove: Brunner-Routledge.

Lilley, M. (2007). My Time. *Therapy, 18*(5), 34–35. See www.mytime.org.uk for further information.

Littlewood, R., & Lipsedge, M. (1989). *Aliens and alienists.* London: Unwin Hyman.

McKenzie-Mavinga, I. (2003). Linking social history and the therapeutic process in research and practice on black issues. *Counselling and Psychotherapy Research, 3*(2), 103–106.

McLeod, J. (2003). *An introduction to counselling*. Maidenhead: Oxford University Press.

Moodley, R. (1998). I say what I like: Frank talk(ing) in counselling and psychotherapy. *British Journal of Guidance and Counselling, 26*(4), 495–508.

Moodley, R. (2000). Counselling and psychotherapy in a multicultural context. Part 2. *Counselling: The Journal of the British Association for Counselling, 11*(4), 221–224.

Moodley, S.R. (2001). Race, ethnicity and cultural representation of 'psychological distress' and its interpretations in psychotherapy. Unpublished doctoral dissertation, University of Sheffield.

Moodley, R. (2003) Double, triple, multiple jeopardy. In C. Lago and B. Smith (Eds.), *Anti-discriminatory counselling practice* (pp. 120–134). London: Sage.

Moodley, R., and Dhingra, S. (1998) Cross-cultural/racial matching in counselling and therapy: White clients and Black counsellors. *Counselling: The Journal of the British Association for Counselling, 9*(4), 295–299.

Moodley, R., & Palmer, S. (2006). Race, culture and other multiple constructions: An absent presence in psychotherapy. In R. Moodley & S. Palmer (Eds.), *Race, culture and psychotherapy* (pp. 11–26). London: Routledge.

National statistics online. (2007). Accessed 20 September 2007, at http://www.statistics.gov.uk/cci/nugget.asp?id=459.

Paley, G., & Lawton, D. (2001). Evidence-based practice: Accounting for the importance of the therapeutic relationship in UK national health service provision. *Counselling and Psychotherapy Research, 1*(1), 12–17.
Palmer, S. (Ed.). (2002). *Multicultural counselling.* London: Sage.
Pedersen, P. B. (1995). Culture-centered ethical guidelines for counselors. In J. G. Ponterotto et al. (Eds.), *Handbook of multicultural counseling* (pp. 34–49). Thousand Oaks, CA: Sage.
Shoaib, K., and Peel, J. (2003). Kashmiri women's perceptions of their emotional and psychological needs, and access to counselling. *Counselling and Psychotherapy Research, 3*(2), 87–94.
Solomos, J., & Back, L. (1996). *Racism and society*. Houndmills: Macmillan.
Spinelli, E. (2001). *The mirror and the hammer*. London: Sage.
Sue, D. W., Arredondo, P., & McDavis, R. J. (1992). Multicultural counseling competencies and standards: A call to the profession. *Journal of Counseling & Development, 70,* 477–486.
Sue, D. W., Carter, R. T., Casas, J. M., Fouad, N. A., et al. (1998). *Multicultural counseling competencies*. Thousand Oaks, CA: Sage.
Thomas, L. K. (1997). Reworking stereotypes for self identity in a black men's psychotherapy group. *Race and Cultural Education in Counselling, 13,* 23–25.
Tuckwell, G. (2002). *Racial identity, white counsellors and therapists*. Buckingham: Open University Press.
Uwahemu, A. (2004). The proxy self – a more acceptable version of me. *Counselling and Psychotherapy Journal, 14*(1), 44–45.
Van Deurzen, E. (2001). *Existential counselling and psychotherapy in practice* (2nd ed.). London: Sage.
Vontress, C. E. (1979). Cross-cultural counseling: An existential approach. *The Personnel and Guidance Journal, 58,* 117–122.
Vontress, C. E. (1982). Social class influences on counseling. *Counseling and Human Development, 14,* 1–12.
Vontress, C. E. (1985a). Existentialism as a cross-cultural modality. In P. Pedersen (Ed.), *Handbook of cross-cultural counseling and therapy* (207–212).Westport, CT: Greenwood Press.
Vontress, C. E. (1985b). Theories of counseling: A comparative analysis. In R. J. Samuda & A. Wolfgang (Eds.), *Intercultural counseling and assessment* (pp.19–31). Toronto: C.J. Hogrefe, Inc.
Vontress, C. E. (1986a). Existential anxiety: Implications for counseling. *Journal of Mental Health Counseling, 8,* 100–109.
Vontress, C. E. (1986b). Social and cultural foundations. In M. D. Lewis, R. Hayes, & J. Lewis (Eds.), *An introduction to the counseling profession* (pp. 215–250). Itasca, IL: Peacock Publishers.

Vontress, C. E. (1988). An existential approach to cross-cultural counseling. *Journal of Multicultural Counseling and Development, 16*(2), 73–78.

Vontress, C. E. (1991). Traditional healing in Africa: Implications for cross-cultural counseling. *Journal of Counseling and Development, 70*, 242–249.

Vontress, C. E. (1996). A personal retrospective on cross-cultural counseling. *Journal of Multicultural Counseling and Development*, 24(3), 156–166.

Vontress, C. E. (2004). Reactions to the multicultural counseling competencies debate. *Journal of Mental Health Counseling, 26*(1), 74–80.

Vontress, C. E., & Epp, L. R. (2001). Existential cross-cultural counseling: When hearts and cultures share. In K. J. Schneider, J. F. T. Bugental, & J. F. Pierson (Eds.), *The handbook of humanistic psychology: Leading edges in theory, research and practice* (pp. 371–388). Thousand Oaks, CA: Sage.

Watson, V. V. V. (2004). The training experiences of black counsellors. Unpublished doctoral dissertation, University of Nottingham.

West, W., & McLeod, J. (2003). Cultural landscapes in counselling and psychotherapy: Introduction to the theme section. *Counselling and Psychotherapy Research, 3*(2), 82–85.

11 Clemmont E. Vontress, African Cultural Imperatives, and Traditional Healing

OLANIYI BOJUWOYE

People are more likely to relate with each other better if they understand one another's cultures. A good understanding of people's ways of being and doing should improve relationship among them. It is from this perspective that I consider Clemmont Vontress's works on African traditional healing as attempts to make people understand and appreciate African cultural practices, especially those associated with healthcare delivery. However, Vontress's passion and contributions in this regard notwithstanding, he remains a Westerner with Western perspectives for evaluating the different phenomena he came across in his African visits, including the responses to his inquiries and the events and people he studied. My aim in this chapter, therefore, is to provide an African perspective on some of Vontress's views on African traditional healing, especially with regard to the contexts in which it occurs and the underlying principles of the practices.

Vontress no doubt contributed to cross-cultural counseling by explicating the relationship between culture and psychology, and in particular 'how culture affects therapeutic helping' (Jackson, 1987, p. 21). Vontress's contention, in this regard, is that 'culture is a human necessity' and that people cannot be described as culturally deprived (ibid.). This assertion emerged from the view that human beings have beliefs and procedures or established ways, by which they cope with their environment or make sense out of life (Vontress, 1996). Consistent with this assertion is Nyasani's (1997) that whether Africans, Asians, or Europeans, people have minds, the products of which are unique cultural edifices and streams that arise from environmental conditionings, adaptations, and long-standing traditions. Since psychology is the study of the human mind, the central ingredient of which is culture, then understanding cultural systems and practices is an important aspect of psychology or its applications (Smith, 1991). Vontress implied this logical relationship of culture and human behavior in the report of his observation of some African immigrants when he stated: 'In the early eighties I became interested in the problems encountered by international students in the United States ... It is difficult for them to adjust to the new culture' (Vontress, 2000, p. 4).

While understanding cultures may foster better inter-racial relationships, it could also entrench a sense of difference. However, while Vontress refuses to be drawn into the argument of the negatives of cultural differences, he prefers instead to highlight the impact of cultural differences on psychotherapeutic interventions (Vontress, 1996). Lindsey (1995) asserts that this impact cannot be ignored, nor can one pretend that psychological knowledge can be applied (as in counseling) in a social vacuum or value-free context. To this Vontress (1996) adds that counselors cannot treat all clients as if they were from the same cultures. They also cannot adopt counseling theories evolved from cultures different from the clients' if their services are to be effective. Vontress's (2003) study of African immigrants in Europe and the United States revealed that they generally do not consult Western caregivers. The reason for the immigrants' behavior is not just fear of disclosing private personal details to strangers; rather, the Africans were convinced that their dominant cultural values would not be reflected in counseling.

Strupp and Hardley (1977) note that in counseling clients are encouraged to confront their belief, ideal, and value systems, to construct images of the world and of themselves, and to adapt to their ecological and social environment. That is to say, if counseling intervention is to be successful, clients must be made to operate from the perspectives of cultural realities they understand or within which they have been brought up. This is because, when in counseling clients are made to operate outside their cultural realities, such helping is unlikely to be seen to contribute to the clients' quality of life. Cultures exert a significant influence over people's thoughts, feelings, and behaviors. Furham (1997) notes further that cultures influence help-seeking behaviors, acceptance of help, and attitudes to overcoming health problems. Furthermore, Moodley (2007) also contends that cultural beliefs about health and illness contribute to the ways in which clients represent and present their psychological distress, and these beliefs also determine cure seeking. A good indication of the ability to empathize with clients and to intervene on their behalf is the adoption of counseling theories that reflect clients' cultural values (Vontress, 1986). The elements of culture which Vontress (1996) indicates should feature in counseling theories include knowledge of clients' cultural imperatives regarding human nature, what constitute difficulties in living, and the methodology of intervention.

African Cultural View of Human Nature

Any therapeutic approach, whether Western or non-Western, adopted in counseling must be based on certain assumptions about human nature, or assumptions regarding the conceptualization of reality by people of a certain culture within their environment. In this connection, Vontress (2000) also agrees that human nature is culturally defined. Each culture has its own perspectives regarding health and disease, or what people of the culture consider as primary causes of ill health and the theory or theories of healthcare delivery. However, in multi-ethnic Africa, Vontress seems rather unsure of a dominant African view of human nature upon which a counseling theory for working with African clients can be based. According to Vontress, 'it is difficult to conceptualize a single view of helping for the Africans themselves, because there are over 2,000 ethnic groups, each culturally different from the other' (Vontress, 1996, p. 164). This contention is certainly contrary to what most African scholars and philosophers believe to be true. For instance, Lassiter (2000) notes that there has existed, and still exists, widespread sub-Saharan African core values, beliefs, cultural themes, and behavior patterns that predate European contact, and it is upon these that the fundamental thought processes and behaviors of contemporary sub-Saharan Africans are based. According to Nyasani (1997), there is such a thing as an African 'mentality,' or 'psyche,' arising from and reflecting a long history of social, cultural, and environmental adaptation and acculturation. Therefore, despite the over 2000 ethnic groups, African philosophers and researchers (Senghor, 1966; Shutte, 1993; Nyasani, 1997; Gyekye, 1988) agree that there are common patterns, or themes, regarding human nature among African cultural groupings. Languages, cultural tools, and methods may differ, but the general underlying principles of most cultural practices of the different African ethnic groups, particularly those pertaining to healthcare delivery, are much the same.

These common themes regarding human nature concern matters of collectivity and spirituality. With regard to collectivity, psychological and moral characteristics pertaining to African identity, personality, and dignity place emphasis on community rather than the individual (Makgoba, 1997). Human nature is socially constructed as people define themselves in relation to others, and the self is a product of, or that which emerges from, relational experiences (Spinnelli, 1994). However, Gyekye (1988) notes that while the dominant entity of African social order is community, that order manifests features of both communality and individuality. Individuals are obviously aware of themselves as individuals, but this is relatively unimportant compared to one's sense of moral duty to the community, which takes precedence over individual interests (Owus-Bempah & Howitt, 1995).

Vontress (2003) rightly recognizes spirituality as an important aspect of the African cultural view on human nature. Africans believe that the universe is not void, but is populated by various elements possessing spirit or a core energy essence binding them together in unity, harmony, and totality. As a result, a firm balance or equilibrium is maintained between all the elements in the universe (Crafford, 1996). This spirit or core energy essence is believed to be unequally distributed among the cosmic elements, resulting in the existence of power relations among them. Thus, some cosmic entities are believed to be more powerful than humans; some humans are also believed to be capable of acquiring more power and becoming more powerful than others.

The general African cultural view of human nature is that it is an interdependent, inseparable whole. Humans are not alone or separated from, but are parts of nature. Humans and the phenomenal world are extensions of each other and influence one another. Taking this notion of collectivity into consideration in any theoretical approaches to counseling African clients should yield some successes.

African Cultural Imperatives Regarding 'Ideal' Human Functioning

Emerging from the notion of the interconnectedness of the phenomenal world is the view of health as synonymous with euphoric harmonious relationships. Good health, or 'ideal' human functioning, is a harmonious relationship with the universe and with local ecology, including plants, animals, and interpersonal relationships (Edwards, 2000). Signs of good health include affluence, wealth, comfort, pleasure, a good harvest, a successful business or career, blissful marital relationships, harmonious relationships with peer groups, neighbors, fellow workers, and one's community. African cultures consider a healthy person as one who integrates into, and contributes to, the community and continues to work at maintaining balance, renewing order, and recreating new forms of harmony (Edwards, 2000). Psychologically healthy persons strive to be in harmony with the forces of nature (human or nonhuman, seen or unseen) impinging on them. The African perspective on health, therefore, has greater meaning, balance, connectedness, and wholeness, both within each individual and also between individuals and their environment (Vontress, 1996).

Ill health is also socially constructed and described as disharmonious relationships. Traditional African cultures view each human as being represented in the physical body and spirit/mind as well as being part of the environment. Or, as Binswanger (1962) puts it, each human exists in a unique physical, interpersonal, and private world. Ill health, therefore, is when there is disharmonious relationship, or break, within oneself (intra-personal or body-mind break). Vontress's (1996) considers this aspect of ill health as leading to difficulties which can be assigned any number of psychological labels. Ill health can also involve disharmonious relationships, or breaks in relatedness, between people (interpersonal break), or between people and their natural environment (Vontress, 1996), or between people and other realities – spiritual entities (God) or ancestral spirits, for instance – as defined by their cultures (Atherton, 2007). Thus, ill health also has wider ramifications and connections with all aspects of human existence, including the social, intellectual, emotional, familial, career, and spiritual aspects of life. This is consistent with Vontress's (2003) existential conception of ill health as disconnections in the psychological, physiological, social, and spiritual aspects of life. This multidimensional view is also consistent with the World Health Organization's (WHO, 1993) view that health is not just the absence of disease and infirmity, but complete physical, mental, social, occupational, and spiritual well-being. Vontress (1996) clustered areas in which people experience difficulties in life into four, including the world of self, or private or intrapersonal world (*eigenwelt*), the world of interpersonal relationships (*mitwelt*), the world of environmental relationships (*umwelt*), and the world of spirit forces (higher power) (*überwelt*).

All dimensions of human existence are explored in traditional healing when ill health is being diagnosed. However, Vontress (2003) is of the view that African traditional healers tend to place more emphasis on the spiritual component of clients' lives. The word 'spiritual' may not necessarily serve as a synonym for religious. However, Owusu-Bempah and

Howitt (1995) disagree with this contention because in many African cultures religion, or the spiritual, and medicine are almost indistinguishable – religion is medicine and medicine is spiritual. Moreover, the pursuit of health for fulfillment of the whole of existence is a religious affair (Mbiti, 1989). From my own understanding, 'spiritual' has many dimensions, as it dominates every aspect of life, religion being one of these. One dimension is self-awareness, gaining insight into, or being in touch with, one's deep inner self. To be in touch with one's inner self is to be in touch with, or to reach deep into, one's spirit, or mind – the citadel where every thought originates, where all forces continually contend, and the realm where resources are cultivated for personal empowerment in dealing with all the contextual forces people have to deal with in everyday living (Bojuwoye, 2001). Being in touch with one's spirit is an indication of integration of body and mind. Without this spiritual aspect of the essence of oneself, it becomes natural to see and feel problems (Tulku, 1975), and African traditional healers help their clients to attain this aspect through meditation, music and dance, and other methods to attain an altered state of consciousness.

Another dimension of 'spiritual' has religious connotations. Africans are very religious and have cultural imperatives incorporating the Supreme Being, or God (the ultimate source of life energy essence), and spirit entities regarded as those of the ancestors (Mbiti, 1989,). These two cosmic entities are believed to have a higher power than humans and are revered for this attribute. The belief is that when a person dies, he/she becomes an ancestral spirit. Death does not make a person cease to belong to his/her social unit (family, clan, tribe, or nation), as the person transformed into spirit (although invisible) continues to reside in the household like everyone else and be involved in the lives of his/her descendants, influencing their behavior (Gumede, 1999; Ngubane, 1977). The roles played by ancestral spirits (believed not to be as powerful as God, but nevertheless more powerful than humans) include being intermediaries between humans and God, or representatives of God, and capable of bringing about good health, wealth, or illness to living humans. Ancestral spirits are believed to be capable of interceding in virtually all aspects of life, including averting illness, assisting in obtaining good fortune, averting natural disasters, and interceding in interpersonal relationship conflicts. Therefore, the need for rapport with a 'higher power,' as Vontress (2003) contends, is a well-established principle within African cultural imperatives.

The notion of appeal to a higher power is associated with the perceived external causes of ill health. The perceived external causes of ill health is consistent with Dryden's (1984) assertion that some cultures view ill health as largely extra-psychic, rather than intra-psychic, and as a reflection of acute or chronic disturbances in the balance of emotional forces in the individual's important relationship system. In this connection, Comaroff (1980) also notes that an aspect of the African cultural view of ill health is that it is an 'affliction' attributable to spiritual entities, human agents, or a 'higher power.' Pillay and Wissenaar (1996) explain this by stating that when people have ill health, experience a medical condition, or undergo other negative life events that they have no direct control over or do not fully understand, they become obsessed with thoughts of being controlled by someone 'out there.' This way of viewing ill health also informs the belief in the intentionality of nature: that nothing happens by chance, and whatever happens to people has meaning and purpose (Ray, 1993). Ill health is the result of the active, purposeful intervention of some powerful cosmic entities – who may be human (a witch or sorcerer), non-human (a ghost or ancestral spirits), or supernatural (a deity) (Ray, 1993). Illnesses, like misfortunes, broken relationships, and physical injuries (even death), are regarded as afflictions, attributable to acts of humans or spiritual entities perceived to have higher powers. Moreover, the belief is that a person's affliction with ill health is meant to serve as a social sanction or as punishment for inappropriate behavior patterns or lifestyle choices resulting from that individual's violations of cultural taboos, failure to adapt to rules-guided behaviors, or refusal to identify with culturally defined realities. In real terms, however, the basic principle underlying this view of ill health is that individual life conditions, lifestyle choices, and behavior patterns can result in ill health. In this connection, some African implicit theories of the causation of ill health parallel those espoused by Western theoreticians (Mpofu, 2007).

To Western critics (van Dyk, 2001; Viljoen, 1997), the African view of ill health as an 'affliction,' or something that does not just happen by chance, implies that sick people are victims who should not be held responsible for their own behaviors, and that personal initiatives in searching for solutions are repressed. This is far from the truth as, in African cultures, people live by rules-guided behaviors. African communalism allows for, and demands, individual expression and accountability, and the family and community expect individuals to take personally enhancing and socially responsible decisions and actions

(Gyekye, 1988). It is in fact more correct to state that this is an African acknowledgment that ill health is associated with dynamic contextual forces, structures, and systems in the environment of people. All negative forces or influences in the environment of people arising from inequalities, injustices, or other forms of unfair social order elicit inner crises of emotions and sensations that disrupt normal consciousness and make people feel powerless or under the control of a 'higher power.' Certainly, the evolution of ill health cannot be separated from broader social issues, economic conditions, and power relations within peoples' contexts, as these contribute significantly to the formation of psychopathology (Hayes, 1986). Human sufferings often arise from group, community, social, cultural, and institutional arrangements, and not necessarily from individual psychopathology (Angelique & Kyle, 2001). Vontress (1996) also concurs with this contention by stating that harsh environmental conditions certainly make people powerless, necessitating rapport with a 'higher power.' However, as Vontress notes, people in the West define a higher power or spirituality differently from the way Africans define them and, although it is not usually acknowledged, people in the West also appeal to a 'higher power' during a time of loss, trials, and tribulations (Vontress, 2003) by praying and meditation.

African Cultural Intervention Strategies

Appeal to a higher power is not the only intervention strategy employed by Africans. On the contrary, many intervention strategies of African cultural healthcare practices parallel those of existential counseling. Vontress notes that African traditional healing incorporates many existential concepts in its philosophies (Epp, 1998). For example, African traditional healing is holistic. Vontress (1996) also describes existential counseling as a holistic intervention strategy focusing simultaneously on the psychological, sociological, physical, and spiritual dimensions of human existence. The African multidimensional view of ill health informs the design of the holistic intervention model of healthcare which facilitates well-being on many levels and in many areas of life, as it involves interactions and the integration of body and spirit/mind, as well as the integration of the individual with his/her environment (Atherton, 2007). The art and science of the holistic intervention model, the type espoused by African traditional healing, is the reconstruction of the physical, social, and spiritual orders of the sociocultural systems (Comaroff, 1980). African traditional healing goes beyond symptom removal to address deeper contextual as well as emotional and spiritual causes of ill health, helping patients realize that certain forces in nature, impacting negatively on people's health, are parts of the essence of life, not to be wished away, but rather to be negotiated and be accommodated (Bojuwoye, 2001).

The basic therapeutic technique of African traditional healing (as in existential counseling) involves good social networks, not only of fellow humans but also of ancestors and deities (higher powers). A common element of all successful therapies is positive interpersonal relationships which are positively related to therapeutic outcomes (Garfield, 1995; Strupp, 1989). The central vehicle for delivering care is the relationship between therapists and clients (Hannigan, Bartlet, & Clilverd, 1997). Vontress also notes that the interpersonal relationship is the most potent therapeutic factor in existential counseling (Epp, 1998). Consistent with the principle of providing care within a broad psychosocial framework, most African traditional healing practices are conducted in groups which bring people together for human interactions to procure health. Parrot (1999) notes that using interpersonal relationships to address health problems is a good strategy, as group interactions guide and facilitate changes in the behavior, cognition, and emotional state of those involved. Vontress (2000) also notes that the African perspective on ill health is that it is a condition affecting not just individuals, but also the families and the collectives to which individuals belong. Being healthy and alive is a collective and communal, rather than individual, matter (Edwards, 2000). Healthcare delivery demands group solidarity, a sense of shared fate or collective responsibility. Making healthcare a group affair also implies that treatment is multidisciplinary, involving many people all working collaboratively together to bring about wellness in different aspects of an individual's life.

Using social activities as intervention strategies (as in African traditional healing) is based on the principle that humans depend on themselves for the development, exercise, and enforcement of their healing power. According to Shutte (1993), the spirit or life energy essence needed for healing is not self-generated but comes through community with other people. Group activities, such as ritual ceremonies and cultural festivals, offer people opportunities to come together for psychoeducation in cultural belief systems regarding health promotion, the development of skills, attitudes, and values in problem sharing, problem solving, decision making, resources sharing, and finding better ways of coping. Group healing facilitates mutual emotional support and enhances self-esteem, and leads to people feeling empowered, or being in control of themselves, and functioning more effectively.

Perhaps a major factor in the potency of African traditional healing is its being characterized by high-energy-level activities including dancing, singing, and praying. Therapies which provide vigorous activities and interpersonal interactions are perceived to be more effective than those which fail to engage the body actively to generate healing energy (Bojuwoye, 2001). Music is an important tool to make therapy active, as it triggers dancing and singing, lifting the spirits of clients and serving as emotional arousal and a strong impetus for the development of powerful morale and the expectation of successful outcomes. Vontress's study of African traditional healing revealed the roles of music to include 'promoting [the] curative process. It profoundly affects muscle tone, body rhythms, and emotions and respiration, heartbeat, digestive peristalses, and brain waves [which] become synchronized … Music draws people together and creates a joyful, and therapeutic sense of unity' (Vontress, 2003, p. 25).

> Music acts as a healing function for [the] individual and the group. A remedy for human imbalance, it facilitates communication with the ancestral spirits and Creator. It harmonizes forces of the visible and invisible worlds, … captures the movements of the human body, its sensations and nature itself … The sound [of music] is the force of change … Music triggers dance and dance is magnetic. They are both contagious and important ingredients for healing. (Vontress, 1999, p. 333)

As people express themselves in dance, their spirits are freed from the contamination of destructive negative emotional feelings, which facilitates self-discovery and the creation of a pleasant, positive, appreciative, and affirming environment (Atherton, 2007). The collective, consensual actions of cultural group dances enhance group consciousness (solidarity), promoting acceptance and appreciation of one another. In this regard, Comaroff (1980) also notes that essential outcomes of African traditional group healing are changes in the dynamics of human relationships from being competitive to being collaborative. As emotions are expressed in dance, catharsis is achieved, and realities from cultural perspectives are accepted as people embrace new values and behaviors in an effort to reduce deviations from existing culturally defined standards.

Integrating Traditional Healing with Mainstream Healthcare Systems

While to Western critics extreme experiences and quick fixes characterize African traditional healing, giving it attractiveness and glamour, the cultural context within which traditional healing works cannot be ignored (Moodley, 2007). Human behavior cannot be divorced from its social, political, economic, and cultural contexts (Govender, 1989). Cultural context is certainly a critical factor in mental health treatment, which makes it necessary to explore the integration of cultural healing practices with mainstream healthcare systems (Moodley, 2007). Integration has great promise for the optimization of cultural resources and indigenous knowledge relevant to health promotion, and this is likely to make healthcare services more acceptable to people with their full participation and at a cost they can afford (Straker, 1994). Context-sensitive practices make care community-oriented, empower community members, and encourage them to become independent and able to take responsibility for improving their own lives and to understand that they are not the victims of environment (Ross & Deverell, 2004). Furthermore, the fact that only a small minority is being served by the Western-oriented healthcare system in Africa makes the integration of traditional healing more imperative, especially for the majority of people, who are geographically and economically inaccessible. Western therapists can also learn from traditional healers because, according to Vontress, '[the] majority of the people in the world consult them … Without them many people would have no medical or psychological services at all. The recognition of this fact led the World Health Organization nearly a quarter of a century ago to recommend that Western health professionals reach out to their traditional counterparts and collaborate with them in the healing enterprise' (Vontress, 2003, p. 26).

Traditional healers bear most of the health burden in Africa (UNESCO, 1994; Vontress, 2005). The actual health-seeking behaviours of Africans also suggest high confidence in the practices of traditional healthcare, as most Africans make use of the services of traditional healers even if they also use Western medicine (Bojuwoye, 2005). No wonder the World Health Organization recommended integration of African traditional healthcare with Western-oriented mainstream health systems as the surest means to achieve total healthcare coverage (Conserveafrica, 2006).

However, there are constraints to the integration of traditional healthcare with mainstream systems. Some of these constraints are due to the traditional healthcare system, while negative attitudes to traditional healthcare by Western-oriented practitioners are also a major problem (Conserveafrica, 2006). Among the drawbacks of traditional healthcare are incorrect diagnosis, imprecise dosage, low hygiene standards, the secrecy of some healing methods and absence of written records about patients (Conserveafrica, 2006). Western-oriented healthcare practitioners tend to focus on risks and pass judgment based on worst outcomes of African healthcare while playing down the efficacy of traditional medicine and expertise of traditional healers (Conserveafrica, 2006). Western critics also describe the cultural settings of traditional healing as dubious and dangerous (Moodley, 2007). Some other people, however, have found African traditional healers to be experienced and skilled in biomedical components of their profession, including an array of biomedical methods and cultural practices ranging from fasting and dieting to herbal therapies, and from bathing and massage to surgical procedures (Conserveafrica, 2006). Vontress also notes that the African traditional healers whom the West disrespects and describes as 'witch doctors' are in fact as effective at bringing health to people as are Western-trained biomedical doctors and psychologists (Epp, 1998). To overcome constraints to integration, therefore, education, training, and research have been suggested (Aids Foundations South Africa, 2006).

With regard to the challenges of insufficient documentation, specific experimentation for verification of traditional healers' claims, and lack of preservation of medicinal extracts for an extended shelf life, it is suggested that government address these issues by establishing institutional and financial support to promote the potential role of herbal medicine in primary healthcare. Conserveafrica (2006) suggests that governments should give priority to the inventory and documentation of various medicinal plants, herbs, cultural materials, tools, indigenous bodies of knowledge, and principles as well as traditional practices relevant to healthcare. It is heartening to note that some of these concerns are already being addressed in some African countries, starting with giving official recognition to traditional healers as important factors in the healthcare sector. For instance, the Traditional Health Practitioners' Bill for the formalization of traditional healthcare is currently in the process of being enacted in South Africa (Inggs, 2007), while this has already been done in Zimbabwe and one or two other African countries (Lazarus, Bojuwoye, Chireshe, et al., 2006). There are also efforts at various levels to organize and mobilize traditional healers for effective practices through training. Packree (2007) also reports that some provincial governments in South Africa have even set up directorates to deal with traditional medicine and healing.

Challenges and Future Directions

The training of traditional healers for capacity building to increase their competences and expand their roles in healthcare promotion at the grass-roots level is being suggested and carried out in South Africa (Aids Foundation South Africa, 2006). Traditional healers need training to understand better the nature of diseases, especially those not within their traditional domain (e.g., HIV/AIDS), to avoid misconceptions and wild claims, and to collaborate with Western-oriented practitioners and university researchers. Inggs (2007) reports that there has been an increase in the funding of scientific and clinical research on traditional medicine by government and research organizations (e.g., South Africa National Research Foundation) to facilitate the registration of traditional medicinal products by the Medicines Control Council of South Africa. Efforts to build the capacity of traditional healers as well as the competence of the biomedical practitioners are ongoing, as many institutions of higher learning have been given money to invest in equipment and to conduct research into and test the claims by traditional healers (Inggs, 2007). Lazarus et al. (2006) also report that a number of universities in South Africa now feature community-oriented psychology courses and supervised practical and internship works in their training programs for psychologists and counselors so that these practitioners can play their roles more effectively.

The traditional African healthcare system's focus is more on the subjective perception of illness, as opposed to the objective psychological processes focused on by the Western system. In this connection, one major challenge for psychologists and counselors could be in the area of research into subjective experiences, including mind-body interventions and the meanings which characterize African traditional healing. The research focus may have to take on postmodern perspectives and do what Atherton (2006) refers to as finding 'modern truth in ancient wisdom.' There certainly would be a need for the reinterpretation, reconstruction, or repositioning of concepts and evolvement of alternative forms of knowledge, approaches, and ways of explaining. For instance, on the theory of ill health, it should be clear to modern-day psychologists and counselors that the 'demons' – the angry ancestral spirits, or human agents, inflicting punishment on people and making them sick – are none other than the contextual factors or the intolerablly harsh socioeconomic conditions in which people live today. That these 'demons' of contextual systems, structures, and forces are responsible for the powerlessness and emotional upheavals people feel. That the healing power people look for in ancestral spirits or a higher power is within individuals and can be activated by the cultivation of appropriate interpersonal relationships and the acquisition of knowledge, skills, attitudes, and values for personal empowerment and for the reassessment of situations, the willingness to make changes, and the adoption of better behavior patterns (coupled with a refusal to be a victim of environment). There abound many traditional ways of encouraging people to rethink human relationships, from being competitive to being collaborative, which researchers would need to look into. African traditional societies also have several resources and or sources of support as well as avenues for learning traditional coping skills. Touch and music therapies, the power of spoken words, narratives, and metaphors to imprint intentions on people – all well established in African traditional healing – need to be studied carefully with a view to exploiting their therapeutic benefits.

Western-oriented health workers (psychologists, public health and social workers) also need training in abilities and skills in community work to identify relevant community-based organizations and develop appropriate strategies (mobilization, advocacy, networking, leadership training, etc.). With the integration of both traditional and Western-oriented health systems would come opportunities for the exploitation of the each culture's unique approaches to understanding health and disease. Integration also gives opportunity for both traditional and Western-trained practitioners to cooperate, work together, and learn from each other, especially about successes and failures, and discover when, how, and to whom to refer cases (Aids Foundation South Africa, 2007).

Conclusion

As the world is becoming more multicultural, ordinarily people of different cultures living together should not suggest problems for healthcare practitioners, but rather a challenge as to how the resources of the different cultures can be pooled for improving human conditions. However, this is not always the case, as Vontress (Epp, 1998) found out; too often people are treated differently, and in many cases harshly, because of the differences practitioners see standing out conspicuously, not the similarities. Vontress's (2000) view is that no matter what conditions people live under, they are all members of the human species, and there is a universal all-encompassing humanness in each of us, and that people should focus more on cross-cultural similarities and the broad patterns by which ideas and knowledge could be shared and human conditions improved. Focusing on what people perceive as the negative aspects of cultural differences can only lead to the separation of human beings, with people standing proudly apart. Vontress, however, is not suggesting that the unique differences in each culture are not important. Rather, his suggestion is that psychologists and counselors should creatively exploit the uniqueness of each culture to the advantage of human beings, and not to their detriment. If care providers are to effect changes in their clients, then they must respect and be tolerant of their clients' cultural value differences. As Vontress (1996) argues, how can people help to heal or be healed if there is no respect and no love for one another? Moreover, if it is realized that every culture has something to contribute to human progress, there would be no such problem of disregard for some certain cultures, but rather trust, faith, and love would prevail between people, which are essential ingredients ensuring healing and effective healthcare (Epp, 1998).

Love for humanity and respect for all cultures are certainly the driving force in Vontress's works and his contributions to cross-cultural counseling. I also believe that these qualities, and not his remote ancestral connections to Africa, are responsible for his passion for African traditional healing, which, in no small way, he has helped to popularize. Very few people can overcome their cultural prejudices and recognize, as Vontress (2000) has demonstrated, that 'we are all alike and different at the same time.' This recognition is what can bring about health and progress for all people.

REFERENCES

Aids Foundations South Africa (2006). Current situation. Accessed 11 May 2006, at http://www.aids.org.za/hiv.htm.

Atherton, K. (2007). *Holistic healing*. Pindari Herb Farm. Accessed 21 May 2007, at http://pindariherbfarm.com/healing/holiheal.htm.

Binswanger, L. (1962). *Existential analysis and psychotherapy*. New York: Dutton.

Bojuwoye, O. (2001). Crossing cultural boundaries in counselling. *International Journal for the Advancement of Counseling, 23*, 31–50.

Bojuwoye, O. (2005). Traditional healing practices in Southern Africa. In R. Moodley & W. West (Eds.), *Integrating traditional healing practices into counseling and psychotherapy* (pp. 61–72). Thousand Oaks: Sage.

Buhrman, M. V. (1990). Psyche and soma: Therapeutic considerations. In G. Sayman (Ed.), *Modern South Africa in search of soul: Jungian perspectives on the wildness within* (pp. 203–218). Boston: Sigo Press.

Comaroff, J. (1980). Healing and the cultural order. The case of Baralong Boo Ratshidi of Southern Africa. *American Ethnologist, 7*, 637–657.

Conserveafrica (2006). Overview of medicinal plants and traditional medicine in Africa. Accessed 27 May 2006, at http://www.conserveafrica.org.uk/medical_plants.pdf/.

Crafford, D. (1996). The African religions. In P. Meiring (Ed.), *World of religions: A South Africa perspective.* Pretoria, South Africa: Kagiso.

Dryden, W. (1984).Therapeutic arenas. In W. Dryden (Ed.), *Individual therapy in Britain* (pp. 1–22). London: Harper & Row Publishers.

Edwards, S. D. (2000). Developing community psychology in Zululand, South Africa. In S. N. Madu, P. K. Baguma, & A. Pritz (Eds.), *Psychotherapy and African reality* (pp. 149–159), Pietersburg, South Africa: UNN Press.

Epp, L. R. (1998). The courage to be an existential counselor: An interview of Clemmont E. Vontress. *Journal of Mental Health Counseling, 20*(1), 1–12.

Frank, J. (1982). What is psychotherapy? In S. Bloch (Ed.), *An introduction to psychotherapy.* New York: Oxford University Press.

Furham, L. (1997). Overcoming neuroses: Lay attributions of cure for five specific disorders. *Journal of Clinical Psychology* 53: 595–604.

Govender, R. (1989). Political psychology and developing countries: Can it make a meaningful contribution? Unpublished paper, University of California, Los Angeles.

Gumede, M. V. (1990). *Traditional healers: A medical doctor's perspective.* Braamfontein, South Africa: Skotaville.

Gyekye, K. (1988). *The unexamined life: Philosophy and the African experience.* Accra: Ghana University Press.

Hayes, G. (1986). Intervening with political psyche, In *Organization for appropriate social services in South Africa* (pp. 44–48). Johannesburg: Organization for Appropriate Social Services in Southern Africa.

Inggs, M. (2007). Plant strippers threaten traditional healing. *Sunday Tribune* (Durban, South Africa), 9 September 2007, 2.

Jackson, M. L. (1987). Cross-cultural counseling at a crossroads: A dialogue with Clemmont E. Vontress. *Journal of Counseling and Development, 66*, 20–23.

Kashima, Y. (2000). Conception of culture and person for psychology. *Journal of Cross-Cultural Psychology, 31*, 14–32.

Lassiter, J. E. (1999). African culture and personality: Bad social science, effective social activism, or a call to reinvent ethnology? *African Studies Quarterly 3*(2), 1. Available at http://www.africa.ufl.edu/asq/v3/v3i3a1.htm.

Lazarus, S., Bojuwoye, O., Chireshe, R., et al. (2006). Community psychology in Africa: Views from across the continent. *Journal of Psychology in Africa, 16*(2), 147–160.

Makgoba, M. W. (1997). *MOKOKO, the makgoba affair: A reflection on transformation*. Florida Hills: Vivlia Publishers and Booksellers.

Mbiti, J. S. (1989). *African religions and philosophy* (2nd ed.). Oxford: Heinemann Educational Books Inc.

Moodley, R. (2007). Replacing multiculturalism in counselling and psychotherapy. *British Journal of Guidance and Counselling, 35*(1), 1–22.

Mpofu, E. (2007). Conduct disorder in children: Presentation, treatment options and cultural efficacy in an African setting. *International Journal of Disability, Community and rehabilitation 2*(1). Available online at http://www.ijdcr.ca/VOL02_01_CAN/articles/mpofu.shtm1.

Ngubane, H. (1977). *Body and mind in Zulu medicine*. London: Academic Press.

Nyasani, J. M. (1997). *The African psyche*. Nairobi: University of Nairobi and Theological Printing Press.

Owusu-Bempah, J., & Howitt, D. (1995). How Eurocentric psychology damages Africa. *The Psychologist*, October 1995, 462–465.

Packree, S. (2007). Traditional healing directorate set up. *Daily News* (Durban, South Africa), 30 August 2007, p. 5.

Parrott, C. (1999). Towards an integration of science, art and morality: The role of values in psychology. *Counselling Psychology Quarterly, 12*, 5–24

Philip, D. R., & Verhasselt, Y. (1994). Health and development: Retrospect and prospect. In D. R. Phillips & Y. Verhasselt (Eds.), *Health and Development* (pp. 301–318). New York: Routledge.

Pillay, A. L., & Wassenaar, D. (1996). Hopelessness and psychiatric symptomatology in hospitalized physically ill adolescents. *South African Journal of Psychology, 26*, 47–51.

Ray, C. B. (1993). Aladura Christianity: A Yoruba religion. *Journal of Religion in Africa, 23*, 266–291.

Ross, E., & Deverell, A. (2004). *Psychological approaches to health, illness and disability*. Pretoria, South Africa: Van Schaik Publishers.

Senghor, L. (1966). Negritude and African socialism. In K. Kirkwood (Ed.), *St Anthony's Papers No. 1* (pp. 16–22). London: Oxford University Press.

Shutte, A. (1993). *Philosophy of Africa.* Rodenbosch: University of Cape Town Press.

Spinnelli, E. (1994). *Demystifying therapy.* London: Constable.

Straker, G. (1994). Integrating African and western healing practices in South Africa. *American Journal of Psychotherapy, 48,* 455–467.

Tulku, T. (1975). *Reflections of mind: Western psychology meets Tibetan Buddhism.* Emeryville, CA: Dharma Publishing.

UNESCO, (1994). Traditional knowledge into the twenty-first century. *Nature & Resources, 30*(2). UNESCO, Paris.

Van Dyk, A. C. (2001). Traditional African beliefs and customs: Implications for AIDS education and prevention. *South African Journal of Psychology, 31*(2), 60–66.

Viljoen, H. G. (1997). Eastern and African perspectives. In W. F. Meyer, C. Moore, & H. G. Viljoen (Eds.), *Personology: From individual to ecosystem* (pp. 591–627). Johannesburg: Heinemann.

Vontress, C. E. (1979). Cross-cultural counseling: An existential approach. *The Personnel and Guidance Journal, 58,* 117–122

Vontress, C. E. (1986). Existential anxiety: Implications for counseling. *Journal of Mental Health Counseling, 8,* 100–109.

Vontress, C. E. (1988). An existential approach to cross-cultural counseling. *Journal of Multicultural Counseling and Development, 16*(2), 73–78.

Vontress, C. E. (1996). A personal retrospective on cross-cultural counseling. *Journal of Multicultural Counseling and Development, 24,* 156–166.

Vontress, C. E. (1999). Interview with a traditional African healer. *Journal of Mental Health Counseling, 21*(4), 326–336.

Vontress, C. E. (2000). Cross-cultural counselling in the 21st century. A keynote address presented at the International Association for Counseling. Thessaloniki, Greece, 4–7 May 2000.

Vontress, C. E. (2003). On becoming an existential cross-cultural counsellor. In F. D. Harper & J. McFadden (Eds.), *Culture and counseling* (pp. 20–30). Boston: Allyn & Bacon.

Vontress, C. E. (2005). Animism: Foundation of traditional healing in sub-Saharan Africa. In R. Moodley & W. West (Eds.), *Integrating traditional healing practices into counseling and psychotherapy* (pp. 124–137). Thousand Oaks: Sage.

World Health Organization (1993). *World health statistical manual*, 1992. Geneva, Switzerland.

12 Clemmont E. Vontress and Cross-Cultural Counseling in the Caribbean

RONALD MARSHALL AND DEONE CURLING

Counseling in the English-speaking Caribbean[1] is a relatively new approach in addressing individuals' problems driven by social, cultural, and situational factors considered beyond their control. Counseling first emerged in the Caribbean around the late 1970s. It is slowly gaining in popularity as many psychologists trained abroad are returning to the region (Ward & Hickling, 2004). Although counseling is not fully developed, it appears to be increasingly used in schools, to deal with family problems, and by individuals seeking the services of a counselor whenever a 'serious' problem arises. There are those, however, who question the role psychology plays within the Caribbean region (Ali & Toner, 2004; Roopnanrine, 1997). In addition, throughout his career Clemmont Vontress (1982) has critiqued the Eurocentric approach to therapy and stated that many outside the Western world are skeptical that someone can significantly influence the destiny of another just by talking.

Vontress (2003), however, teaches us that in non-Western societies, such as the Caribbean, it is believed that the root cause of psychological and physical distress lies in the disconnection of the client's psychological, physiological, social, and spiritual worlds. Understanding human problems in this way closely relates to Vontress's approach to cross-cultural counseling. Counseling, therefore, can be a very effective interventionist tool to address emotional and situational problems emanating from social interaction. The manner in which this is played out in the Caribbean is of particular interest here. In this respect, throughout the discussion we are going to explore Vontress's work by examining the mainstream counseling approach in the Caribbean and investigate the concept of psychological surrendering and how culture, class, and race factor into it.

Counseling in the Caribbean

Counseling in the Caribbean should be understood in context of its history and culture. The Caribbean has a legacy of slavery, indentureship, and colonization that had effectively seen white elites capture power and subsequently control the development of the Caribbean and the direction of its islands. The Caribbean was left with a legacy of social problems that have been passed down from generation to generation, and this filters into the psychological make-up of a people feeling inadequate (Ward & Hickling, 2004). These social problems tend to challenge family dynamics, parent-child attachment, difficult relations between sexes, underdevelopment, and economic disadvantage (ibid.). The use of Western models of counseling needs to be seriously reviewed in order to determine their applicability and suitability to the region. As Corey (2005) eloquently expresses it, 'Our human qualities and experiences have influenced us' (p. 17).

The history and culture of the Caribbean people construct who they are as individuals, and this needs to be understood within the counseling setting. In addition, the variegated structure of Caribbean societies, with race and class intertwined, opens the door to answering many questions about the relationship between counseling and the social setting in which it is immersed. It was in the slavery period that the colour/class system characteristic of the region emerged (Henriques & Manyoni, 1977). From emancipation and the independence of the islands years later came a motley collection of various cultures within the framework of race and class, where light skin gets social preference and dark-skinned individuals face numerous challenges.[2] Moreover, meaningful psychological and counseling insights could be gleaned from stereotypical roles and how these hinder or solve problems arising out of race- and class-based interactions between individuals. In this respect, the counselor–client relationship needs to be examined in order to fully understand the critical role race and class tend to play in the therapeutic alliance.

Individuals caught within a race/class/culture vortex cannot be easily accommodated by traditional counseling; even as the presence of the practitioner of traditional European counseling foists this aberration upon the culture (a practice readily 'accepted' in the region because of the ethnic mix of Caribbean societies, which invariably adopts various cultures with relative ease). According to D'Ardenne and Mahtani (1989), traditional Western 'psychotherapy is essentially

Eurocentric, ethnocentric, individualistic, patriarchal and social-class oriented.' Counselors trained in traditional Eurocentric practices may transmit the superior/inferior, development/underdevelopment perspective that is characteristic of white culture. While this may continue to be the practice in European and Western societies in which blacks are minorities, in the Caribbean this practice must be seriously examined. For instance, although the vast majority of people from the Caribbean are of African, East Indian and, and other ethnic groups, whites still have considerable sway economically, even though their political aspirations have receded.

Counseling in a Multicultural Setting

The popular Caribbean saying used through out the region, 'Out of many comes one,' suggests that out of many peoples, races, and ancestors has emerged a single people illustrating the concept of assimilation. However, the integration of many people has failed to address the power relations that are inherent in the polarity of integration. Moodley and Curling (2006) explain that the theory of multiculturalism has challenged the concept of assimilation, and as the term suggests, it is a multiple articulation of varied, contradictory, and contested ideas and explanations for complex human behaviors, functions, rituals, and ceremonies. The diverse Caribbean population is a kaleidoscope of interaction between people of varying culture, socioeconomic class, race, ethnicity, sexual orientation, ability, and religion/ spirituality. To conduct counseling in a multicultural setting is to acknowledge these differences. Multicultural counseling occurs when counselors are able to engage in difficult dialogues related to class, race, gender, religion, disability, and sexual orientation. For the therapy to be successful, therapists need to examine their own unconscious complex human behaviors and recognize their own learned stereotypes and prejudices that they uphold in relation to the difference of 'the other.' What must be recognized as well are the institutions around which these psychotherapeutic outcomes are produced – namely, the family, the workplace (including the work ethic), religion, marriage, and the education system.

Ramirez (cited in McLeod, 1998) has suggested that a 'common theme running through all cross-cultural counseling is the challenge of living in a multi-cultural society' (p. 173). One important approach noted by the author is to concentrate on the connection between personal problems and the politics or social realities of the client. He explains that an individual in this instance is not seen purely as a person having psychological problems, but as an active member of a culture. These sentiments are echoed by Vontress (1979) when he explains that culture can turn against us when we internalize the subliminal negative messages constantly being sent our way from a dominant culture.

The social aspects of identity become embedded in the history of geographic movement and the inevitable positive and negative encounters that occur as a result. Moreover, 'today, as in the past, people move freely about the face of the earth ... [and] in spite of the heterogeneity of contemporary societies, psychotherapeutic professionals are expected to provide equally competent services to those who need them' (Vontress, 1985, p. 1). He notes that little attention has been paid to the construction of new theories designed to facilitate cross-cultural helping. One of the most challenging tasks for cross-cultural counselors, according to Vontress, is an accurate psychosocial assessment of clients. Strange and unfamiliar cultural surroundings may provoke anxiety and frustration. As Vontress explains:

> How counselors actually help clients is one of the most confusing aspects of counseling and is reflected as such in the psychotherapeutic literature. Words such as techniques, processes, procedures, skills, tactics, and strategies are often used interchangeably in referring to a partial or complete methodology. How cross-cultural counselors help clients cannot be separated from their perception of human nature, how people acquire culture, and the definition of what constitutes bizarre or unacceptable behavior. (Vontress, 1985, p. 22)

In fact, 'the cultural expansion of the profession [cross-cultural counseling] has ... caused counselors to become more flexible in their approaches to counseling' (Vontress, 1986, p. 243). The author explains that people become so much a part of their culture that they tend to respond almost automatically to it. Culturally different clients, he warns, may come into conflict with the counselor when they remain unaware of the behaviors required of them in unfamiliar environments.

Counseling is known in the Western world as a process that helps individuals who are psychologically healthy resolve personal concerns. According to Krumboltz, it 'consists of whatever ethical activities a counselor undertakes in an effort to help the client engage in those types of behavior which will lead to a resolution of the client's problems' (cited in George & Cristiani, 1995, p. 2). Nevertheless, Gopaul-McNicol (1998) explains that Caribbean peoples tend to believe that solving problems is internally orientated; the only outsiders who are permitted to intrude in their lives outside the family structure are priests, ministers, or spiritual healers. Therefore, individuals seek the services of a counselor as a last resort when others have failed them.

Hence, Vontress warns us, when a Caribbean individual from a lower socioeconomic class makes the decision to engage in counseling, which is based on middle-class values, 'the cross-cultural psychotherapeutic atmosphere is contaminated by psychological pollutants over which they (the counselors) have little control' (Vontress, 1982, p. 347). The author was speaking specifically about the race-class problem faced by blacks in the United States and the problem of finding a resolution in the therapeutic environment. However, in the Caribbean, while 'blackness' takes on a different meaning, the implications following a clash of values resonate with the same intensity.

Psychological Surrendering

Although clients come from all social strata, counselors generally are middle-class in their values, lifestyle, speech, and general view of the world. From the nature of their professional training, they tend to assume that their clientele upholds the same middle-class values and that the theories and techniques they learned in professional schools should suffice across all social classes (Vontress, 1982). Taking into account this approach, Vontress suggests that there must be an element of psychological surrender for the therapeutic alliance to occur. He continues that psychological surrendering entails five dimensions: the rapport between client and counselor, the client's trust of the counselor, one's ability to listen to what is offered to them, the client's willingness to self-disclose, and ('though a negative factor in psychological surrendering') the client's resistance. Vontress clarifies:

> Counseling is most productive when clients psychologically surrender themselves to the process. Clients' reluctance or failure to do so is embodied in concepts such as acting-out behavior, negative transference, provocativeness, resistance, and blocking. In general, these labels suggest that clients are at fault for hindering efforts on their own behalf. This view of the problem is unfortunate because it tends to absolve counselors from further attempts to help people who need it the most – lower class people. (Vontress, 1982, p. 347)

For instance, individuals from a lower socioeconomic class are made to go into settings[3] where they feel ill at ease; are placed in situations that contradict, even poke fun at, the things that are 'achievable,' but which remain outside their reach. Many professional services, such as counseling, operate out of convenient locations, but others, in order to avoid cramped surroundings, are found in exclusive neighborhoods.[4] These settings produce a certain amount of unease, as the client has to step out of his/her familiar social environment to one considered 'better'; thus, the psychotherapeutic atmosphere changes. So also would diagnosis, prognosis, and intervention (see Vontress, 1982). To overcome this problem, adjustment to the counselor–client relationship must be made. Lennard and Bernstean (1970) suggest that 'counselors should explain to clients what they are planning to do, how they will do it, expected benefits to be derived from the process, what the counselor's role is, and what is expected of the client.'

Gopaul-McNicol (1998) proposes that counselors also need to personalize the therapeutic relationship, for instance, consider making home visits to build trust between themselves and their clients. This may be important to consider because, as Vontress (1982) notes, 'many lower-stratum clients are reluctant to surrender themselves psychologically because they are unable to trust their counselors. They cannot believe firmly or have complete confidence in the veracity, honesty, integrity, reliability, and justice of middle class people who declare an interest in helping them' (p. 349).

In the Caribbean region, this behavior is particularly prevalent, since class distinctions are determined by one's type of culture, associations, and place of residence, among other things. In Guyana, lower socioeconomic clients find it extremely difficult to access the more highly qualified and much valued upper-class counselors, even when they mimic higher socio-economic values. This is because in Guyana ethnic distinctions are so prevalent that sensitivity of class and race come into most social encounters and co-equal social relations are difficult to initiate. Vontress and Epp (2001) explain that in order to begin the therapeutic relationship clients must feel that the therapist truly cares for them as human beings:

> Over the years, my colleagues have come to see me as an iconoclast because I reject the notion of therapeutic objectivity and professional distance and declare them to be anti-therapeutic ... I believe that we must genuinely care about our clients as fellow human beings. I have come to despise the professional games and bureaucracy that we dispense as our

> means of helping others. No wonder clients often come to hate counseling centers; these organizations often reflect the insensitivity of the clients' world instead of offering a place of refuge and healing. (Vontress & Epp, 2001, p. 383)

Empathy as a significant aspect of psychological surrendering may become an elusive goal. In the therapeutic relationship, clients are searching to feel counselors' empathy toward them before they are able to surrender. If the client is outside the counselor's community, it becomes more challenging for the client to trust that the counselor has empathy for his/her situation. Vontress explains that 'the more different counselors are from their clients in terms of social class and race, the more difficulty they have in empathizing with those they are expected to help; the inability to empathize with another being is immediately felt by the other' (Vontress, 1982, p. 349). The therapeutic alliance between counselors from a different social class and their clients becomes an added challenge. Genuine empathy from the counselor becomes the link that bridges the gap.

Cultural, Class, and Race

The therapist may experience some challenges in getting their views across to the client, who by their lack of understanding and inadequate vocabulary finds themselves in an awkward position. The counselor may not grasp the full extent of his/her client's issue. They may have a different perspective on interpreting the problem, a lack of understanding of the cultural significance of the dilemma and of the context in which the issue occurred, and inappropriate methods to address the problem. This may be especially difficult if there is 'class posturing.'[5] The client must skillfully pick his/her way through the ensuing dialogues because they are caught between ideologies, philosophies, and perceptions. According to Vontress (2003), clients need to feel that counselors understand where they are coming from. The degree to which counselors with Eurocentric values could positively intervene in a client's psychological make-up against a class/race background points to a test of their skills and experience in working within cosmopolitan cultures, such as the Caribbean. As Vontress (2003) expresses it: 'The ability of therapists to speak the client's ethnic or national language is the first indication of their ability to empathize with them and to intervene on their behalf' (p. 25).

Culture within counseling plays a significant role in the therapeutic alliance. Gollnick and Chinn (1998) state that 'intercultural misunderstandings occur even when no language barrier exists and large components of the major culture are shared by the people involved' (p. 8). At the same time, however, the social constructs of culture, class, and race 'are essential elements within which the identity of the client is negotiated and the inter-subjective relationship is constructed' (Moodley & Palmer, 2006, p. 11). The question is whether, in psychologically surrendering themselves, clients in the Caribbean, originating from lower socioeconomic backgrounds, facilitate the counseling process and reap the expected benefits. As mentioned earlier, clients who fail to psychologically surrender themselves tend to be seen as behaving negatively (Vontress, 1982). This reaction may spill out into the wider society and have serious consequences for the resolution of conflict, particularly from a class-race perspective. This situation may ignore the hidden aspects of individual problems and lead to their 'negotiated' outcome in other spheres of social activities. Hence, counselors should not readily judge 'anti-social' behaviour in terms of individual pathology, since it may deprive them of important understandings of the clients' world (Lago, 1996).

One way to deal with this is for counselors to view their clients as cultural representatives and as individuals, taking into consideration the facts of body movements, nonverbal language, and proximal behavior. Vontress (2003) advises counselors to create a cultural profile on each of their clients. This helps in understanding the extent to which the client's culture shapes, directs, and influences who they are. In the Caribbean, ever-present in counselor-client encounters is the individual's ancestral lineage – whether they are pure Afro-Trinidadian, Afro-Jamaican, or East Indian, or Mixed.[6] But there are many aspects of cultures that both client and counselor may be less aware of: nonverbal communication, attitudes towards words, attitudes towards commitments, attitudes towards authority, and perceptions of professionalism, among others (Lago, 1996).

'Personal talk,' class, and cultural alignments play a central role in the counseling relationship. Since, people are 'not inclined to talk "personal talk" to people who show disrespect by refusing to reciprocate' (Vontress, 1982, p. 350), the client–counselor interaction could stumble and stall, because counselors are trained to hold back their personal self within the engagement with clients. Hence, Caribbean counseling attempts to deal with normal, as well as unusual, patterns of interactions that are thrown up by differences in culture and class intersections, mediated by skin colour and stature.

Counselors have recognized the association between culture and class for quite some time (Vontress, 1986). In the United States, 'members of racial and ethnic groups are often concentrated at the lower levels of stratification systems' (Rothman, 1999, p. 61). However, although there are aspects of political domination of some groups (Blacks, Mexican-Americans, and Latinos) in the United States, the same does not appear in the Caribbean. In the United States, there is the overarching 'American culture,' even as cultural differences are evident. No such qualification exists in the Caribbean. Focusing on Central and South America, Vontress (1986) points out that large groups tend to absorb a minority group until differences or distinctions are no longer noticeable. In the 1970s, the Caribbean region experienced Black Power consciousness and expressed sentiments that called for the removal of 'whites' in top executive and occupational positions. At the same time, trade unions called for governments to take greater control of their economies. Commitment to change tends to vary from country to country. But any movement away from the metropolitan value system warrants appropriate treatment modalities (Foulks, 1980).Thus, as far as diagnosis is concerned, defining the problem in Caribbean society takes the form of understanding how the environment (culture, class, and race) manifests itself in different ways depending upon a group's cohesion or dividedness.

Since the Caribbean is migration-prone, as well as pluralistic to varying degrees,[7] it is in the interests of the counselor to obtain fresh insights into behaviors of individuals, since the dynamics of the social situation are always in flux. A case in point is the deportees from the United States and Canada. Some individuals who have spent a great portion of their lives in North America and are sent back to the Caribbean experience a form of culture shock. They return 'home,' but find themselves in a 'strange' culture where people tend to 'look down' on them. Therefore, what we observe externally may be the unresolved manifestation of inward social and psychological dissonance, which finds individual expression in a complex web of social interactions that have created a network of suspicion, tension, anxiety, subservience, and feelings of 'inferiority,' 'incompetence,' and even 'resistance.'

Another example in which the dynamics of culture, class, and race play themselves out is the Caribbean family, one of the many institutions that may perpetuate the complex social interactions that are mirrored in negative counselor–client interactions. In the Caribbean, a family has traditionally meant a network of people, not just two parents and their children (Hodge, 2002, p. 475). Although this form of family organization is dominant in the Caribbean, it is not dominant in relation to the values of the middle class. Thus, families are often faced with the conflicting values, demands, and rules of different dominant-dyad priorities which, combined with socioeconomic stresses and other cultural pressures, may result in family disorganization and weakening of attachment ties, social isolation, and marginalization (Cook-Darzens & Brunod, 1999, p. 433). For instance, over the years, matriarchy and single parenting were viewed as 'bad' for the society and even pathologized by Western psychotherapy, since observers believed that they were responsible for a number of social ills.

However, matriarchy and the extended family are the strength and backbone of Caribbean people's psychological well-being. The matriarch tends to be the female elder in the home. The expression 'Yu mother house' used to refer to a person's home even when the mother in question has a male partner living in the household (Hodge, 2002, p. 482). This shows that the matriarch of the family is respected by all its members and the community at large. Mammy, Granny, Ma, or Mama, as she is affectionately referred to in the Caribbean, tends to be the nurturer of family members' psychological well-being, as well as of members within the extended family. According to Rawlins's (2002) study, the family provides individuals a sense of security against loneliness, mental instability, poverty, and physical ill health

This powerful network, the family, is at the heart of the Caribbean client. Vontress (2001) warns that in collective societies such as the Caribbean's, the heads of families assume a powerful and respectful role. It is a good idea for counselors to ask clients whether there are people at home or elsewhere who should be consulted regarding the presenting of problems and their solutions. This is true throughout various family classes in the Caribbean; decisions that affect an individual tend to be made with the consultation of all the family members (Rawlins, 2002, p. 280). The therapist must understand that within a collective society individualism is not valued as it is in Western regions, and needs to respect the fact that Caribbean people speak in terms of 'we' not 'I.' Decisions are made in the context that all family members will be well taken care of. For example, self-care is usually referred to in the context of how it benefits the family as a whole and not just the individual (Curling, Chatterjee, & Massaquoi, 2008). The family becomes the first teacher of how culture, class, and race play out within the individual.

The Countdown to Psychotherapeutic Provision

This chapter's concern is with how ex-colonial multi-ethnic entities continue to pose social and psychological problems to individuals who themselves are members of different cultural backgrounds, and who compete for legitimization within the social spaces they occupy. Group expectations reinforce the culture of groups, thus providing them with their distinctiveness. Class represents one aspect of cultural variation, since a class's members have a common advantage over other groups, that is, they 'are more able to manipulate their environments than those with no such advantage' (Vontress, 1986, p. 221).

The counselor must be armed with the notion that in ex-colonial, multicultural societies, class and culture are important, since they touch significant aspects of psychotherapy such as normative behaviors, notions about the characteristics of a help giver, diagnoses across culture, and intervention strategies (Vontress, 1986). Thus, the behaviors, thoughts, and values of clients must be seen through a cultural prism (Lidz, 1976).

Once Caribbean society recognizes that there lies a deeper urge for understanding their social relations, where class and race preside, this holds a wide understanding for Vontress's work. Counselors in the Caribbean who were trained abroad need to know the history of various races and how they live and function in the society. The subject/personal and relational world of the client, and how he/she effects a 'cure,' can be culturally constructed in a multicultural setting. The culture *within* which a person operates is a complex and difficult one and has implications for counselors, but the counselor seldom observes the client acting within his/her own cultural context (McLeod, 1998).

The question is how do counselors trained abroad deal with clients from the developing Caribbean, or how do locally (or regionally trained) counselors work with people migrating into the Caribbean? Vontress throws some light on this problem. He invites our attention to two main issues in the United States that could be applied to the Caribbean situation: client preference for counselors and test bias. In regards to the first, it is felt that counselors from the dominant group are ineffective with minority racial groups. In regards to the second, it is believed that counselors and psychologists working with mature clienteles do not take the time and money to develop standardized psychometric instruments to translate tests into the language of their clients. In other words, these instruments are not subject to cultural revision or adjustment from time to time.

In addition, teachers and students must realize that 'minority' does not mean 'inferiority.' Given that those with economic power tend to confront most of their social challenges, counselors must be culturally sensitive to the social consequences of their intervention and kinds of prognosis (Vontress, 1986).

Conclusion

The emergence of a new set of social relations structured upon psychotherapeutic relevance entails psychological adjustments that recognize the principles of psychotherapy and psychoanalysis in order to inform social interaction and self-development. This adjustment is important for 'freeing up' social spaces that are polluted by subjective negative internalized states. In developing societies such as the Caribbean's, class and race are effective tools that structure social interactions. Here is where research into counseling minorities can make a big difference. This is not simply a matter of minority clients having to sort out issues amongst themselves. It has to do with different races and ethnicities living side by side within ex-colonial developing territories, and the implication of these past experiences that are still relevant in contemporary Caribbean societies. In the Caribbean, unlike other regions of the world, culture is not easily defined. It is a concoction of European and American values and ideologies, reinforced by the reactions to cultural and political dominance (subtle as they may be) in song, dance, and dress. These are important factors to consider when addressing efficient and effective cross-cultural counseling in the Caribbean. At the same time, the ability of the counselor to draw from different cultures is a major asset in bridging the gap between theory and practice. Ways to accomplish this inlude encouraging research into disadvantaged groups in the national community and getting accustomed to using language that is culturally acceptable, as well as those that are specific to various sub-groups within the population. Also, counselors should be exposed to varied counseling techniques with a view to finding the correct mix of skills that would make the difference between pretence and presence. In this context, we would have applied the lessons learned from Vontress's work, as it addresses the question of psychotherapeutic surrendering.

NOTES

1 The Caribbean is a region of many cultures and nationalities. These are small ex-colonial territories still smarting from the lingering social and psychological effects of slavery and indentureship and, to some extent, the effects of Crown Colony governing. Independence (with specific reference to the English-speaking Caribbean) was granted to these countries in the mid-to-late twentieth century and it is believed by some observers that when sugar was no longer 'king,' the economic future of these islands was in doubt. Ethnicity, or the cultural aspects of living, is of particular importance, for it determines access to the means of production, namely, wealth, political power, and prestige (Yelvington, 1993). These factors, it is argued, find themselves in the counselor–client interaction and have implications for the future of counseling in the Caribbean.
2 Skin colour in the Caribbean is a derivative of slavery and the colonial experience. Whites ruled these countries and designated anything that was 'black' or associated with black, including skin colour, as inferior. After emancipation of the slaves the values of the white planter class, including skin colour (such as shades of white, or approximating white), were considered to be of greater social value. Thus, a lighter skin colour indicated a higher social status and darker skin colour was associated with lower social status.
3 'Settings,' in this instance, means the type of adornment on the walls – the paintings, the quotations from prominent figures (known or unknown to the client) – the ambiance, and the body language of the counselor (whether it is accepting or condescending), and how all of these transmit values that may make the client feel uncomfortable, or 'out of place.'
4 In the Caribbean island of Trinidad, most of the professions jostle for space in the urban city centre. Counselors in the suburbs stand out as having special skills tailored to the needs of a special clientele. Although clients come from all social strata, counselors 'are middle class in values, lifestyle, speech and general view of the world' (Vontress, 1982, p. 346).
5 'Class posturing' means posing as a member of another group and imitating their mannerism, especially in situations when the individual needs to be accepted by the group perceived as possessing a higher status than the one he/she currently belongs to.
6 Mixed persons are those who have at least one parent who is either pure African or pure East Indian, or who themselves are children of mixed unions. These individuals are assuming increased social significance, as

they represent the embodiment of the appreciation, understanding, and 'tolerance' of different cultures and groups.

7 In Trinidad, Guyana, and Suriname, individuals tend to vote on the basis of ethnicity or class. A party considered an African party will tend to attract voters of African descent and voters with an East Indian descent. One perceived to be an 'East Indian party' tends to attract or is expected to receive a sizeable portion of the East Indian vote. According to plural theory, individuals meet in the marketplace, but cohere around their own set of values.

REFERENCES

Ali, A., & Toner, B. (2004). A cross cultural investigation of emotional abuse in Caribbean women and Caribbean-Canadian women. *Journal of Emotional Abuse: Interventions, Research and Theories of Psychological Maltreatment, Trauma and Nonphysical Aggression, 5*, 125–140.

Cook-Darzens, S., & Brunod, R. (1999). An ecosystemic approach to improving mother–infant attachment in a Caribbean matrifocal society. *Contemporary Family Therapy, 21*(4), 433–452.

Corey, G. (2005).Theory and practice of group counseling (7th ed.). California: Thomson Brooks/Cole.

Curling, D., Chatterjee, S., & Massaquoi, N. (2008). Women's transitional locations as a determinant of mental health: Results from a participatory action research project with new immigrant women of colour in Toronto. Unpublished manuscript.

D'Ardene, P., & Mahtani, A. (1989). *Transcultural counselling in action.* London: Sage.

Foulks, E. F. (1980). The concept of culture in psychiatric residency education. *American Journal of Psychiatry, 137*, 811–816.

George, R. L. & Cristiani, T. S. (1995). *Counseling: Theory and practice* (4th ed.). Boston: Allyn & Bacon.

Gollnick, D., & Chinn, P. (1998). *Multicultural education in a pluralistic society* (5th ed.). New Jersey: Prentice-Hall, Inc.

Gopaul-McNicol, S. (1998). Caribbean families: Social and emotional problems. *Journal of Social Distress and the Homeless, 7*(1), 55–73.

Henriques, H., & Manyoni, J. (1977). Ethnic group relations in Barbados and Grenada. In UNESCO (Ed.), *Race and class in post-colonial society: A study of ethnic group relations in the English-speaking Caribbean, Bolivia, Chile and Mexico* (pp. 55–110). United Kingdom: UNESCO.

Hodge, M. (2002).We kind of family. In P. Mohammed (Ed.), *Gendered realities: Essays in Caribbean feminist thought* (pp. 474–485). Mona, Jamaica: University of the West Indies Press.

Lago, C. (1996). *Race, culture and counseling*. Philadelphia: Open University Press.

Lennard, H. L., & Bernstein, A. (1970). *Patterns in human interaction*. San Francisco: Jossey-Bass.

Lidz, T. (1976). *The person: His and her development throughout the life cycle* (rev. ed.). New York: Basic Books.

McLeod, J. (1998). An introduction to counselling. Philadelphia: Open University.

Moodley, R., & Curling, D. (2006). Multiculturalism. In Y. Jackson (Ed.), *Encyclopedia of multicultural psychology* (p. 325). Thousand Oaks, CA: Sage.

Moodley, R., & Palmer, S. (Eds.) (2006). Race, culture and psychotherapy: Critical perspectives in multicultural practice. London: Routledge.

Rawlins, J. (2002). Middle-Aged and Older Women in Jamaica. In P. Mohammed (Ed.), *Gendered realities: Essays in Caribbean feminist thought* (pp. 277–288). Mona, Jamaica: University of the West Indies Press.

Roopnanrine, J. (1997). Toward integration: Diverse issues in examining Caribbean families. In J. Roopnanrine (Ed.), *Caribbean families: Diversity among ethnic groups* (pp. 305–314). London, Eng.: Greenwood Publishing.

Rothman, R. (1999). *Inequality and stratification*. New Jersey: Prentice Hall.

Vontress, C. E. (1979). Cross-cultural counseling. An existential approach. *Personnel and Guidance Journal, 58*, 117–122.

Vontress, C. E. (1982). Social class influences on counseling. *Counseling and Human Development, 14*, 1–12.

Vontress, C. E. (1985). Theories of counselling: A comparative analysis. In R. J. Samuda, & A. Wolfgang (Eds.), *Intercultural counseling and assessment: Global perspectives* (pp. 19–31). Toronto: C. J. Hogrefe.

Vontress, C. E. (1986). Social and cultural foundations. In M. D. Lewis, R. Hayes, & J. Lewis (Eds.), *An introduction to the counselling profession* (pp. 215–250). Itasca, IL: Peacock Publishers.

Vontress, C. E. (2003). On becoming an cross-cultural counselor. In F. D. Harper & J. McFadden (Eds.), *Culture and counseling* (pp. 20–30). Boston: Allyn & Bacon.

Vontress, C. E., & Epp, L. R. (2001). Existential cross-cultural counseling: When hearts and cultures share. In K. J. Schneider, J. F. T. Bugental, & J. F. Pierson (Eds.), *The handbook of humanistic psychology: Leading edges in theory, research, and practice* (pp. 371–388). Thousand Oaks, CA: Sage.

Vontress, C. E., & Jackson, M. L. (2004). Reactions to the multicultural counseling competencies debate. *Journal of Mental Health Counseling, 26*(1), 74–80.

Ward, T., & Hickling, F. (2004). Psychology in the English speaking Caribbean. *The Psychologist,17*, 442–444.

Yelvington, K. (1993). *Trinidad ethnicity.* Knoxville: University of Tennessee Press.

PART FOUR

Clemmont E. Vontress – Multiple Identities, Multiple Pathways, and Beyond

13 Clemmont E. Vontress and the Ongoing Cultural Crisis in Counseling

ROY MOODLEY

In the last four decades, Clemmont Vontress has been pivotal in bringing culture to the consciousness of the counseling world (see, for example, Vontress, 1962, 1963, 1976, 1979, 1982, 1986, 2003, 2008). While Vontress and his allies have now formed a large community of multicultural and cross-cultural counselors, the issues of culture[1] and of its associated concepts of race[2] and ethnicity still remain relatively marginal in mainstream counseling and psychotherapy (Carter, 1995; Moodley, 1999a, 2007). The research and writing in this field is often restricted to a small group of scholars who attempt to make inroads into a profession that itself is problematized by theoretical apartheid – numerous theories and diverse methodologies and practices. Moreover, multicultural counseling too has been dynamically changing over the last decade. From its early beginnings of culture meaning race and ethnicity, it has now shifted to include other marginalized groups, such as those marked by gender, sexual orientation, social class, and disability (see Robinson, 2005, for discussion). This notion of multicultural diversity has offered an interesting and creative paradigm shift in the way that culture was originally conceived in the counseling profession; at the same time, the notion of diversity has also complicated and confused an already problematic area of multicultural counseling theory and practice. While it seems that the complication is centered around the idea of the inclusiveness of gender, sexual orientations, class, and disability in multicultural counseling theory and practice, the issue has more to do with the dilution of race and racism in counseling and psychotherapy (Helms, 1994). As Helms argues: 'It is by no means clear that the same competencies required to deliver effective services to clients for whom racial group membership is central are equally appropriate for clients for whom

Other social identities (for example, gender, age, or religion) are more central' (Helms, 1994, p. 163; see also Pope-Davis & Liu, 1998). Clearly, Helms highlights the pitfalls of an intersectional analysis within which the specificities of race, gender, ethnicity, and sexual orientation can be lost in the attempt to synthesize differences. This situation to some degree was experienced by the women's movement in claiming a universal theory but ultimately being critiqued by black, lesbian, disabled, and working-class women for not taking account of particular contexts and oppressions (Moodley, 2007).

The diversity movement has also resulted in a variety of oppressed and marginalized groups currently competing with and sometimes against each other for space, time, and other material and metaphorical resources in the counseling profession. Furthermore, this contested arena of diversity has reinforced many of the prevailing notions that accompany competing groups. In other words, marginal groups have become insular and apartheid-like in their approach to theory and practice. This has led to counselors and clients being labeled in relation to their race, gender, sexual orientations, social class, disability, religion, and age. Indeed, such a system of labeling has resulted in therapy services being delivered under particular categories: for example, African American therapy, Asian American counseling, Euro-American counseling psychology, gay and lesbian therapy, and Afrocentric counseling. At the same time, all these marginized groups under the rubric of diversity seek inclusion in multicultural counseling and psychotherapy. Since multiculturalism is untheorized (Willett, 1998), and at times fails to articulate a radical approach in terms of racism, imperialism, sexism, and economic oppression (Moodley, 1999 a,b), it has not offered much in terms of clinical theorizing, practice, and research. Indeed, it seems to have created further splitting, fragmentation, and marginalization of much of the theory and practice of counseling and psychotherapy with minority clients. On the other hand, Clemmont Vontress has been clear from the outset that his brand of counseling is cross-cultural, and not multicultural, counseling (personal communication, October 2007), because multicultural counseling has become a complicated, problematic, and ideological arena for doing therapy and alleviating suffering. As Vontress says, 'Whereas multicultural counseling during the civil rights movement tended to focus on differences, I was committed to getting black clients to recognize that they are human beings just like everybody else ... I needed to develop a philosophical vantage point that would enable me and other counselors to bridge cultural differences, not to perpetuate or increase them' (Vontress, 2003, p. 23).

Throughout his research and writing Vontress has emphasized that while cultural difference should be acknowledged and worked through in the counseling process, it must not take precedence over the presenting issues and the client's distress and pain. This has been Vontress's position throughout his career, arguing for culture as a central core of the client's subjectivity, while at the same time recognizing that therapy could be limited by it. Throughout his writings Vontress has encouraged counselors to listen to the client's pain and discomfort before generating interpretations based on race, culture, and ethnicity.

In this chapter, I will explore Vontress's ideas on culture and counseling and show that they are still critical to the development of counseling and psychotherapy for a 21st century. To contextualize this discussion I consider the notion of culture and cross-cultural counseling, the trouble with multiculture, and the consequent crisis in multicultural counseling. Finally, the chapter considers the evolution towards diversity counseling and what this process means for the future of culture and counseling.

Centering Culture in Counseling

Clemmont Vontress sees culture as the heart and soul of all counseling relationships, and as such it must be at the center of therapy. The notion of culture itself is not specific or clearly defined, being so indeterminate that it can easily be filled in with whatever preconceptions a theorist brings to it (see Halton, 1992; Taylor, 1871). Taylor, for example, includes knowledge, belief, art, morals, law, custom, and any other capabilities and habits acquired by individuals as members of society in his definition of culture. Related terms such as subculture, popular culture, counterculture, high culture, ethnic culture, organizational culture, mass culture, political culture, feminist culture, deaf culture, and others are indicative of the complexity, dynamism, and evolving nature of the concept of culture within the disciplines of the humanities and the social sciences (Moodley, 2007). The concept of culture should not be treated as a global entity, but as far as possible be disaggregated into a number of discrete variables (values, ideologies, beliefs, preferences) to avoid any vagueness, multiple meanings, and circular definitions.

The global characterization of culture offers methodological difficulties when an attempt is made to link it causally with phenomena in individual behavior (Smelser, 1992), or when culture represents itself as civilization that produces and reproduces the Other (see Bhabha, 1999; Said, 1978, 1993; Spivak, 1988, for discussion). Moreover, when ethnic cultures are interpreted through the imaginative minds of ethnographers and anthropologists such as James Frazer (1922), Bronisław Malinowski (1922, 1932), Margaret Mead (1928, 1930), Ruth Benedict (1935), and Clifford Geertz (1973), the concept of ethnic culture become the illusionary projections of Western thought. The latter point is particularly important in understanding counseling and psychotherapy with ethnic minority patients. A contemporary critique of psychiatry would contend that the psychiatric discourse tends to link culture with now outdated pseudoscientific theories on 'race' and culture (see Thomas & Sillen, 1972). These approaches have often resulted in particular treatments for black and ethnic minority patients, some of which would now be seen as racist (see Fernando, 1988). Clearly, the concept of culture permeates many discourses and disciplines.

While there is very little agreement among the cultural commentators about the meaning of culture, there is a general acceptance that culture is a process that is not static but constantly changing in time and space within a given society (Moodley & Curling, 2006). If it is 'stripped of its dynamic social, economic, gender and historical context, culture becomes a rigid and constraining concept which is seen somehow to mechanistically determine peoples' behaviour and actions rather than provide a flexible resource for living, for according meaning to what one feels, experiences ... The rigid conceptualisation of culture ... obscure[s] the similarities between broadly defined cultural groups and the diversity within a cultural group' (Ahmad, 1996, p. 190). Furthermore, Ahmad argues that culture has often been used as a decoy to divert attention away from factors such as social inequalities and racism in the lives of ethnic minority communities. At the same time, 'race,' culture, and ethnicity are clearly ideologically constituted and as such 'carry with them material consequences for those who are included within or excluded from them' (Bulmer & Solomos, 1996, p. 781). It is precisely this contention that Vontress makes in his writings and which has given rise to his controversial position in the new multicultural counseling movement.

In this respect, Vontress is regarded as one of the pioneers, bringing into consciousness the personal and the universal. Vontress's ideas concerning culture, ethnicity, and race have been instrumental in removing the (colour) bar that kept black and other ethnic minority communities away from counseling and psychotherapy. His ideas filtered through the theory and research to build what is now the current new form of multicultural counseling, although Vontress himself rejects the concept of multicultural counseling, preferring the category cross-cultural counseling to identify the practice of counseling with ethnic minority clients. Vontress's anthropological definition of culture has been in conflict with the post-structuralist notion of opening up the cultural definition to a wide and varied landscape so that everything and anything can be part of the concept of culture, collectively constructing it as multiculture. Upadhya (2002) has noted that many anthropologists 'thought that multiculturalism vulgarises the key anthropological idea of cultural relativism by essentialising cultural difference[;] multiculturalism also appeared to posit equality among cultures – a premise that neglected relations of hierarchy and domination among different societies' (p. 172; see also Roseberry, 1989).

For Vontress ethnicity and culture are the social glue that holds our sense of identity together. The cultural space in which we locate ourselves, or find ourselves located, becomes validated through belief and value systems, ethical codes, moral and political standpoints, style and taste, social practices, epistemic knowledge, habits, and expectations. Taken together, these cultural signifiers reinforce, if not impose upon us, a perception of reality of the world and its peoples, and our place within it. For Vontress, the sense of having a defined and validated ethnic culture is vital to our ability to be and become ontologically grounded subjects, for without it we risk not just social, group, familial, and community exclusion but a pathological condition wherein our sense of place within humanity itself is open to question.

Vontress's message to counselors and psychotherapists throughout his work is to be consciously aware that black and ethnic minority clients are at a major disadvantage because of the exclusionary way in which dominant white culture has denied them access to resources because of their skin color. This, indeed, can get played out in the therapy room through transference and countertransference.

The Trouble with Multicultural Counseling

Multiculturalism covers a wide spectrum of meanings, ideas, ideologies, and practices, many of which date to colonial times. However, its contemporary usage, particularly in counseling psychology and psychotherapy is relatively new, dating back to the 1960s, and has always been highly controversial. The term is politicized, contested, and laden with ideological projections and ethnic-group investments. These power dynamics reflect its amorphous character and, consequently, its capacity to influence a variety of arenas, from political debates to individual subjectivities. For example, Parekh (2006) defines multiculturalism as a perspective that is composed of a creative interplay of the 'cultural embeddness of human beings, the inescapability and desirability of cultural diversity and intercultural dialogue, and the internal plurality of each culture ... to illuminate the insights and expose the limitations of others and create ... a vital in-between space, a kind of immanent transcendentalism, from which to arrive at a less culture-bound vision of human life and a radically critical perspective' (pp. 338–339).

Throughout the postcolonial period multiculturalism has become associated with visible minority groups, immigration from developing countries, diaspora, and inner-city living. Other terms that by association attach themselves to multiculturalism include ethnicity, postcolonial, Third World, advantaged, disadvantaged, social mobility, cross-cultural, intercultural, trans-cultural, and ethno-cultural. The literature on multiculturalism can be confusing, not least because the term is so open to subjective interpretation. Many of the leading scholars, for example, have discussed multiculturalism purely with an ethnic minority focus, thus limiting multiculturalism to the racial and ethnic domains (for example, Parekh, 2006; Tapp, 2000). Meanwhile, Hardy and Laszoloffy (1992) remind us of the 'theoretical myth of sameness,' which overlooks the important fact that individuals need to be understood within a broader scope than simply their race or ethnicity.

In the West, at least through the influence of capitalism a particular type of multiculturalism tends to emerge which may not benefit those at the lowest rung of the socioeconomic level. Rodrigues (2002), writing from a Marxist perspective, questions the economic blindness of multiculturalism and argues that not enough attention is paid to the relations between culture and economy. As he states: 'If a society is conceived as made of several communities with very distinct cultural aspirations, then the possibility of resisting big capital will be the lowest. Further, multiculturalism by constructing communities which are necessarily fragmented, with a minimum level of agreement across them, if at all, are not able to offer a resistance that classes and class blocs can muster' (p. 116). According to Turner (1994), multiculturalism is part of a decentering process grounded in the organization of capitalism (transnational labour, commodity and capital markets, and corporate structures), which makes people turn to ethnic and cultural identity as a means of mobilizing themselves for the defense of their social, political, and economic interests. This, Turner argues, has led to control or protection of social groups within the state. In this way multiculturalism serves to unify the nation state as an 'imagined community' of tolerant persons who are accepting of other people to make multiculturalism a point of national pride, but does not call into question the continued hegemony of the dominant cultural community (Walcott, 2003).

In this regard, Vontress has criticized the narrow definition of multicultural counseling in the North American context, which traditionally refers to the four major ethnic groups, namely, African American, Asian American, Latino/a American, and Native American (Vontress & Jackson, 2004; see also Pedersen, 1991 and Speight et al., 1991). Furthermore, Vontress also argued against any particular form of counseling for each of the minority groups mentioned above. For example, he rejected the idea of Afrocentric counseling as a specialized way of doing therapy with African Americans. As Vontress says, 'We must be careful about generalizing about superficial commonalities which necessitates a particular brand of counseling. It would seem unreasonable, for instance, to talk about an Afrocentric model of counseling for African Americans' (Vontress, 1996, p. 164). Clearly, Vontress's point seems to be that the preoccupation of multicultural counseling with highlighting differences without critically examining how they can become sites of negativity and stereotyping has led to his rejection of this theory. And he is not alone in this respect. For example, the cultural philosopher Zizek (1997) argues that'multiculturalism is a disavowed, inverted, self-referential form of racism, a "racism with a distance" – it "respects" the Other's identity, conceiving the Other as a self-enclosed, "authentic" community towards which he, the multiculturalist, maintains a distance rendered possible by his privileged universal position' (p. 22).

Diversity and the Ongoing Cultural Crisis in Counseling

Many scholars are increasingly drawn to the term 'diversity,' largely because it seems to speak simultaneously of both exclusion and inclusion, of socially differentiated groups, individual identity representations, and a multitude of subject positions and orientations, including those connecting to sexuality, race, religion, and disability. Importantly, the term 'diversity' implies neutrality, relativism, and, therefore, a sense of the apolitical, while multiculturalism suggests a complex if not unstable mixture of assimilation and difference. Diversity as a concept that is synonymous with multiculturalism tends to appear much later in the literature, evolving as a result of the confusions and complexities surrounding multiculturalism.

In its current form diversity includes the 'Big 7' social identities or marginalized groups in multicultural counseling, that is, those involving race, gender, sexual orientation, class, disability, age, and religion (see Moodley & Lubin, 2008, for discussion). If counselors are not conscious of these 'other' identities in therapy, the quality of therapy becomes compromised due to the omission of critical aspects of an individual's unique identity and sense of self. The Big 7 social identities have now become standard ways of thinking about the new multicultural counseling in the context of diversity (see Moodley & Lubin, 2008). Counselors would need to be clinically competent to understand specific cultural issues without having to box clients into particular social categories (for example, viewing a client singularly in terms of race, i.e., a 'black man,' as opposed to understanding the complexity of identity variables that go into the client's make-up, i.e., a black, gay, hearing-impaired, working-class, elderly, man). If such a client is not acknowledged for his/her multiple social identities then the counselor may fall into the trap of stereotyping, due to presumed cultural knowledge instead of a true appreciation of the complexities of diversity (Taylor, 2000).

Some argue that sexual diversity and disability are very different from race and ethnicity in terms of clients and their 'subjective distress' in therapy. These scholars and practitioners are concerned that there will be further marginalization of issues of race and racism (Helms, 1994). Others argue that all disadvantaged groups experience discrimination and that there is no need to differentiate them, suggesting for the need to collapse and integrate race, gender, class, sexual orientation, and disability (Robinson, 2005). Many scholars also allude to the fact that multicultural counseling has been expropriated by white middle-class multiculturalists to indulge in their own issues of marginality, such as gender, sexual orientation, or disability, resulting in the further marginalization of race, culture, and ethnicity issues in counseling and psychotherapy. In other words, white social marginalities are being substituted for critical race, ethnicity, and culture issues in the theory and practice of multicultural counseling.

In terms of Vontress's work, there appears to be no disengagement with black and ethnic minority women, LGBTQ, disabled clients, and the poor. Conversely, he has argued for the inclusion of all marginalized identities and not the fragmentation of such subdivisions that the multicultural movement has created, such as Afrocentric Counseling for Africa American clients, Asian Counseling for Asian American clients, and so on.

Moreover, counselors must recognize the importance of examining the intersection and convergences between an individual's gender, racial, ethnic, class, and sexual-orientation identities, since no one identity takes precedence over the others in an individual's inner world (Moodley, 2003). The counselor's own awareness and perceptions of him/ herself as complex, multidimensional beings are critical in developing 'cultural empathy' (Ridley & Lingle, 1996). The need to see the client as complex and more than his or her race or ethnicity has been Clemmont Vontress's message throughout his career. For example, he writes: 'People are multicultural in the sense that we are all products of many cultures' (1996, p. 164). Vontress also argues for a deeper insight into the issue of identity by asking all counselors to first see the humanness and the unfolding tragedies and subjective distress in clients, then any difference that they represent. As Harper and McFadden (2003) point out:

> Counseling professionals must stop to think about culture and counseling in a divergent, creative, practical, real-life, real-time, and futuristic way ... This means addressing the controversial issues that face (us) ..., for example, terrorism, racism, religious conflict, racial and ethnic violence, ... human injustice, AIDS and other diseases, the human impact of globalization and natural disasters, and alcohol and other drug addiction. (p. 388)

Conclusion

If, as Pedersen argues, all counseling is multicultural (Pedersen, 1991), then cross-cultural or multicultural counseling is not a specific approach of therapeutic intervention but a philosophy of practice that can easily be embedded into any one of the 400-plus therapeutic approaches (Garfield & Bergin, 1994). The perception that multicultural and diversity counseling is a specific therapeutic approach reduces the chances that all counselors and psychotherapists will become culturally competent in the 'Big 7 stigmatized identities' in therapy. The crisis has led mainstream counselors and psychotherapists to stay away from the race, class, culture, ethnicity, sexual orientation and disability debate, conveniently step aside claiming a lack of training in cultural competencies, and allow the multiculturalists to work through the splitting and fragmentations. Whether the fissures and cracks are therapeutically beneficial for clients who seek counseling is difficult to predict. Unless all counseling becomes multicultural, the dominant white cultures will view multicultural diversity as a minoritized practice and one that is different from the mainstream monocultural therapeutic approaches. While many clinicians have become more aware of the need to emphasize context, the importance of subjective meanings, and holistic perspectives (Moodley & Lubin, 2008), very much in accord with Vontress's philosophy, we still find the profession developing along apartheid-like paradigms, within which individuals and groups are separated and segregated by race, gender, sexual orientation, class, disability, age, and religion. Over his forty years of research and writing, Vontress has maintained a core humanistic philosophy which has remained constant throughout the crisis that cross-cultural counseling has found itself in, that is, that all clients must be treated as human beings irrespective of race, gender, class, sexual orientation, disability, and so on. This core value of counseling will remain long after the politics of identity has been displaced or replaced with perhaps another ideological variable that attempts to diagnose the suffering of the subject.

NOTES

1 Culture and ethnicity, just like race, have been problematized by their ambiguous usage in various spaces and in different times. Social construction theorists claim that these concepts are products of specific histories and geopolitical experiences. Sometimes they are used as 'empty signifiers' covered in ideological meanings that promote particular self-interests but do nothing for black and ethnic minority groups (Moodley, 1998; Gates, Jr, 1986).

2 In the written word or text, race is often presented within single or double quotation marks – 'race' or "race" – to strongly suggest that race is not a biological or natural category but a socio-historical concept (Du Bois, 1897; Appiah, 1986, 1989). Surrounding it with quotation marks has become popular practice, as Mason observes: 'Almost every monograph, article or text book now found it necessary to make extensive use of the inverted comma whenever the word "race" appeared' (Mason, 1996, p. 796). This

practice may appear to have allowed for a more socio-political conceptualization without the biological attachments, but has in fact drawn attention to it, in such a way that the single or double quote marks have created a double bind, on the one hand, freeing the term but also at the same time legitimizing it, and thus giving it a reality and a theoretical background that does not exist.

REFERENCES

Ahmad, W. I. U. (1996). The Trouble with Culture. In D. Kelleher & S. Hillier (Eds.), *Researching cultural differences in health* (pp. 190–219). London: Routledge.

Benedict, R. (1935). *Patterns of culture* (7th ed.). London: Routledge & Kegan Paul, 1961.

Bhabha, H. K. (1999). Liberalism's sacred cows. In Susan Moller Okin, *Is multiculturalism bad for women*? Princeton: Princeton University Press.

Bulmer, M., & Solomos, J. (1996). Introduction: Race, ethnicity and the curriculum. *Ethnic and Racial Studies, 19*, 777–788.

Carter, R. (1995). The influence of race and racial identity in psychotherapy. New York: Wiley.

Fanon, F. (1952). *Black skins, white masks* (C. L. Markmann, Trans.). New York: Grove Press, reprint 1967.

Fernando, S. (1988). *Race and culture in psychiatry*. Kent: Croom Helm.

Fernando, S. (Ed.). (1995). *Mental health in a multi-ethnic society: A multidisciplinary handbook*. London: Routledge.

Frazer, J. G. (1922). *The golden bough: A study in magic and religion*. London: Macmillan Press.

Garfield, S. L., & Bergin, A. E. (1994). Introduction and historical overview. In A. E. Bergin & S. L. Garfield (Eds.), *Handbook of psychotherapy and behavior change* (3–18). Chichester: Wiley.

Geertz, C. (1973). *The interpretation of cultures*. New York: Basic Books.

Halton, E. (1992). The cultic roots of culture. In R. Munch & N. J. Smelser (Eds.), *Theory of culture* (pp. 29–63). Berkeley/Los Angeles: University of California Press.

Hardy, K. V., & Laszoloffy, T. A. (1992). Training racially sensitive family therapists: Context, content, and contact. *Family in Society, 73*(6), 364–370.

Harper, F. D., & McFadden, J. (2003). Conclusions, trends, issues, and recommendations. In F. D. Harper & J. McFadden (Eds.), *Culture and counseling: New approaches* (pp. 379–393). Boston: Allyn & Bacon.

Helms, J. (1994). How multiculturalism obscures racial factors in the therapy process: Comment on Ridley et al. (1994), Sodowsky et al. (1994), Ottavi et al. (1994), & Thompson et al. (1994). *Journal of Counseling Psychology, 41,* 162–165.

Helms, J., & Richardson, T. Q. (1997). How 'multiculturalism' obscures race and culture as differential aspects of counseling competency. In D. B. Pope-Davis and H. L. K. Coleman (Eds.), *Multicultural counseling competencies* (pp. 60–79). Thousand Oaks, CA: Sage.

Laungani, P. (1999). Client centred or culture centred counselling? In S. Palmer & P. Laungani (Eds.), *Counselling in a multicultural society* (pp. 133–152). London: Sage.

Malinowski, B. (1922). *Argonauts of the western Pacific: An account of native enterprise and adventure in the archipelagoes of Melanesian New Guinea.* London: Routledge.

Malinowski, B. (1932). *The sexual life of savages in North-Western Melanesia: An ethnographic account of courtship, marriage, and family life among the natives of the Trobriand Islands, British New Guinea.* London: Routledge.

Mead, M. (1928). *Coming of age in Samoa.* Harmondsworth: Penguin.

Mead, M. (1930). *Growing up in New Guinea.* Harmondsworth: Penguin.

Moodley, R. (1999a). Challenges and transformation: Counselling in a multicultural context. *International Journal for the Advancement of Counselling, 21,* 139–152.

Moodley, R. (1999b). Psychotherapy with ethnic minorities: A critical review. *Changes, International Journal of Psychology and Psychotherapy, 17,* 109–125.

Moodley, R. (2007). (Re)placing multiculturalism in counselling and psychotherapy. *British Journal of Guidance and Counseling, 35*(1), 1–22.

Moodley, R., & Curling, D. (2006). Multiculturalism. In Y. Jackson (Ed.) *Encyclopedia of multicultural psychology.* Thousand Oaks, CA: Sage.

Moodley, R., & Lubin, D. B. (2008). Developing your career to working with diversity. In S. Palmer & R. Bor (Eds.), *The practitioner's handbook.* London: Sage.

Parekh, B. (2006). *Rethinking multiculturalism: Cultural diversity and political theory* (2nd ed.). Basingstoke, Hampshire: Palgrave Macmillan.

Pedersen, P. (1991). Multiculturalism as a fourth force in counseling. *Journal of Counseling and Development, 70,* 4–250.

Pope-Davis, D. B., & Liu, W. M. (1998). The social construction of race: Implications for counseling psychology. *Counselling Psychology Quarterly, 11,* 151–161.

Ridley, C. R., & Lingle, D. W. (1996). Cultural empathy in multicultural counseling: A multidimensional process model. In P. B. Pedersen, J. G. Draguns,

W. J. Lonner & J. E. Trimble (Eds.), *Counseling across cultures* (4th ed., pp. 21–46). Thousand Oaks, CA: Sage.

Robinson, T. L. (2005). *The convergence of race, ethnicity, and gender: Multiple identities in counseling* (2nd ed.). Upper Saddle River, NJ: Pearson/Merrill/Prentice Hall.

Rodrigues, V. (2002). Is there a case for multiculturalism? In K. Deb (Ed.), *Mapping multiculturalism*. New Delhi: Rawat Publications.

Roseberry, W. (1989). Multiculturalism and the challenge of anthropology. *Social Research, 59*(4), 841–858.

Said, E. W. (1978). *Orientalism*. London: Routledge & Kegan Paul.

Said, E. (1993). *Culture and imperialism*. London: Chatto & Windus.

Smelser, N. J. (1992). Culture: Coherent or incoherent. In R. Munch & N. J. Smelser (Eds.), *Theory of Culture* (pp. 3–28). Berkeley/Los Angeles: University of California Press.

Speight, S. L., Myers, L. J., Cox, C. I., & Highlen, P. S. (1991). A redefinition of multicultural counseling. *Journal of Counseling and Development, 70*, 29–36.

Spivak, G. C. (1988). Can the subaltern speak? In C. Nelson & L. Grossberg (Eds.), *Marxism and the interpretation of culture*. Urbana: University of Illinois Press.

Tapp, R. B. (Ed.) (2000). *Multiculturalism*. New York: Prometheus Books.

Taylor, R. L. (2000). Diversity within African American families. In D. H. Demo, K. R. Allen, & M. A. Fine (Eds.), *Handbook of family diversity* (pp. 232–251). Oxford: Oxford University Press.

Taylor, E. B. (1871) *Primitive culture: Research into the development of mythology, philosophy, religion, art and custom*. London: Murray, reprint 1920.

Thomas, A., & Sillen, S. (1972). *Racism and psychiatry*. USA: Citadel.

Turner, T. (1994). Anthropology and Multiculturalism. In D. T. Goldberg (Ed.), *Multiculturalism: A Critical Reader*. Cambridge, MA: Blackwell.

Upadhya, C. (2002) Culture wars: The anthropological debate on multiculturalism. In K. Deb (Ed.), *Mapping Multiculturalism*. New Delhi: Rawat Publications.

Vontress, C. E. (1962). Patterns of segregation and discrimination: Contributing factors to crime among Negroes. *Journal of Negro Education, 31*, 108–116.

Vontress, C. E. (1963). The negro against himself. *Journal of Negro Education, 32*, 237–252.

Vontress, C. E. (1976). Racial and ethnic barriers in counseling. In P. Pederson, W. J. Lonner, & J. G. Draguns (Eds.), *Counseling across cultures*. Honolulu: University Press of Hawaii.

Vontress, C. E. (1979). Cross-cultural counseling: An existential approach. *The Personnel and Guidance Journal, 58*, 117–122.

Vontress, C. E. (1982). Social class influences in counseling. *Counseling and Human Development, 14*,1–12.

Vontress, C. E. (1986). Social and cultural foundations. In M. D. Lewis, R. Hayes, & J. A. Lewis (Eds.), *Introduction to the counseling profession*. Itasca, IL: Peacock.

Vontress, C. E. (2003). On becoming an existential cross-cultural counselor. In F. D. Harper & J. McFadden (Eds.), *Culture and counseling*. Boston: Allyn & Bacon.

Vontress, C. E. (2008). Existential therapy. In J. Frew & M. D. Spiegler (Eds.), *Contemporary psychotherapies for a diverse world*. Boston: Houghton Mifflin/ Lahaska Press.

Vontress, C. E. & Jackson, M. L. (2004). Reactions to the multicultural counseling competencies debate. *Journal of Mental Health Counseling, 26*(1), 74–80.

Vontress, C. E., Johnson, J. A., & Epp, L. R. (1999). *Cross-cultural counseling: A Casebook.* Alexandria, VA: American Counseling Association.

Walcott, R. (2003). *Black like who? Writing black Canada*. Toronto: Insomniac Press.

Willet, C. (1998). *Theorising multiculturalism: A guide to the current debate.* Oxford: Basil Blackwell.

Zizek, S. (1997). Multiculturalism, or, the cultural logic of multinational capitalism. *New Left Review, 225*, 28–51.

14 Privileging Multiple Converging Identities in Counselling and Clemmont E. Vontress

TRACY L. ROBINSON-WOOD

Conceptualizations of diversity are influenced by one's gender, race, and cultural identities. Written predominantly by racially diverse and heterosexually identified men, the early writings of cross-cultural counseling and psychology in the United States privileged race and cultural identities. Given the legacy and current reality of racism in America and the stratification of racial groups, this is understandable. Yet, as native-born people of color, immigrants, White women and men, gay and transgender people, and people with disabilities began writing from their personal, cultural, and clinical experiences, gender, sexual, and disability identities were made central to the literature. Increasingly, a focus on spirituality is found.

Diversity in counseling has evolved from this initial and limited focus on race and culture to intersections with multiple, visible, and invisible identities, such as class, disability, sexuality, spirituality, and ethnicity.[1] The evolution of diversity in counseling would not be possible without the pioneering work of Clemmont Vontress, who paved a path of attending to multiple and converging identities. With an enduring message of existential inclusion, he held fast to an unswerving recognition of how human beings are more similar than different. 'No matter the conditions under which people live, they still must adjust to the fact that they are human beings' (Jackson, 1987, p. 22). His scholarship on cross-cultural counseling was foundational to the profession's expanded constructions of diversity and seeing clients whole.

Seeing clients whole refers to the counselor's ability to attend to clients' multiple identities. Attention to the whole self during the clinical encounter is not dependent, as Clemmont Vontress said, on a bag of 'tricks of the trade, the mechanics of counseling' (Jackson, 1987, p. 23), but on the existential encounter between the client and the counselor. Vontress saw the relevance of existential counseling for all people, particularly those whose lives were without meaning. He said, 'Existential counseling is a rich and profound approach to helping clients of all cultures find meaning and harmony in their lives' (Epps, 1998, p. 2). Attending to the simultaneous and dynamic intersections of the client's and the counselor's race, ethnicity, gender, and other primary identity constructs within counseling is core to the existential encounter. With an intentional gaze at the pioneering work of Clemmont Vontress, this chapter explores the meaning and importance of privileging multiple identities within counseling and therapy. Diversity discourses are defined and their impact on multicultural practice is explored. Questions are posed for the profession to grapple with that emerge from a critical look at subtle discourses on diversity. Vontress's work, particularly as it relates to existential counseling, provides the lens through which this discussion occurs.

Multiple Identities and Privilege

Vontress conceptualized five concentric and interacting cultures as foundational to the development of most people: 'the universal, the ecologic, the national, the regional, and the racial-ethnic' (Jackson, 1987, p. 22). Each person coexists within visible and invisible group identities that have various levels of socially constructed status such as being a young, attractive White lesbian or being a Black able-bodied heterosexual, Christian man. Effective therapy does not deny these cultures between client and therapist, but acknowledges the multiple and concentric identities that constitute the self.

Despite the emphasis of multicultural counseling, an ecological framework in which personal/environment interaction, culture, ethnicity, family, collective society, history, and spirituality are fundamental to understanding the client (Robinson-Wood, 2009), forces interfere with the intent of multicultural counseling, such as differences.[2] Vontress said, 'It is a matter of common experience that one finds it more difficult to establish empathy with those who are different from himself' (Vontress, 1969, p. 274). Undoubtedly, people are more similar as human beings than they are different. Yet differences and their socially constructed meanings are not insignificant.

Much has been invested in equipping counselors and psychologists, primarily White people, with tools to be culturally competent in cross-cultural situations. A plethora of beautifully written articles, special editions, and tomes exist on multiculturalism and cultural diversity with the collective aim of this important work to improve the quality of therapy for clients and enhance client healing. In an effort to improve multicultural competence among mental health professionals, the multicultural counseling and psychology literature includes an extensive examination of socially constructed difference, multicultural competencies and guidelines, cultural worldviews, values, power, oppression, cultural encapsulation, privilege, supervision models, training, racism, racial identity models, acculturation, assimilation, and more. Amid all of this important and transformative work, the current dialogue on diversity and multiculturalism is more fragile than it needs to be. This fragility is problematic given our profession's reliance on both the message and the meaning of diversity.

Race functions as a grandmaster status in society. As a social construction, race has the power to eclipse other identities that are just as potent to identity construction. Omni and Winant (2006) argued that although particular meanings, myths, and stereotypes about race can and indeed do change, 'the presence of a system of racial meanings and stereotypes, of racial ideology, seems to be a permanent feature of U.S. culture' (p. 23). To illustrate this point, I will share a true story. A Black man dressed in a sweatshirt and jeans stands behind a White woman at an ATM on a Saturday morning in a crowded mall. He notices her clutching her purse, looking back at him nervously. She appears to be concerned about being robbed. His status as a prominent heart surgeon is invisible, unknown to her – visible is his Blackness and maleness. The socially constructed meanings of these identities are criminality and dangerousness. A Black woman or a white man standing behind her would not have aroused this same level of concern. Suggesting that anyone would arouse similar concerns does not support an honest examination of one's proximity to race-based discourses created from living in a society constructed on the basis of skin color and racial categories.[3]

One of the challenges facing us is an understanding of to whom diversity refers. While there is no confusion about the inclusion of people of color among the diverse, it appears not to include White people. Newman (2007) observed that whiteness is unremarkable and unexamined, yet it is against whiteness that discussions about diversity occur. White people are not required to think about race as core to their identity, yet discourses about Whiteness exist. Lipsitz (2005) said 'whiteness is everywhere in American culture, but it is very hard to see ... As the unmarked category against which difference is constructed, whiteness never has to speak its name, never has to acknowledge its role as an organizing principle in social and cultural relations' (p. 402).

Without being named in the dialogue, White people, particularly those who do not have a marginalized identity (being gay, disabled, female, poor), are sent a message that they do not need to be engaged in and embraced by the work of diversity. We know this not to be true and yet, where do White people who are not gay, female, low-wage earning, or disabled go to explore their White privilege? More importantly, what is the motivation for doing so? Discourses about Whites as well as other race discourses show up and affect the profession, our students, clients, and counselors.[4] It is important that White people who choose to get up close to their White skin privilege not be perceived as extraordinary. Otherwise, the underlying discourse is that there is something special about Whites when they explore race and challenge racism.

Discourses in Diversity

Discourses refer to forms of speech and carry meaning. They are not often articulated or named, but they lurk about and infiltrate the convention halls, classrooms, therapy rooms, and counseling publications. Dominant discourses are often unconscious. People may not be aware of where they are located within and positioned by certain discourses. Location means 'identifying where one resides in this society on a continuum from privilege to oppression in relation to various contextual aspects of the self, such as ethnicity, gender, sexual orientation, religion, and class status' (Vasquez & Magraw, 2005, pp. 66–67). Discourses can be subtle yet hold enormous power. Having White-looking or light skin, being male, having wealth, heterosexuality or the semblance thereof, sounding like one is a native-born English speaker, looking young, thin, and having both a mentally and physically able body are the bases by which people are appraised in America. Status is attributed to these characteristics.

In the United States there is a dominant discourse that persons who have membership in groups socially constructed as holding value are valued and valuable. Worth is defined by what one does, how one looks, and the amount of money one earns due to society's valuation of youth, productivity, ability, and material gain. Vontress (1991) pointed to the culture in which people are socialized as determining the beliefs they hold about the nature of their and other people's problems and how they should be solved.

Stigmatized groups often find themselves pushing back against conventional and stereotypical ways society uses to define them. Stigma refers to objectification, whereby people are rendered members of categories rather than possessors of individual characteristics. Stigma, however, is not interchangeable with deficiency. Having an identity that society marginalizes (e.g., being disabled) is not the same as a disabled person internalizing an inferior identity. Able-body discourses frame men who are disabled as asexual, dependent, and not masculine (Robinson, 2005). A man who is a paraplegic is framed by the marginalization of this identity. Subsequently, the man may be viewed within the dominant culture as not whole, devalued by the stigmatized identity within an able-bodied valuing society. Individuals in stigmatized statuses are presumed to mirror the image of the social creation. Other identities invisible to the eye – father, partner, friend, son, uncle, worker, golfer, church member – inform a client's coping skills, sense of identity, heightened vulnerability, and problem resolution. Culturally informed values are at the core of students' confusion regarding why a person would remain disabled if given a choice to be able-bodied. While life might be easier if one were free of a disability, it need not be a better life given that the self is uniquely created and nurtured by living with a disability.

Despite the reality of multiple identities, people do not always choose which status is most important to others (Ore, 2006).[5] Persons who are stigmatized are viewed as feeling stigmatized and being the problem (Rosenblum & Travis, 2006), although the problem is homophobia, religious intolerance, and racism. Clearly, identity statuses in and of themselves are insufficient to explain or predict one's proximity to discourses.

Protecting Privilege and Fear of Difference

Clemmont Vontress neither silenced nor minimized the importance of examining race in multicultural work, and yet he upheld the universality of all humans. His message was to courageously call things as they are without forgetting our connections and responsibility to one another. Yet, a sole focus on similarities does not explicate the ways in which unearned privilege instills and perpetuates difference and inequality. A classroom discussion of gender privilege (apart from its intersections with race, disability, sexuality, and age) does not evoke the same level of dissonance as a discussion about White privilege among my White graduate students. That White women who are able bodied, heterosexual, thin, and middle-class have more social power than White women who are large-bodied, or non-gender-conforming lesbians, or poor reduces the comfort level in the room. While it is not unusual for women of color to contend with racism first and then develop their gender identities later, for White women, the reverse is often true. If it does occur, an awareness of sexism in their lives precedes an awareness of White privilege.

Therapists need to be mindful of the press of dominant discourses on themselves and clients and, at the same time, remain open to discovering which of their clients' multiple and intersecting identities is the clinical focus. Every fall, at colleges across America, there are students of color who explore their emotional interest in and sexual attraction to people of their same gender. What does privileging exploration of the sexual self mean for the college student of color? Does this mean the student is underdeveloped in his/her racial or ethnic identity? Could it possibly mean that the student is further along in his/her ethnic identity development, having had more community support to explore Puerto-Rican or Chinese culture? Coming-out to a conservative religious family as a lesbian woman represents a developmental challenge, and for many, a crisis. In time, an integration of multiple identities hopefully takes place. To the extent that a young woman is feminine-appearing and attractive (a social construction of gender), the coming-out process may be more difficult because it is unsuspected. A prevailing discourse regarding sexuality is that feminine women are sexually attracted to men and do not look gay. That gay men or lesbian women can be spotted because of overtly feminine or masculine non-gender conforming appearance is a discourse rampant in our culture.

Beneath the surface of multicultural relationships is privilege and oppression, flowing like an underground river (Zetzer, 2005). This is not a place from which meaningful and transformative therapy can occur. The able-bodied therapist cannot join with the disabled client if a belief exists that the client would be better off as an able-bodied person. The White therapist cannot join with her Black client if she has not examined her White privilege or is uncomfortable talking about race or insists on talking only about race. The Black therapist cannot join with a Black client if she expects her client to think about race the way he or she does.

Among some clients of color, identities other than race have more salience. Each person of color, although a product of the American culture, has learned to cope with their status as a person of color differently (Vontress, 1996). Vontress (2004) reminded us that counselors must strive not to impose race on clients, but attend to the significance that the client attaches to race as an issue in their lives. The counselor's countertransference is showing when he expects his clients of color to feel as he does about racial issues.

Despite theoretical knowledge and multicultural competence in cross-cultural contexts, has a counselor earned the right to help clients explore loss, fear, and conflict if they have never received therapy themselves or are unwilling to seek counseling? As counselors, we bring our whole selves, attitudes about suffering, rage, disappointment, success, arrogance, insensitivity, and empathy. Beliefs and memories about sex, obesity, money, culture, abortion, politics, infidelity, God, and divorce sit with counselors as they sit with clients. Leadership to initiate conversation about difficult topics is a manifestation of our competence and yet a counselor's unexamined life intimidates the existential encounter. Multiculturally competent counseling and therapy neither resembles nor reinforces the dominant discourses of society that perpetuate a client's subjugation.

Existential Connections

Early in his career, Clemmont Vontress recalled that he once asked a young Black male student how he felt about this and that. In frustration the student exploded, 'What's all this "how do you feel stuff?" I feel like you feel when something like that happens to you' (Lee, 1994, p. 68). By listening to clients' words and silence, the invisible can be made visible. Both spirituality and therapy involve the telling and hearing of one another's stories, and each helps clients learn to accept themselves, release hurts and resentments, confront guilt, identify and modify destructive patterns of thinking and behaving, acknowledge shortcomings, and forgive self and others (Burke & Miranti, 2000). Berliner (1995) said, 'Both psychological growth and spiritual conversion draw the person out of old ways of being, through the deaths such letting go requires, and into liberated forms of life consistent with one's true self' (p. 113).

Discomfort with things spiritual is a challenge for some counselors and psychologists. Many people, therapists included, have suffered from harsh religious teachings that 'lead us to regard all religion and all spirituality as harmful and unnecessary' (West, 2000, p. 17). Some clinicians are uncomfortable with their own as well as their clients' spiritual expressions due to a lack of exposure to and familiarity with healthy spirituality. Others have not developed this identity and may deem it peripheral to clinical competence.

Along with friendship, love, and work, spirituality is central to life. Despite this, there are barriers to an inclusion of spirituality into therapy. Unresolved issues in the therapist's life, lack of clarity about spirituality as a mysterious and deep phenomenon, as well as fear of imposing values, may lead a counselor to maintain silence. Spirituality is a dimension of multiculturalism; yet, the lack of training about spirituality within therapy is a problem (Hall, Dixon, & Mauzey, 2004). Part of multicultural competence is the ability of counselors to integrate spirituality into therapy, yet what counselors-in-training are being taught about spirituality is a significant gap in the research (Young, Wiggins-Frame, & Cashwell, 2007). The belief that spirituality cannot be studied and should not be studied has contributed to its absence in research (Miller & Thoresen, 2003).

Multicultural competence includes counselors' ability to integrate clients' spiritual lives into the therapy process. As counselors committed to clients' healing, we have a sacred responsibility to honor the therapeutic event as a place of healing where we gather around the silence, speak, and are heard. By invoking the universal, Vontress stated, existential counseling focuses on the 'eternal issues of love, loveliness, suffering, and death that each of us face daily … It is applicable to all problems-in-living; but it is especially appropriate when one's client feels lost in the movement of a life without meaning' (Epps, 1998, p. 2).

Creating Community and Being Allies in Therapy

As mental health professionals, we are called to be allies with our clients. Vasquez and Magraw (2005) said: 'An ally is someone who gets in the way of oppression. An ally intervenes from a place of privilege to stop mistreatment from occurring. An ally is someone who takes action when witnessing racism, sexism, homophobia, and the like' (p. 73). This mutuality represents an intimate space that two people inhabit together as human beings within, and governed by, a professional context. As a counselor learns of his or her client's stories, becoming an ally is a component of a connective capacity.[6] The counselor asks,

'How does your loss impact your thoughts about your future?' 'What is helpful to you as you reflect on your experiences of change?'

Helpers, amidst their personal challenges, have an ethical and professional responsibility to use their full lives for clients' therapeutic benefit, and yet to what extent is this help compromised when, among some counseling professionals, a reluctance exists to receive therapy? An unwillingness to utilize the gifts of our profession alienates counselors from clients and the therapy process. There are tremendous benefits in receiving psychotherapy from a competent professional to explore family-of-origin issues, relationship quality, losses, successes, resentments, goals, dreams, nightmares, early trauma, and the like. As a profession we are called upon to be mentally healthy. Clemmont Vontress described mental health as more than the absence of psychological symptoms. 'It is being in balance and harmony with one's inner self, with one's friends, family, and colleagues; with one's physical environment and with one's spirituality' (Epps, 1998, p. 7). Part of being multiculturally competent professionals is living examined, authentic, healthy, and reflective lives. This requires the ability to know where we are in proximity to discourses about race and other sources of difference.

Parker Palmer (2004), Quaker, educator, and writer, discusses circles of trust, a tradition among Quakers known as clearing committees. Circles of trust are places where people can be alone together. Their 'singular purpose is to support the inner journey of each person in the group, to make each soul feel safe enough to show and speak its truth, to help each person listen to his or her inner teacher' (p. 54). With circles of trust the people gathered on the outside of the circle know only to ask questions of the seeker. Community is critical to the sacred and is at the heart of a 'connective capacity' whereby people feel in relationship with one another (Palmer, 1999). If the connective capacity is missing, being a woman or a therapist of color does not ensure that one is able to work effectively with other women or clients of color.[7]

Challenges and Future Directions

Race is arguably the dominant and most dissonance-provoking dimension of the current discourse on multicultural issues. One of the risks associated with expanding diversity to include other dimensions, albeit essential, is a tendency to avoid the inclusion of race and instead focus on gender or sexual-orientation diversity. Although minimizing race does not dismantle racism or move the pioneering work of Clemmont Vontress forward, newer dimensions of diversity are perceived by some to be less legitimate and thought of as trespassing on the terrain and turf of race and ethnicity.

Both the American Counseling Association and American Psychological Association have espoused a commitment to diversity. These professional organizations, to which the majority of counselors and psychologists belong, have enormous power, as do the boards affiliated with them that accredit counseling and psychology programs. If racial diversity were more than an espoused value, how do APA-affiliated graduate programs with 100% White faculty receive a stamp of approval cycle after cycle from the APA? After the reports, visits, and sanctions, has the spirit of and commitment to diversity been honored when other dimensions of diversity are valued over racial diversity? Why does the National Counseling Exam taken by students to become licensed as professional counselors de-emphasize sociocultural-foundation questions but other core domains are more prevalent, such as career development and family theory? A message is sent that sociocultural foundations are less important.

People of privilege are able to opt out of struggle against oppression if and when they choose (Wildman and Davis, 2006) and although it is important that all counselors unpack their skin, race, gender, sexuality, class, and other privileges, it is important not to admire one group for examining their privilege.

Conclusion

Empathic therapy is a gift in that it can help people move toward wisdom, peace, and sanity in their lives following tragedy and crises. The existential encounter between therapist and client, not reliance on therapeutic techniques, is the most significant therapeutic ingredient. Clemmont Vontress taught us this. At its best, therapy is a holding environment for the client (Kegan, 1982). It represents an existential space where the client can go and bring all of who he or she is, where multiple selves, visible and invisible, are welcomed and received.

Racial similarities between a client and a counselor do not guarantee the experience of a holding environment. At the same time, differences do not negate it. The experience of having another listen to one's story is extremely therapeutic. In hearing others' stories, we are more able to touch our own and learn from them.

NOTES

1 Invisible identities are those that are not visible to the counselor or expressed by the client, and include sexuality, disability, class, spirituality, addiction, divorce, and trauma. Experiences that influence a client's identity development, as well as the unconscious realm, have considerable significance in the client's life and problem presentation.
2 The counselor's countertransference, lack of multicultural competence, as well as clients' attitudes about the counselor or fears about the therapeutic event are among the factors that can interfere with therapeutic effectiveness.
3 In presentations on privilege where I have told this story, I repeatedly get White people who tell me that they are uncomfortable with anybody standing behind them. I ask them to think about this in terms of the following: would a small child, a person in a wheelchair, a person with a seeing-eye dog, or an elderly person with a cane evoke feelings of discomfort while they are transacting business at an ATM?
4 Discourses about whiteness include Whites as smart, capable, and qualified, and unsure allies in the fight against racism.
5 It is imperative that we disentangle the difference between immutable identities – being black, being gay, being female – and the consequences of socially constructed meanings about differences, such as racism, homophobia, and sexism.
6 These questions can support a client through loss and transition and signal to the client that she is not walking through her journey alone.
7 Although some clients may prefer counselors who share gender or race, this similarity alone is not sufficient to provide a connective capacity.

REFERENCES

Berliner, P. M. (1995). Soul healing: A model of feminist therapy. In M. Burke & J. Mirant (Eds.), *Counseling: The spiritual dimension* (pp. 113–125). Thousand Oaks, CA: Sage.

Burke, M. T., & Miranti, J. (2001). The spiritual and religious dimensions of counseling. In D. Locke, J. Myers, & E. Herr (Eds.), *The handbook of counseling* (pp. 601–612). Thousand Oaks, CA: Sage.

Cashwell, C. S., & Young, J. S. (2004). Spirituality in counselor training: A content analysis of syllabi from introductory spirituality courses. *Counseling and Values, 48*, 96–109.

Duerk, J. (1994). *Circle of stones: Woman's journey to herself.* San Diego, CA: Lura Media.

Epps, L. R. (1998). The courage to be an existential counselor: An interview of Clemmont E. Vontress. *Journal of Mental Health Counseling, 20,* 1–12.

Fukuyama, M. A., & Sevig, T. D. (1999). *Ingegrating spirituality into multicultural counseling.* Thousand Oaks, CA: Sage.

Goodman, J. (2001). Basic counseling skills. In D. Locke, J. Myers, & E. Herr (Eds.), *The handbook of counseling* (pp. 237–256). Thousand Oaks, CA: Sage.

Hall, C. R., Dixon, W.A., & Mauzey, E. (2004). Spirituality and religion: Implications for counselors *Journal of Counseling & Development, 82,* 504–507.

Hill, P.C., & Pargament, K.I. (2003). Advances in the conceptualization and measurement of religion and spirituality: *American Psychologist, 58*(1), 64–74.

Ingersoll, R. E. (1995). Spirituality, religion, and counseling: Dimensions and relationship. In M. Burke & J. Mirant (Eds.), *Counseling: The spiritual dimension* (pp. 5–18). Thousand Oaks, CA: Sage.

Jackson, M. L. (1987). Cross-cultural counseling at the crossroads: A dialogue with Clemmont E. Vontress. *Journal of Counseling and Development, 66,* 20–2.

Jordan, J. (1997). A relational perspective for understanding women's development. In J. Jordan (Ed.), Women's growth in diversity (pp. 9–24). New York: The Guilford Press.

Kaplan, A. G. (1987). Reflections on gender and psychotherapy. In M. Braud (Ed.), *Women and therapy* (pp. 11–23). New York: Haworth Press.

Kegan, R. (1982). *The self in transformation.* Cambridge, MA: Harvard University Press.

Lee, C. C. (1994). Pioneers of multicultural counseling: A conversation with Clemmont E. Vontress. *Journal of Multicultural Counseling & Developmen*t, *22,* 66–76.

Lipsitz, G. (2005). The possessive investment in Whiteness: Racialized social democracy and the 'White problem in American studies.' In T. Ore (Ed.), *The social construction of difference and inequality: Race, class, gender and sexuality* (pp. 402–413). Boston: McGraw Hill.

Mencher, J. (1997). Structural possibilities and constrants of mutuality in psychotherapy. In J. Jordan (Ed.), *Women's growth in diversity* (pp. 110–119). New York: The Guilford Press.

Miller, W. R., & Thoresen, C. E. (2003). Spirituality, religion, and health: An emerging research field. *American Psychologist, 58*(1), 24–35.

Newman, D. M. (2007). Identities and inequalities: Exploring the intersections of race, class, gender, and sexuality. Boston: McGraw Hill.

Omni, M., & Winant, H. (2006). Racial formations. In T. Ore (Ed.), *The social construction of difference and inequality: Race, class, gender, and sexuality* (pp. 19–29). Boston: McGraw Hill.

Ore, T. E. (2006). Maintaining inequalities: Systems of oppression and privilege. In T. Ore (Ed.), *The social construction of difference and inequality: Race, class, gender, and sexuality* (pp. 199–223). Boston: McGraw Hill.

Palmer, P. J. (1999). A vision of education as transformation. In S. Glazer (Ed.), *The heart of learning: Spirituality in education* (pp.15–32). New York: Putnam.

Palmer, P. J. (2004). *A hidden wholeness: The journey toward an undivided life.* San Francisco, CA: Jossey-Bass.

Powell, L. H., Shahabi, L., & Thoresen, C. E. (2003). Religion and spirituality: Linkages to physical health. *American Psychologist, 58*(1), 36–52.

Robinson-Wood, T. L. (2009). *The convergence of race, ethnicity, and gender: Multiple identities in counseling*. 3rd edition. New Jersey: Merrill Prentice Hall.

Robinson, T. L., Watt, S. K. (2001). Where no one goes begging: Gender, sexuality, and religious diversity. In D. Locke, J. Myers, E. Herr (Eds.), *Handbook of counseling* (pp. 589–599). Thousand Oaks, CA: Sage.

Robinson-Wood, T. L., and Braithwaite-Hall, M. (2005). Spirit matters: Women, spirituality, and clinical contexts. In M. Mirkin, K. Suyemoto, & B. Okun (Eds.), *Psychotherapy with women: Exploring diverse contexts and identities* (pp. 280–296). New York: The Guilford Press.

Rosenblum, K. E., & Travis, T. C. (2006). The meaning of difference: American constructions of race, sex, and gender, social class, and sexual orientation. Boston: McGraw-Hill Humanities.

Schultz-Rooss, R. A., & Gutheil, T.G. (1997). Difficulties in integrating spirituality into psychotherapy practice, *Journal of Psychotherapy Practice and Research, 6*, 130–138.

Suyemoto, K. L., & Kim, G. S. (2005). Journeys through diverse terrains: Multiple identities and social contexts in individual therapy. In M. Mirkin, K. Suyemoto, & B. Okun (Eds.), Psychotherapy with women: Exploring diverse contexts and identities (pp. 1–41). New York: The Guilford Press.

Swinton, J. (2001). *Spirituality and mental health care: Rediscovering a 'forgotten' dimension.* London and Philadelphia: Jessica Kingsley Publishers.

Vasquez, H., & Magraw, S. (2005). Building relationships across privilege: Becoming an ally in the therapeutic relationship. In M. Mirkin, K. Suyemoto, & B. Okun (Eds.), *Psychotherapy with women: Exploring diverse contexts and identities* (pp. 64–83). New York: The Guilford Press.

Vontress, C. E. (1969). Cultural differences: Implications for counseling. *Journal of Negro Education, 38*, 266–275.

Vontress, C. E. (1991). Traditional healing in Africa: Implications for cross-cultural counseling. *Journal of Counseling & Development*, *70*, 242–249.

Vontress, C. E. (1996). A personal retrospective on cross-cultural counseling. *Journal of Multicultural Counseling & Development*, *24*, 156–166.

Vontress, C. E. (2004). Reactions to the multicultural counseling competencies debate. *Journal of Mental Health Counseling*, *24*, 74–80.

West, W. (2000). Psychotherapy and spirituality: Crossing the line between therapy and religion. London: Sage.

Wildman, S. M., & Davis, A. D. (2006). Making systems of privilege visible. In T. Ore (Ed.), *The social construction of difference and inequality: Race, class, gender, and sexuality* (pp. 563–569). Boston: McGraw Hill.

Young, J. S., Wiggins-Frame, M., & Cashwell, C. S. (2007). Spirituality and counselor competence: A national survey of American Counseling Association members. *Journal of Counseling & Development*, *85*(1), 47–52.

Zetzer, H. A. (2005). White out: Privilege and its problems. In S. Anderson & V. Middleton (Eds.), *Explorations in privilege, oppression, and diversity* (pp. 3–16). Belmont, CA: Brooks/Cole.

15 African American Women, Race and Gender Politics, and the Work of Clemmont E. Vontress[1]

CARMEN BRAUN WILLIAMS

Multiculturalism, a powerful force in the counseling profession, has infused counseling theory, research, and practice with new perspectives on race, class, gender, and other sociopolitical dimensions of identity, and has offered insight into how dynamics of power, domination, and subordination affect human psychology (D'Andrea, 2005; Jackson, 1995; Sue, Ivey, and Pedersen, 1996). As such, multiculturalism has effected a paradigmatic shift in psychological theory about race and other cultural variables – a shift from simplistic 'deficiency' analyses to appreciation for more nuanced renderings of the psychology of people of color.

This fluid and dynamic conceptual landscape is augmented by multiculturalism's recent sway toward a multifaceted examination of complex and overlapping social identities and away from analyses of single social dimensions, such as race, in isolation from others (Constantine, 2002). Constantine (2002) stated: 'Current models of mental health care often do not allow for the processes by which individuals with multiple oppressed identities arrive at a positive overall sense of cultural identity' (p. 211). Recent multicultural counseling literature has begun to redress this problem of fragmentation of cultural identity (Constantine, 2002; Croteau, Talbot, Lance, & Evans, 2002; Harley, Jolivette, McCormack, & Tice, 2002). This shift offers a more viable framework for understanding the complexity of the lives of African American women.

A more nuanced examination of cultural identity can be traced to the foundational work of Clemmont E. Vontress. Through his articulation of multicultural counseling from a holistic, existential perspective, Vontress laid the groundwork for later exploration of cultural identities as multiple and overlapping rather than as rigid and fixed. His analysis of individuals as whole human beings rather than as fragmented parts (Vontress, 1986, 1996; Vontress & Epp, 2001), foreshadowed the examination of cultural variables in relationship to one another rather than as compartmentalized (Constantine, 2002; Croteau et al., 2002; Harley et al., 2002; Hays, 1996; Moradi & Subich, 2003).

This conceptual shift has significance for counseling African American women, and offers an alternative to earlier psychological perspectives on people of color. Much of the early theory on race in psychology (largely centered on formulations of African American culture and psychology) was characterized by a 'deficiency' perspective. That is, African American culture and people generally were portrayed negatively, as unhealthy and 'culturally deprived,' in comparison with European Americans (Vontress, 1996). Compulsive comparisons of African Americans to European Americans in the early literature served to reinforce the position of European American culture as normative, the standard to which all people of color were held – and against which, psychologically speaking, they paled in comparison (Allport, 1982; Hall, 1997; Kardiner & Ovesey, 1962).

These biases persisted for decades. By the mid-1970s, not coincidentally as African Americans and other students of color were entering and completing graduate programs in psychology in greater numbers than before, psychology and counseling[2] theory and research, still written largely from a Eurocentric perspective, gradually reconsidered its view of people of color as monolithic and culturally deprived. Vontress was an early observer of this shift: 'The whole counseling profession has grown as a result of [an] increased level of understanding of humanity. Over the last ten or fifteen years, writers interested in cross-cultural counseling have discussed many variations in counseling that are made necessary by the cultural differences of clients' (Vontress, 1986, pp. 243–244). Thus, multicultural counseling theory and practice, which was delving into areas such as racial identity development, the psychological impact of social oppression, and the effects of race on psychotherapeutic outcomes, began to situate people of color within a more complex, multilayered, and richly hued cultural context. In other words, people of color began to construct theory in which their cultural patterns and experiences were located at the center of culturally syntonic analyses.

The current emphasis in counseling on cultural competency can be traced to this shift from people-of-color-as-*object* of Eurocentric bias to people-of-color-as-*subject* and author of their own narratives. This subjective perspective enabled a more contextual study of cultural identities and experiences which exposed vital cultural elements that contribute to psychological well-being (Helms & Cook, 1999). Operating from a new perspective, multicultural counseling theory virtually exploded with writing that defined and elucidated the experiences of people of color from a perspective of strength rather than weakness, and from a standpoint of wholeness and health rather than pathology (Helms & Cook, 1999; Vontress and Epp, 2001).[3]

In this chapter, Vontress's contributions to a more holistic understanding of the multiple identities of African American women will be examined. Vontress's emphasis on wholeness is in stark contrast to theoretical perspectives, such as feminist and afrocentric, which present fragmented views reflecting race and gender as single, isolated variables rather than overlapping. The shortcomings of feminist and afrocentric theories' single-variable analyses, and their genesis in identity politics, will be discussed. This chapter will conclude with a case scenario illustrating multiple identities, and an analysis of the case through the holistic perspective of Vontress's model.

Race and Gender Identity Politics

African American women's lives have been affected, to a noteworthy extent, by identity politics (Comas-Diaz & Greene, 1994). Identity politics, criticized by some as 'fragmentary approaches of previous attempts at redressing inequalities' (Chantler, 2005, p. 241) for focusing on a single social dimension (e.g., race *or* gender), have insinuated themselves into counseling theory and practice by way of afrocentric and feminist counseling approaches. That statement is not intended as an indictment of these approaches.[4] Indeed, psychological theory inevitably is influenced by sociopolitical forces. As Vontress stated, 'Politics influence everything in life' (as cited in Jackson, 1987, p. 23). 'In counseling, cultural and social class status are important, because nearly every aspect of the enterprise is influenced in some way by them. Counselors and clients are products of their respective cultures' (Vontress, 1986, p. 223).

Thus, political and social forces – and the power dynamics and inequities embedded therein – have shaped our sociocultural realities and, inevitably, our theories.[5] Eurocentric perspectives, with their marginalization of people of color and women and placement of White men at the center of analysis, are reflections of how prevailing social constructs are mirrored in counseling and psychology theory. Our responsibility as theorists, researchers, and practitioners is to understand the sociopolitical context of theory building and practice and to be mindful of the biases underlining our work.

Political influences notwithstanding, Eurocentric theory has not been without merit with regard to people of color. Psychoanalytic theories, cognitive/behavioral theories, and humanistic/existential theories have contributed valuable concepts and treatment modalities that have been applied cross-culturally in appropriate ways. Likewise, afrocentrism and feminism, despite their limitations, have offered important psychological antidotes to racism and sexism. As Chantler (2005) acknowledged, 'Identity politics have played a crucial role in spotlighting processes and experiences which are frequently overlooked and marginalized, and by bringing into the public domain what are often considered personal and isolated issues' (p. 241). However, despite afrocentric and feminist assertions of the existence of a monolithic 'Black culture' and 'women's culture,'[6] and proposed corresponding psychological traits, these perspectives have limited utility for guiding therapists working with African American women to address the nuances of and intersections between cultures.

The Paradox of Afrocentric and Feminist Psychology

Afrocentric psychology and feminist psychology, both outgrowths of identity politics, presented race and gender, respectively, from a standpoint of strength rather than deficiency. The paradox, however, is that each perspective, while purporting to offer positive psychological portrayals of African Americans and women, was mired in a one-dimensional view of African American women (Williams, 1999, 2006). Despite their significance as affirming alternatives to Eurocentric counseling ideologies, it is ironic – but hardly surprising – that these theories were themselves guilty of being one-dimensional with regard to race and gender. Specifically, early feminist theory focused on White women (Bohan, 1993; Comas-Diaz & Greene, 1994; Landrine, 1995; Reid, 1993), not *all* women, and afrocentric theory centered on the experiences of African American men with little attention to gender differences (e.g., Asante, 1992; Nobles, 1991; White, 1984). In both theories African American women were, for the most part, invisible.

The limitations of afrocentric and feminist theories set the stage for the emergence of womanism (Walker, 1983), or Black feminism. In a ground-breaking treatise, Collins (1990) criticized the 'prominent masculinist bias' in the extant Black social, political, and psychological writings. She argued for an examination of Black women's resistance to oppression as a framework for understanding modes of empowerment cultivated by Black women for psychological survival in dehumanizing historical circumstances (Collins, 1990). In other words, she argued for a strength-based approach to understanding Black women's psychology that acknowledges interlocking cultural identities. Consequently, Black feminist theory gained some traction in the 1990s as an antidote to the shortcomings of afrocentric and feminist psychologies by formulating race, class, sexual orientation, and gender as interwoven and dialectical (Collins, 1990).

Vontress's Model and African American Women

Vontress's theoretical work reflects a deep appreciation of the need to view clients in a holistic manner. Unlike afrocentric and feminist approaches, Vontress's concept of concentric and intersecting cultures (Vontress, 1986) offers a viable framework for understanding African American women's multiple identities. Specifically, Vontress described individuals as 'being composed of multiple cultural influences rather than being culturally monolithic' (Vontress and Epp, 2001, p. 372). Elaborating on this premise, Vontress stated, 'It is antitherapeutic to stereotype clients who appear to represent national, cultural, or racial groups. People with ancestral roots in Europe, Asia, Africa, the Middle East, the Americas, and other parts of the world defy the simple classifications that their superficial racial characteristics would indicate' (Vontress & Epp, 2001, p. 381).

Given the tendency toward the compartmentalization of race and gender in afrocentric and feminist theories, Vontress's emphasis on wholeness and integrity of self was and remains a promising lens through which to view the fluid, evolving identities of African American women. Although Vontress explored race and racism, he did not directly examine the interaction of race and gender and its implications for the counseling process. This is a shortcoming, to be sure. However, a shortcoming, as Vontress himself stated, does not make a theory misguided, only incomplete. It is the author's contention that enough elasticity exists within Vontress's framework to extend his discussion to the interaction of race and gender, and to examining the meaning of that interaction for African American women.

If it is critical, as the author argues in this chapter, to understand that African American women's identities are not one-dimensional, not shaped just by race, and not just by gender, but also by the dynamic interaction between the two variables (Greene, 1994; Jordan, J. M., 1997; Jordan, J. V., 1997; Landrine, 1995), then it is significant that Vontress provides a framework for appreciating these multiple identities. Indeed, his framework rests on the notion of intersecting cultural influences. According to Vontress, 'Most people are products of five concentric and intersecting cultures: (1) universal, (2) ecological, (3) national, (4) regional, and (5) racio-ethnic,' each of which is influential to varying degrees, with the strength of those influences changing through various developmental stages (Vontress, 1986, p. 216). The fluidity of identity and the space that is created for unique manifestations of identity within each individual, even when race and gender are constant, are powerful constructions in Vontress's model.

According to Vontress (1986), 'universal culture' rests on the notion of biological and behavioral commonalities; for example, the human need for water, sleep, and shelter. 'Ecological culture' examines the interaction of human beings with their natural environment. 'National culture' encompasses the influences of worldview, language, and cultural institutions on identity. 'Regional culture,' with its rural, urban, agricultural, and industrial differences, addresses the influence of geographic place on the human experience. And, finally, 'racio-ethnic culture' considers the impact of domination and subordination – power and privilege – on race and ethnicity. Vontress noted the significance of power dynamics for African Americans in stating that African Americans' 'racial difference is clearly visible. The dominant racio-cultural group responds negatively to this difference. As ostracized Americans, their cultural difference is forced upon them' (Vontress, 1986, p. 221). Thus, power is an important variable, especially the power to define another person's reality.

Vontress explained that these five cultures are 'neither entirely separate nor equal'; rather, they are interactive in their influences upon individuals (Vontress, 1986, p. 216). Consequently, because identity is a reflection of unique patterns of cultural influences, within-group differences are as notable – and perhaps more significant – than between-group differences. Vontress thus introduced into multicultural counseling consideration of the interplay between multiple variables. Furthermore, he appreciated the reality of endless possibilities for the relative importance of one or more variables over others in the course of individuals' lives. The culturally competent counselor is cognizant of the myriad possibilities and the consequent importance of exploring each client's narrative as unique to her.

In the following case scenario, Naima, a successful young African American woman, seeks assistance for identity issues. The case illustrates the pitfalls of segregating race and gender, and of defining someone's reality for her. It concludes with a discussion that illuminates the therapeutic promise in applying Vontress's concentric cultures model to working with African American women struggling with the complexities of multiple identities.

Case Scenario[7]

Naima, a 30-year-old African American woman,[8] is director of a White senior citizens center, a leadership position from which she derives considerable satisfaction. She is the first African American administrator at the center, and one of few women on the entire administrative staff. Naima feels a sense of pride and accomplishment in earning the director position in a male-dominated organization. She is acutely aware of daily racist microaggressions (Constantine, 2007; Sue et al. 2007), but feels confident in her ability to handle them skillfully. She received strong family messages about her worth as an African American, and consequently feels a sense of racial pride and confidence in a White world.

Naima is in psychotherapy with Peter, a White male counselor whose peers consider to be culturally competent. Peter operates under several reasonable assumptions about Naima's experience at the senior center; namely, that her colleagues and clients harbor negative assumptions about Naima's competence as a Black woman, and that these assumptions are revealed covertly and indirectly rather than openly. Peter inquires about racism at the center, and Naima acknowledges that, while some of the remarks from the seniors are stereotypical and uninformed, she cares about these individuals, believes they care about her, and thus dismisses their remarks as naive ignorance.

Naima reports that she has encountered no overt racism. She explains that she has been in her position less than three months and is developing productive working relationships with the staff. Although a few of her colleagues have been slow to warm up to her, she has no idea whether to attribute their distance to her newness in the position, to the fact that she is a Black woman, or to their personalities. However, she adds that, if her colleagues are harboring negative assumptions about her abilities and doubts about her competence, she expects that her performance as director, and the positive impact she believes her leadership will have on the organization, will dissipate their concerns.

Peter has difficulty believing Naima is as unfazed as she reports to be about what sounds to him like overt racism from her clients and covert racism among her colleagues. Peter worries that her nonchalance will lead to her being blindsided and unable to handle overt racism when it occurs. He suggests that Naima offer training in cultural competence for her staff. Naima believes Peter's suggestion is premature; 'I need to wait and see what emerges as a problem before I implement solutions.'

Naima has had few opportunities to excel in a male-dominated environment, and therefore feels less sure of how to handle assumptions and stereotypes about women's competence. She describes the African American community where she lives as one in which positions of status – church leaders, political leaders, and civic officials – are held by men. While women in her community are respected, their role is viewed as one of support, not leadership. Consequently, Naima is anxious that sexist assumptions about women's abilities, including those from her own community, may limit her. For her, sexism is a more difficult challenge than racism. As Peter listened to Naima speak of her background and consequent insecurities as a Black woman, he realized that he had made the mistake of singling out race as the primary issue for Naima. He quickly learned to appreciate that the interplay of racism and sexism was more at the heart of Naima's need for counseling.

Application of Vontress's Model to the Case

In the case scenario, it is clear that the therapist, in his genuine attempt to be helpful to his client, was operating from an assumption that racism is separate from and more salient than sexism for Black women clients. It was Naima's persistence in telling Peter a more nuanced story about the impact of community and familial messages about 'women's place' on her view of herself as a leader among men that allowed him to appreciate a bigger picture involving the interplay of racism and sexism.

Vontress's model directly assists us with developing a more holistic perspective from which to consider multiple identities when working therapeutically with Black women. Vontress stressed the complexity and multifaceted nature of cultural influences. He cautioned against assuming, as Peter did in the case example, that race or any other cultural variable is isolated from others in clients' lives:

> It is untenable to suggest that individuals are templates of any collectivity. Although they may each emerge from an identifiable community, they individually perceive the reality of that and other communities differently. Mental health counselors ought to be concerned with how clients respond to the physical, psychological, social, and spiritual environments that influence their existence. (Vontress & Jackson, 2004, p. 78)

All elements of Vontress's model of concentric cultural circles, from attention to environmental and psychological factors, to universal and racio-ethnic factors, are relevant for Black women. Each of the five cultural influences in Vontress's model is applied to the case scenario in the following discussion.

Vontress's depiction of 'universal culture' (Vontress, 1986), with its attention to biological and behavioral commonalities among human beings, can help Peter appreciate Naima's reliance on the bond that she has developed with her clients and most of her staff. In her view, this emotional bond undercuts racism. Vontress's model helps us to appreciate the power of human connection across racial and gender differences (Vontress, 1986, 1996; Vontress and Epp, 2001).

Application of Vontress's 'ecological culture' (Vontress, 1986), which examines the human–environment interaction, might have prompted Naima's therapist to explore aspects of her family and community of origin vis-à-vis her current milieu: how they differ, what elements they have in common, and how her experiences in one milieu could inform her in the other. Applying Vontress's framework, Peter might have asked Naima to describe the landscape of her familial and social environment – her largely African American world – and how it was emotionally, aesthetically, and physically similar to and different from her present professional world. The images Naima drew could have formed the basis for creating visual 'anchors' – powerful mental images from both worlds – that Naima could take with her as she navigated the physical and psychological terrain of her worlds.

'National culture' (Vontress, 1986), with its emphasis on the influences of worldview, language, and cultural institutions on identity, is another element of Vontress's model that has distinct relevance to Naima's situation. For example, to address her concern about how her success as a woman will be perceived by the men and women in her community, Peter could assist Naima to take to her community the same skills that she used to develop the powerful interpersonal connections and trust with her senior citizens. She was able to develop these relationships despite their racial biases. In the same manner, she could use her already cultivated personal connections with people in her community to mitigate the biases they may harbor about her ability to lead as a woman.

The application of 'regional culture' from Vontress's model (Vontress, 1986) could have helped Naima to understand the influence of geographic place on her experience as a Black female. In a manner similar to the utility of 'ecological culture,' Naima's development as a leader could be aided by an understanding of the strengths she derived from her community, with its culture of hard work, determination, and reliance on the strength of familial and communal networks.

Vontress's 'racio-ethnic culture' (Vontress, 1986) offers a window into understanding the impact of domination and subordination – in terms of both race and gender. Dynamics of domination and subordination are evidenced within both Naima's community and her current professional milieu. Naima's success as an African American woman is a testimony to her adroitness in transcending many of the limitations inherent in these milieus, yet she remains somewhat conflicted about her success. Naima might feel considerably supported through a discussion with Peter of African American women role models – strong and capable women found in Black women's history and literature – who transcended racial and gender limitations within their communities and assumed prominent leadership positions. Such a discussion rests on therapists' knowledge of African American women's culture and history – or, at the very least – begs the cultivation of a broad network of competent and diverse colleagues on whom therapists may call for consultation and creative interventions concerning cultural and identity issues.

Considered together, the elements of Vontress's concentric and intersecting cultures offer therapists a strategy with which to integrate the seemingly disparate socio-psychological factors of clients' presenting problems. Even more importantly, his model offers therapeutic possibilities for African American women for whom the segmentation of race and gender into single and isolated dimensions of identity would be a disservice. Vontress's model is a welcome antidote to such segmentation and enables the therapeutic process to embrace the multiple identities of African American women.

Challenges and Future Directions

A challenge in counseling African American women and other women of color is embracing the reality that neither gender nor race alone determine identity (nor, for that matter, do other cultural variables such as class, sexual orientation, spirituality, and ability status determine identity when examined separately). Mainstream counseling theory, despite progress over the past several decades, remains limited heuristically relative to African American women.

Since African American women live as individuals for whom race and gender – and other sociopolitical variables – intersect, it is critical that counseling theories and training programs explore these intersections if they are to be relevant to the treatment of African American women. Approaches such as afrocentrism and feminism, which – due to their genesis in identity politics – tended to isolate race from gender, should be applied by therapists only with due mindfulness of their limitations. As such, the limitations of existing theory must be made more explicit.

Contributing to the problem of identity fragmentation is the manner in which multicultural counseling training is conducted in many graduate programs. Multicultural counseling programs with pedagogical practices that compartmentalize cultures by introducing them sequentially (for example, teaching Black culture one week, Latino culture the next, then social class, then sexual orientation, then disability, ...) miss the mark.[9] Unless such approaches make it explicitly clear that this method is a contrivance for training purposes and not reflective of real people's lives – and make some effort at helping trainees sort through the overlapping layers of cultural variables – they run the risk of launching cohorts of novice counselors ill equipped to understand, let alone address, the often competing cultural pressures and fluidity of identity that real clients experience and seek help with in psychotherapy.

Vontress's concept of concentric and interacting cultures transcends compartmentalized approaches to theory, training, and practice. Vontress does not offer a template for working with African American clients – or clients from any other cultural group. And that is precisely the point. In a response to debate about the American Multicultural Counseling and Development multicultural counseling competencies, Vontress and Jackson (2004) commented on the 'undue emphasis placed on race' and assert that 'mental health counselors should look at all factors impacting a client's situation. Race may or may not be one of them'

(p. 76). In this author's experience, race often becomes, if not the sole variable in case discussions of African American clients, the most salient and defining variable. This is a narrow, simplistic perspective that, as illustrated in the case of Naima, does an injustice to Black clients. It is also a reflection of the power inherent in defining another person's reality.

Yet students often want templates. They often are anxious about working with clients who are culturally different. They may, like Peter in the case scenario, non-consciously operate from sets of assumptions – some of which may derive from their multicultural counseling courses – about how one is to interact with or what questions one should ask African American clients. A challenge for counselor educators and trainers is to resist the temptation to fall back on lists of cultural attributes and the illusion of prescriptive practices. In the words of Vontress and Jackson,

> Instead of promoting a psychotherapeutic model that stereotypes people, we recommend strengthening current efforts to highlight the individual uniqueness of all clients, regardless of their cultural backgrounds … Mental health professionals should guard against generalizing about the group to which clients are presumed to belong. The focus should always be on clients, not on a group with which they may or may not identify. (Vontress & Jackson, 2004, p. 78)

Conclusion

This chapter has focused on multiple cultural pressures experienced by African American women as a prototype for the exploration of intersecting and conflicting cultural variables for other persons of color. The author applauds the multicultural work of Vontress with its notion of concentric and overlapping cultures. The chapter discussed the relevance of his model for addressing multiple cultural influences in psychotherapy with African American women. A limitation of this chapter is its examination of only two of the cultural variables – race and gender – that affect African American women's lives. Despite this limitation, the author is optimistic that, given the political and historical centrality of race and gender to African American women's identity,[10] the reader will find heuristic value and relevance from the discussion for other critical dimensions of social and psychological identity.

NOTES

1 This article is a significant expansion of a previous article by the author published in 2006: Multiple stigmas in psychotherapy with African American women: Afrocentric, feminist, and womanist perspectives, in R. Moodley & S. Palmer (Eds.), *Race, culture and psychotherapy: Critical perspectives in multicultural practice* (pp. 177–188) (London: Routledge).
2 The author, although cognizant of historic distinctions between the terms and the professions of counseling and psychology, uses them interchangeably in this chapter. With regard to theories of race and gender and their impact on psychotherapy, both the psychology and counseling professions have been consistent in their limitations.
3 It is hardly surprising that the writing of 'insiders,' those who live and breathe their cultural experiences, will reflect a different set of assumptions from those of 'outsiders.' In the author's view, both perspectives offer insight and both, inevitably, contain bias.
4 See the paper, cited above, by the author for a more complete discussion of oppressive and regulatory aspects of identity politics.
5 It is the author's belief that theorists and therapists, as products of our cultures, are limited in our ability to step outside our culture and understand the myriad ways in which culture informs our perspectives. This, simply, is the nature of how culture shapes what we perceive as reality. However, once our biases are revealed – revelations most often prompted by encounters with and challenges from those who experience different realities from our own – it behooves us to examine our assumptions, or at least to acknowledge them, rather than continue to offer them as 'truth.'
6 The use of quotation marks around the language of 'Black culture' and 'women's culture' is meant to indicate the problematic nature of essentialist constructions within Afrocentric theory and feminist theory that do not account for huge psychological variations among Blacks and among women. There is neither a static 'Black culture' nor a static 'women's culture,' and there are no universal 'Black traits' or 'women's traits.'
7 This case scenario is based on an actual case presented to the author by a supervisor of an African American woman in a leadership position in a predominantly White church.
8 In this case scenario, African American and Black are used interchangeably.
9 This approach to teaching multicultural counseling and psychology reinforces the problematic and essentialist view that cultures are static and that skin color (and gender, and sexual orientation, and class …) presupposes adherence to a fixed set of cultural values, beliefs, and behaviors.

10 This statement is not intended to minimize the profound influences of myriad other social variables on the experience of African American women. African American lesbians, for example, must negotiate assumptions associated with race and gender, and simultaneously traverse a cultural terrain laden with landmines associated with cultural conceptions of sexual orientation. The author's focus on race and gender reflects her areas of expertise, no doubt shaped largely by their salience in her own life experiences.

REFERENCES

Allport, G. (1982). *The nature of prejudice* (4th ed.). Reading, MA: Addison-Wesley.

Asante, M. K. (1992). *Afrocentricity.* Trenton, NJ: Africa World Press.

Bohan, J. S. (1993). Regarding gender: Essentialism, constructionism, and feminist psychology. *Psychology of Women Quarterly, 17*, 5–21.

Chantler, K. (2005). From disconnection to connection: 'Race,' gender, and the politics of therapy. *British Journal of Guidance and Counselling, 33*(2), 239–256.

Collins, P. H. (1990). *Black feminist thought.* New York: Routledge, Chapman & Hall.

Comas-Diaz, L., & Greene, B. (1994). *Women of color: Integrating ethnic and gender identities in psychotherapy*. New York: Guilford.

Constantine, M. G. (2002). The intersection of race, ethnicity, gender, and social class in counseling: Examining selves in cultural contexts. *Journal of Multicultural Counseling and Development, 30*, 210–215.

Croteau, J. M., Talbot, D. M., Lance, T. S., & Evans, N. J. (2002). A qualitative study of the interplay between privilege and oppression. *Journal of Multicultural Counseling and Development, 30*, 239–258.

D'Andrea, M. D. (2005). Continuing the cultural liberation and transformation of counseling psychology. *The Counseling Psychologist, 33*, 524–537.

Greene, B. (1994). African American women. In L. Comas-Diaz & B. Greene (Eds.), *Women of color: Integrating ethnic and gender identities in psychotherapy* (pp. 10–29). New York: Guilford.

Hall, C. C. I. (1997). Cultural malpractice: The growing obsolescence of psychology with the changing U.S. population. *American Psychologist, 52*, 642–651.

Harley, D. A., Jolivette, K., McCormack, K., & Tice, K. (2002). Race, class, and gender: A constellation of *positionalities* with implications for counseling. *Journal of Multicultural Counseling and Development, 30*, 216–238.

Hays, P. A. (1996). Addressing the complexities of culture and gender in counseling. *Journal of Counseling and Development, 74*, 332–338.

Helms, J. E., & Cook, D. A. (1999). *Using race and culture in counseling and psychotherapy: Theory and process.* Boston: Allyn & Bacon.

Jackson, M. L. (1987). Cross-cultural counseling at the crossroads: A dialogue with Clemmont E. Vontress. *Journal of Counseling and Development, 66*, 20–23.

Jackson, M. L. (1995). Multicultural counseling: Historical perspective. In J. G. Ponterrotto, J. M. Casas, L. A. Suzuki, & C. M. Alexander (Eds.), *Handbook of multicultural counseling* (pp. 3–16). Thousand Oaks, CA: Sage.

Jordan, J. M. (1997). Counseling African American women from a cultural sensitivity perspective. In C. C. Lee & B. L. Richardson (Eds.), *Multicultural issues in counseling: New approaches to diversity* (pp. 51–63). Alexandria, VA: American Counseling Association.

Jordan, J. V. (Ed.) (1997). *Women's growth in diversity: More writings from the Stone Center*. New York: Guilford.

Kardiner, A., & Ovesey, L. (1962). *The mark of oppression*. New York: W.W. Norton.

Landrine, H. (Ed.) (1995). *Bringing cultural diversity to feminist psychology: Theory, research, and practice.* Washington: American Psychological Association.

Moradi, B., & Subich, L. M. (2003). A concomitant examination of the relations of perceived racist and sexist events to psychological distress for African American women. *The Counseling Psychologist, 31*, 451–469.

Nobles, W. W. (1991). African philosophy: Foundations for Black psychology. In R. L. Jones (Ed.), *Black psychology* (pp. 47–63). Berkeley, CA: Cobb & Henry.

Reid, P. T. (1993). Poor women in psychological research: Shut up and shut out. *Psychology of Women Quarterly, 17*, 133–150.

Sue, D. W., Capodilupo, C. M., Torino, G. C., Bucceri, J. M., Holder, A. M. B., Nadal, K. L., & Esquilin, M. (2007). Racial microaggressions in everyday life: Implications for clinical practice. *American Psychologist, 62*(4), 271–286.

Sue, D. W., Ivey, A. E., & Pedersen, P. B. (1996). *A theory of multicultural counseling and therapy.* Pacific Grove, CA: Brooks/Cole.

Vontress, C. E. (1986). Social and cultural foundations. In M. D. Lewis, R. L. Hayes., & J. A. Lewis (Eds.), *The counseling profession* (pp. 215–250). Itaska, IL: Peacock Publishers.

Vontress, C. E. (1996). A personal retrospective on cross-cultural counseling. *Journal of Multicultural Counseling and Development, 24*, 156–166.

Vontress, C. E., & Epp, L. R. (2001). Existential cross-cultural counseling: When hearts and cultures share. In K. J. Schneider, J. F. T. Bugental, and J. F. Pierson (Eds.), *The handbook of humanistic psychology: Leading edges in theory, research, and practice* (pp. 371–388). Thousand Oaks, CA: Sage.

Vontress, C. E., & Jackson, M. L. (2004). Reactions to the multicultural counseling competencies debate. *Journal of Mental Health Counseling, 26,* 74–80.

Walker, A. (1983). *In search of our mothers' gardens.* New York: Harcourt, Brace, Jovanovich.

White, J. L. (1984). *The psychology of Blacks.* Englewood Cliffs, NJ: Prentice-Hall.

Williams, C. B. (1999). African American women, afrocentrism, and feminism: Implications for therapy. *Women & Therapy, 22,* 1–19.

Williams, C. B. (2006). Multiple stigmas in psychotherapy with African American women: Afrocentric, feminist, and womanist perspectives. In R. Moodley & S. Palmer (Eds.), *Race, culture and psychotherapy: Critical perspectives in multicultural practice* (pp. 177–188). London: Routledge.

16 Reclaiming the Spirit: Clemmont E. Vontress and the Quest for Spirituality and Traditional Healing in Counseling

PATSY SUTHERLAND AND ROY MOODLEY

Historically, counseling and psychotherapy has been part of the philosophical traditions of European religion and spirituality. However, for much of the 20th century these concepts have been disavowed in psychology, but less so in psychoanalysis and psychotherapy since Freud's and Jung's psychoanalytic concepts of religion, spirituality, and the mind have had enormous and enduring influence in the field (Miller & Thoresen, 2004). While some scholars valued the examination of religion and spirituality in psychology, Richards and Bergen (1997) argue that psychology as a whole located itself within a 19th-century naturalistic science that is based on deterministic, reductionist, and positivist assumptions that viewed religious and spiritual beliefs and practices negatively. However, this view has markedly changed in the last decade. Research and scholarship on spirituality and counseling psychology has been growing at an enormous rate (see Richards & Bergen, 1997; Hayes & Cowie, 2005; Abernethy, Houston, Mimms, & Boyd-Franklin, 2006; Gurney & Rogers, 2007). Indeed, while the interest in, and research on, spirituality and religion have never been entirely excluded from counseling psychology, Kier and Davenport (2004) argue that such research has focused primarily on the Judeo-Christian majority with very little attention been given to other religious and spiritual beliefs and practices. This is a familiar problem with counseling and psychotherapy research generally, even though findings may not be generalizable from one group to another. This is not surprising, since historically counseling psychology has been a predominantly Eurocentric, ethnocentric, and individualistic preoccupation (Moodley, 1999). Clearly, a different and more inclusive approach is needed to take into account not only issues of diversity in counseling psychology but also how spirituality and traditional healing are part of the treatment process. Toward this end there has been some significant research that attempts to consider a new synthesis between religion, spirituality, and traditional healing and counseling, extending notions of health and well-being to include concern for the body, mind, and spirit (see, for example, Vontress, 1991, 1999, 2005; Moodley, 1999; Fukuyama & Sevig, 1999; Moodley & West, 2005; Moodley, Sutherland, & Oulanova, 2008). Despite this integrative activity, many counselors and psychologists, rather than engage in the training or experience needed to fully understand this key area of client diversity, continue to sustain their historic ambivalence (Russell & Yarhouse, 2006).

However, the same cannot be said of Clemmont Vontress, one of the pioneers of cross-cultural counseling. On the contrary, Vontress has been one of the leading members of the movement toward including spirituality and traditional healing into counseling and psychotherapy. Vontress has attempted not only to address the neglect of spirituality in counseling, but also advocate for the inclusion of traditional healing in psychology. According to Vontress (1971a) the attitude of many counseling psychology researchers and scholars is that counseling is counseling, implying that individuals are more alike than they are different, hence, the many differences that are found in society were not taken into consideration (see, also Vontress, 1986, 1991, 1999). Furthermore, Vontress argues that the usual tendency for mainstream counseling theorists to ignore spirituality is another key limitation to the field of counseling and psychotherapy. Ivey, D'Andrea, Ivey, & Simek-Morgan (2007) cite Vontress (1995) who states, 'People cannot be segmented into parts, as if the pieces are somehow unrelated to the whole. My research in West Africa has convinced me that the spiritual dimension of human beings impacts the physical, psychological and social aspects of living' (Ivey et al., p. 19). Indeed, Clemmont Vontress is one of the few theorists to clearly state that the spiritual/religious 'uberwelt'[1] is critical to understanding the individual, as well as his or her culture (Ivey et al., 2007). Elsewhere, Ivey states that counseling issues of Native American Indians, African Americans, Asian Americans, Latinos, and Jews are all closely related to the cultural and spiritual traditions of these communities (see Littrell, 2001), which suggests that culture, spirituality, religion, and traditional healing are critical areas of exploration and expansion in the future development of counseling psychology.

Hence, the work of Clemmont Vontress seems particularly important to explore in this respect; his approach to counseling and psychotherapy in contexts of cross-cultural exchange reflects a clear viewpoint on several of these issues. The aim of this chapter is to introduce the ideas of Vontress on cross-cultural counseling, particularly on the intersection of religion, spirituality, and traditional healing in the field of counseling psychology and psychotherapy. We follow this discussion by exploring Clemmont Vontress's quest for spirituality and traditional healing as a personal and existential journey. Finally, we discuss how Vontress's ideas on spirituality and traditional healing can contribute to the transformation that is taking place in the field of counseling and psychotherapy today. First, we begin with a look at the issues of historical wounding through racism and the legacy of slavery.

Historical Wounding, Culture, and Society

Individuals live in relationship to a cultural, social, political, and economic, as well as a spiritual, frame of reference. According to Vontress,

> We require the respect, direction, love, and affection of parents, elders, departed loved ones and potent spiritual entities. The spirit world connects us with those who, although already come and gone, still reside in us, because of memory, genetic contributions and cultural indoctrination. In many cultures, departed ancestors are considered invisible and valuable members of the family. Their wisdom sustains and directs the lives of the living. (1996, p. 162)

This statement may seem radical and contentious from the viewpoint of Western counseling and psychotherapy (Ivey et al., 2007). Several authors have argued that spirituality and the link with the past are rarely associated with here-and-now action-oriented counseling and therapy (see Duran & Duran, 1995; Parham, White, & Ajamu, 1999; Moodley & West, 2005). Nevertheless, there is a basis for Vontress's ideas in the work of Carl Jung. Jung (1958) valued the examination of religion and spirituality in psychology; his notion of the collective unconscious epitomizes a basis for much of what is deemed spiritual. Moreover, Koss (1988) compared Spiritist[2] healing with Jungian psychotherapy and concluded that they share a number of ideas and practices that are basic to effective healing processes. In both cases, the client's distressful but unconscious desires, fears, and feelings are brought to consciousness to bring about resolution and promote psychological development.

Regardless of whether Vontress's views of spirituality are congruent with our own worldview or not, it is nonetheless true that the spiritual notions he suggests are embedded in many cultures around the world, albeit in different ways (Ivey et al., 2007). Many people from the Aboriginal, African, African American, Asian, Caribbean, Chinese, Japanese, and several other communities would find counseling and psychotherapy deficient without the inclusion of spiritual and religious concepts and traditions immersed into the helping process (Fukuyama & Sevig, 1999). As an example of including the spiritual dimension in counseling, Ivey et al. (2007) suggest that we consider the anger that many African Americans feel as they experience various forms of racism in present-day society. This anger can become internalized, affecting the body, mind, and spirit. Vontress makes the connection between spiritual and bodily ailment in his discourse on middle-class African American men; he states:

> It's terribly fascinating to try to understand why these Black men die in their sleep more than any other men. I maintain it's because they are working in the mainstream culture around White people and have to suppress their hostility during the day. It's only when they are sleeping at night that their system allows their hostility to express itself, and it expresses itself very often in sleep. This helps to explain why there's such an inordinate number of Black middle-class men who die in their sleep at night. (cited in Lee, 1994, p. 71)

These reflections resonate with Vontress's early work on historical hostility, a theme which he notes 'has fascinated me for a long time' (Vontress, 1996, p. 159). His concept of historical hostility is influenced by Carl Jung and the notion of the collective unconscious. According to Vontress, Jung insisted that while human beings are products of their personal histories, they are also products of the collective and universal heritage of the human species; psychological traces or archetypes of previous generations motivate, shape, and influence the development of future generations. Correspondingly, historical hostility describes the unique collective psychology of African Americans as a result of their exposure to slavery, discrimination, and the unrelenting, albeit unconscious, fear of unequal treatment by the majority culture. Vontress (1996) contends that many events in history demonstrate a cultural and spiritual bond between people who have endured collective injustices transgenerationally at the hands of a perceived common oppressor whose continuous discriminatory actions can trigger their collective rage. From this reading, it becomes increasingly clear that this issue may not be without personal implications for Clemmont Vontress, an African American male. It appears that in many ways his current theoretical and therapeutic positions may be a reflection of his own existential wounding and quest for spirituality and healing which may have ultimately led him in search of spirituality and African traditional healing practices.

In Search of Spirituality and Traditional Healing

Vontress believes that spirituality is pivotal to any authentic multicultural encounter. He describes spirituality as the need to search for meaning and connection with others, as well as the transcendent force of the universe (Epp, 1998). This search may have led Vontress to his study of African traditional healing practices. Intrigued by the reports about the effectiveness of Tobie Nathan's ethnopsychiatry,[3] Vontress spent several years researching Nathan's work to learn how he was able to combine Western psychotherapeutic methods with the traditional healing practices used by African and other non-Western healers. Vontress shares Nathan's view that there is a great deal that Western counselors can learn from traditional healers in other parts of the world, and highlights the need to establish collaboration with these healing systems: 'The world needs this collaboration ... Without traditional healers, many people will have no medical or psychological services' (Vontress, 2003, p. 26). Vontress's work on spirituality, based on several trips to the African continent over the past 25 years, exemplifies the richness of the traditional etiologic theories and ensuing therapies that have been used in African cultures for centuries. Supported by rich and compelling evidence from his investigations, Vontress first describes the clinical work of African healers, who are categorized under six headings: indigenous doctors, herbalists, fetish men, mediums, religious healers, and sorcerers (Vontress, 1991, 1999, 2005). In his work Vontress attempts to show how traditional healers aim to restore harmony and equilibrium through natural, spiritual, and psychological healing. Furthermore, Vontress draws attention to the relevance of his studies by elaborating on the African worldview, as well as the healing relationship, diagnostic procedures, and intervention strategies of these healing systems and their implications for the advancement of counseling and psychotherapy in cross-cultural contexts.

According to Vontress (2005), the African worldview is deeply entrenched in animism,[4] the view that everything in the universe is of one source, mind, and will and that the world is animated by spiritual entities. Similarly, Bojuwoye (2005) suggests that two aspects of the traditional African worldview are germane to health care, the interconnectedness of phenomenal worlds (which inform collective living) and spirituality. Traditionally, Africans also believe that the body, mind, and spirit are all connected, and whatever affects one, impacts the other. From this perspective, illnesses and disorders are perceived as arising from natural, social, spiritual, or psychological disturbances that create imbalance which can be expressed in the form of physical or mental ill health (du Plessis, 2003). Moreover, many Africans believe that there are numerous causes for illness; humans, as well as supernatural and ancestral spirits are often perceived as causal agents (Bojuwoye, 2005). At first glance, these beliefs and healing systems may appear to be at odds with Western approaches to health and well-being. However, Vontress adds,

> The culture in which people are socialized determines the beliefs that they hold about the nature of their problems and the way they may be solved ... The belief in animism acts as a powerful force on the traditional African's understanding of difficulties in life. The notions that every object and being has a spirit and that the 'dead' pass into an invisible dimension influence not only the healer's diagnosis of problems brought to him but also the patient's willingness to accept the analyses of them. (1991, p. 249)

In addition to addressing crucial health and mental health concerns, another function of traditional healing practices is that of minimizing the trauma of acculturation (Press, 1978). Western approaches to well-being can be a threatening solution to an already sufficiently threatening problem. Traditional healers tend to be from their client's own culture and may exhibit familiar behavior and attitudes, not the least of which may be the client's own language. When they interpret problems in cultural terms, a label is assigned that has familiar implications and a predictable course of treatment. Even in instances where the healer may use interventions in which the content or symbolic impact may be unknown to the client, the intent and common basis for the procedure are often compatible with his or her worldview (Press, 1978). Vontress (2005) cites NGOMA, (2003) who states that 'the most effective therapeutic agents are those who embody the culture of their clients. In a sense, the client's culture is the healing instrument' (p. 133).

Reclaiming the Spirit through Decolonizing the Mind and Body

Vontress's notion of historical hostility, as previously described, is closely related to the concepts of received transgenerational hatred (Apprey, 1999), post-traumatic slave syndrome (Leary, 2005), and transgenerational trauma, which represent attempts to find a fitting clinical term that captures the urgency of the irrefutable historical fact of African Americans, Caribbeans, and Africans in the Diaspora. This historical fact often manifests itself in the form of transgenerational haunting[5] (Apprey, 1999) and self-hatred (Vontress, 1962, 1963, 1966, 1971a, 1971b). For example, although African Americans are significant contributors to American life, they are often debased by a White dominant culture that perceives them as inferior, and subliminally reinforces that inferiority (Vontress, 1996). Consequently, Blacks tend to reject themselves because they cannot help but internalize the negative self-concept that is unrelentingly hammered into their psyches. While this self-hatred is usually unconscious and veiled to those afflicted by it, for Clemmont Vontress it is all too apparent. He explains:

> Being a reflective young person, I recognized the absurdity of a situation in which my race determined my destiny instead of my intelligence and character. I was constantly searching for answers to soothe the psychological pain that an inferior social status engenders ... There is an enormous wellspring of pain that builds when one's intelligence can bring one forward and one's race becomes an undeserved penalty. (Epp, 1998, p. 2)

This psychological pain and spirit injury has resounding implications for Clemmont Vontress and those of African heritage who were torn from the world of their ancestors and forced to adapt to a culture that dehumanizes them on a daily basis. Furthermore, Apprey (1999) suggests that we 'think of a broken line, a cut, a gap, rupture, lost ancestry and the wound of an absence in the African American lineage' (p. 133). What attempts are made to mend the wound of such absence and loss? For Clemmont Vontress it seems to involve a personal and professional search for healing and of going back and reclaiming through African traditional healing and spirituality. This sentiment was echoed by Moodley (2008) at the Toronto Decolonizing the Spirit Conference:

> I think that it is my spirit that is free in me, that attempts to find a way to be free, and in that notion of finding freedom or in the act of wanting to

> rise above the shackles, the oppressive structures within which it constructs itself, I think is an act of spirituality ... I think that's our journey, maybe of recovering, of reclaiming who we are ... of reclaiming the spirit that is imposed on by the colonized body and mind.

Thus, it seems that spirituality and African traditional healing represent not only an approach to health and well-being, but also a tool for survival, resistance, reclaiming truths, and healing. It becomes increasingly clear that Vontress's work on spirituality, traditional healing, and multicultural counseling and psychotherapy may be heavily influenced by his relationship with his own woundedness and the need to heal the spirit-injuries stemming from slavery, racism, and cultural degradation. This is evident in Vontress's willingness to maintain a consciousness of, and engage with the parts of, himself that is continuously wounded in his work as a counselor; in other words, himself as the wounded healer. Whether these wounds are physical, emotional, or existential, Koss-Chioino (2006) contends that they must often be confronted during transactions with distressed clients.

Throughout his work, Vontress emphasizes the need for psychotherapeutic interventions that address the particularized needs of individuals of African descent, as well as other culturally diverse clients. Correspondingly, Apprey (1999) argues that while there are many psychotherapeutic approaches for understanding the impact of historical trauma, counselors and clinicians working with the African American community must speak to the issue of how the historical anguish associated with the exilic condition[6] is internalized, reenacted by future generations, and adapted so that any sense of homecoming or at-home-ness is shattered or compromised. He continues: 'There must first be many profiles of understanding of the actual injury. There must be an understanding of how the aggrieved community has stored in their communal memory those psychological hurts, those feelings of humiliation and changing historical accounts of the actual injuries' (p. 140). These reflections help to elucidate the critical role of spirituality and traditional healing practices, and the importance of Vontress's contribution and its implications for multicultural counseling and psychotherapy. According to Vontress (1996), 'one of the most challenging problem is trying to get people to love themselves when the national culture constantly sends out the subtle message that they are not worthy of love – which undermines even the most impassioned therapeutic positive regard' (p. 158). Indeed, Vontress's valuable contribution helps to form a foundation for the development of a multifaceted framework for multicultural counseling and psychotherapy.

Implications for Counseling and Psychotherapy

Vontress's resolve in taking into account the cultural shaping of psychological distress and the need to use therapeutic interventions specific to the client's culture is consistent with his view of the connection between culture and psychic structure. As mentioned earlier, the culture in which people are socialized determines the beliefs that they hold about the nature of their problems; consequently, healing practices are also by-products of such a worldview. Over time, each population develops its own worldview. Vontress argues that it is passed from one generation to the next, consciously and unconsciously, and that conceptualizations of health and illness are vital components. While there has been a significant increase in the scholarly attention devoted to spirituality, traditional healing, and cross-cultural communication, most attempts at cross-cultural therapy have been ineffective due to the lack of a shared reality (Vontress, 2001). Western practitioners are often frustrated when working with non-Western clients whose values and beliefs systems differ; they often perceive these values, beliefs, and traditional healing systems as obstructions to health care (Carrazana, DeToledo, Tatum, Rivas-Vasquez, Rey, & Wheeler, 1999). Vontress cites Torrey (1986), who suggests that counselors need to find ways to be therapeutic without imposing their psychotherapeutic 'science' on people who are socialized in spiritually oriented societies. We contend that such imposition is reminiscent of colonialism and can potentially be retraumatizing for many culturally diverse individuals. Furthermore, Moodley, Sutherland, and Oulanova (2008) suggest that counselors must be willing to accommodate clients who engage in the process of dual interventions, that is, traditional healing alongside conventional counseling and psychotherapy. Such dual interventions address the mind-body-spirit holism that many clients seek.

It therefore follows that an understanding of the spiritual connection can help counselors in improving not only clients' thinking but also their bodily functioning (Chissel, 2000; Chopra & Simon, 2001; Moodley & West, 2005). Vontress (1991) argues that Western counselors who focus exclusively on the psychological component are more likely to misdiagnose the problems of their non-Western clients. Is it not reasonable to conclude that people who believe that their problems derive from the displeasure of departed ancestors are likely to be affected by that belief? While psychological measures may be used to recognize the presence of a psychological imbalance, such information by itself may not be as valuable without some insight into the source of the disturbance (Vontress, 1991). To this end, counselors must be willing to explore the traditional beliefs that their clients hold about the root causes of their difficulties. Vontress reinforces the importance of the meaning one attributes to one's life, as well as the situations one comes across. Through such meaning making, we are able to redefine our existence and create more effective ways of making sense of who we are, our relationship with others, and our being-in-the-world (Ivey et al., 2007).

Vontress's work is integral to understanding the central role of religion, spirituality, and traditional healing practices in the lives of many diverse clients. Although he focused predominantly on African healing systems, the worldview of the African people regarding illness and health has important parallels to many non-Western cultures. For example, Caribbean cultures are deeply rooted in spiritual dimensions; many individuals from the Caribbean believe that mental health problems are caused by spells, spirits, and demons, and that such problems represent a punishment for wrongful deeds (Laguerre, 1987; Nicolas, DeSilva, Grey, & Gonzalez-Eastep, 2001; Waldron, 2003). Because illness is linked to spirituality and religion, healing is often obtained through spiritual means. Therefore, it is imperative for counseling professionals to understand and respect these beliefs. This requires a culturally sensitive healthcare delivery system, culturally sensitive counselors and practitioners, adequate counselor training, linguistically appropriate health messages, and health care staff that include indigenous community practitioners (Vontress, 1991, 2005; Bayne-Smith, 1998).

Conclusion

The connections between religion and spirituality and illness and healing concerns are as old as human history (Bou-Yong, 2001). In many cultures around the world, the spiritual or traditional healer remains an important resource for many individuals seeking relief from suffering and for restoring health and well-being. Nonetheless, the field of counseling psychology has historically neglected the spiritual dimension of human consciousness and the important role it plays in determining the ways in which people conceptualize distress by adhering to causality principles and scientific orientations. Despite the history of tension between these two fields, there is a resurgence of interest in religious, spiritual, and traditional healing practices and therapy. In this regard, the work of Clemmont Vontress is particularly influential. Throughout his work, Vontress argues for the inclusion of the spiritual dimension in counseling and psychotherapy. Such integration has the potential to not only eliminate some of the barriers that prevent minority groups from accessing counseling, but also to truly transform theory, research, and practice in multicultural counseling and psychotherapy.

In order to achieve substantive change, however, Vontress argues that it is necessary to incorporate worldviews that challenge universal assumptions in counseling psychology. Furthermore, counselors and therapists should consider the implications of their choice of diagnostic tests, constructs, and psychotherapeutic interventions, which may ignore cultural realities and resources that empower clients. This will require a major shift in the perception of religious, spiritual, and traditional healing beliefs and practices as psychopathologies. Vontress's work reveals that these beliefs and practices stem from healing systems that are rich with strategies, many of which can be successfully incorporated into therapy. Clearly, the transformative benefit of integrating religion, spirituality, and traditional healing into counseling and psychotherapy lies in the simultaneous pursuit of cultural competence in clinical practice, education, training, and research, and consideration of how clients respond to the physical, psychological, social, and spiritual environments which influence their existence. According to Vontress and Jackson (2004), the therapist whose objective is to only address the psychological concerns of his/her client may, in so doing, neglect the most important therapeutic consideration – the spiritual.

NOTES

1 Vontress & Epp (2001) define the 'Uberwelt' as the spirit world, and suggest that this realm may also comprise intangible feelings of the here and now which bind the human community together in mutual understanding with a potent, though invisible, emotional adhesive. These intangible feelings include love, devotion, empathy, respect, and altruism.

2 Spiritism or Espiritismo refers to a popular healing tradition in Puerto Rico. Its ritual practices center around working with spirits. Mediums

become possessed by these spirits and through visions they are able to heal individuals presenting with a wide range of health and social problems (Koss-Chioino, 2005).

3 The term used by Nathan to describe the intervention methods he uses for counseling African immigrants and their families (Vontress, 2003).

4 Bojuwoye (2005) defines animism as the belief that the world is animated by spiritual entities, a belief that is characteristic of the traditional African worldview. When someone dies the person is believed to transform into an ancestral spirit who is actively involved in the lives of the person's descendants and able to influence their behavior.

5 In Maurice Apprey's (1999) work on transgenerational hatred in the African American community, he writes about the transfer of destructive aggression from one generation to the next. Such a transfer may reveal a shift from suicide in one generation to murder, incest, or physical abuse in the next. Apprey suggests, 'It is as if the injured group has accepted the message that they do not deserve to live and therefore must die in one way or the other. At the very least that injured group may exist in a reduced form such as living but living a most unproductive life.'

6 People of African descent have had to struggle with the realities of forced migration from their homeland and of being forced to adopt a foreign identity, which at once debased and dehumanized them as a result of the colonial encounter (Oluruntoba-Oju, 2006).

REFERENCES

Abernethy, A. D., Houston, T. R., Mimms, T., & Boyd-Franklin, N. (2006). Using prayer in psychotherapy: Applying Sue's differential to enhance culturally competent care. *Cultural Diversity and Ethnic Minority Psychology, 12*(1), 101–114.

Apprey, M. (1999). Reinventing the self in the face of received transgenerational hatred in the African American community. *Journal of Applied Psychoanalytic Studies, 1*(2), 131–143.

Bayne-Smith, M. (1998). Health promotion in New York City's Caribbean community: Implications for health professionals. *Wadabagei: A Journal of the Caribbean and Its Diaspora, 1*(1), 141–158.

Bojuwoye, O. (2005). Traditional healing practices in Southern Africa: Ancestral spirits, ritual ceremonies, and holistic healing. In R. Moodley & W. West (Eds.), *Integrating traditional healing practices into counseling and psychotherapy*. Thousand Oaks, CA: Sage.

Bou-Yong, R. (2001). Culture, spirituality, and mental health: The forgotten aspects of religion and health. *The Psychiatric Clinics of North America, 24*(3), 569–579.

Carrazana, E., DeToledo, J., Tatum, W., Rivas-Vasquez, R., Rey, G., & Wheeler, S. (1999). Epilepsy and religious experiences: Voodoo possession. *Epilepsiu, 40*(2), 239–241.

Chissel, J. T. (2000). *Pyramids of power: An ancient African American centered approach to optimal health*. Baltimore: Positive Perceptions Publications.

Chopra, D., & Simon, D. (2001). *Grow younger, live longer*. New York: Three Rivers.

du Plessis, K. (2003). Turning to tradition. *Perspective: African Journal of HIV/AIDS, 5*, 102–107.

Duran, E., & Duran, B. (1995). *Native American post colonial psychology*. Albany: State University of New York.

Epp, L. R. (1998). The courage to be an existential counselor: An interview of Clemmont E. Vontress. *Journal of Mental Health Counseling, 20*(1), 1–12.

Fukuyama, M., & Sevig, T. D. (1999). *Integrating spirituality into multicultural counseling*. Thousand Oaks, CA: Sage.

Gurney, A. G., & Rogers, S.A. (2007). Object-relations and spirituality: Revisiting a clinical dialogue. *Journal of Clinical Psychology, 63*(10), 961–977.

Hayes, M. A., & Cowie, H. (2005). Psychology and religion: Mapping the relationship. *Mental Health, Religion & Culture, 8*(1), 27– 33.

Ivey, A. E., D'Andrea, M., Ivey, M. B., & Simek-Morgan, L. (2007). *Theories of counseling and psychotherapy* (6th Ed.). Boston, MA: Allyn & Bacon.

Jung, C. (1958). *Psychology and religion*. New York: Pantheon.

Kier, F. J., & Davenport, D. S. (2004). Unaddressed problems in the study of spirituality and health. *American Psychologist, 59*(1), 53–54.

Koss, J. D. (1988). Pyschodynamic interpretations of psychiatric illness: Perspectives from analytical psychology. *Journal of Analytical Psychology, 36*, 341–355.

Koss-Chioino, J. D. (2006). Spiritual transformation, ritual healing, and altruism. *Zygon, 41*(4), 877–892.

Laguerre, M. S. (1987). *Afro-Caribbean folk medicine*. South Hadley, MA: Bergin & Garvey Publishers.

Leary, J. D. (2005). *Post traumatic slave syndrome: America's legacy of enduring injury and healing*. Milwaukie, Oregon: Uptone Press.

Lee, C. (1994). Pioneers of multicultural counseling: A conversation with Clemmont E. Vontress. *Journal of Multicultural Counseling and Development, 22*, 66–78.

Littrell, J. M. (2001). Allen E. Ivey: Transforming counseling theory and practice. *Journal of Counseling and Development, 79*(1), 105–118.

Miller, W. R., & Thoresen, C. E. (2004). Spirituality, health, and the discipline of psychology. *American Psychologist, 59*(1), 54–55.

Moodley, R. (1998). I say what I like: Frank talk(ing) in counseling and psychotherapy. *British Journal of Guidance & Counseling, 26*(4), 495–507.

Moodley, R. (1999). Challenges and transformations: Counseling in a multicultural context. *International Journal for the Advancement of Counseling, 21*, 139–152.

Moodley, R. (2008). Decolonizing the spirit panel.At Decolonizing the spirit: Making indigenous spirituality visible in research learning and praxis conference, OISE, University of Toronto, Canada.

Moodley, R., Sutherland, P. & Oulanova, O. (2008). Traditional healing, the body and mind in psychotherapy. *Counseling Psychology Quarterly*, 21(2), 153–165.

Moodley, R. & West, W. (Eds.) (2005). *Integrating traditional healing practices into counseling and psychotherapy*. Thousand Oaks, CA: Sage.

NGOMA. (2003). *Indigenous healing in South Africa: An overview.* Accessed 12 November 2003, at http://www.wits.ac.za/izangoma/part1.asp.

Nicolas, G., DeSilva, A. M., Grey, K. S., & Gonzalez-Eastep, D. (2001). Using a multicultural lens to understand illnesses among Haitians living in America. *American Journal of Orthopsychiatry, 77*(4), 702–707.

Oloruntoba-Oju, O. (2006). The redness of blackness: Revisiting Derek Walcott's mulatto aesthetics. *Caribbean Quarterly, 52*(1), 12–25.

Parham, T. A., White, J. L., & Ajamu, A. (1999). *The psychology of blacks: An African centered perspective* (3rd ed.). Upper Saddle River, NJ: Prentice Hall.

Press, I. (1978). Urban folk medicine: A functional overview. *American Anthropologist, 80*(1), 71–84.

Richards, P. S., & Bergin, A. E. (1997). *A spiritual strategy for counseling and psychotherapy*. Washington: American Psychological Association.

Russell, S. R. & Yarhouse, M. A. (2006). Training in religion/spirituality within APA-accredited psychology predoctoral internships. *Professional Psychology: Research and Practice, 37*(4), 430–436.

Torrey, E. F. (1986). *Witchdoctors and psychiatrists: The common roots of psychotherapy and its future.* New York: Harper & Row.

Vontress, C. E. (1962). Patterns of segregation and discrimination: Contributing factors to crime among Negroes. *Journal of Negro Education, 31*, 108–116.

Vontress, C. E. (1963). The Negro against himself. *Journal of Negro Education, 32*, 237–241.

Vontress, C. E. (1966). The Negro personality reconsidered. *Journal of Negro Education, 35*, 210–217.

Vontress, C. E. (1971a). *Counseling Negroes*. Boston: Houghton Mifflin.

Vontress, C. E. (1971b). Racial differences: Impediments to rapport. *Journal of counseling psychology, 18*, 7–13.

Vontress, C. E. (1986). Social and cultural foundations. In M. D. Lewis, P. Hayes, & J. A. Lewis (Eds.), *An introduction to the counseling profession* (pp. 215–250). Itasca, IL: Peacock.

Vontress, C. E. (1991). Traditional healing in Africa: Implications for cross-cultural counseling. *Journal of Counseling and Development, 70*(1), 242–249.

Vontress, C. E. (1995). The philosophical foundations of the existential-humanistic perspective: A personal statement. Washington: George Washington University.

Vontress, C. E. (1996). A personal retrospective on cross-cultural counseling. *Journal of Multicultural Counseling and Development, 24*(3), 156–166.

Vontress, C. E. (1999). Interview with a traditional African healer. *Journal of Mental Health and Counseling, 21*(4), 326–336.

Vontress, C. E. (2001). Cross-cultural counseling in the 21st century. *International Journal for the Advancement of Counseling, 23*(2), 83–97.

Vontress, C. E. (2003). On becoming an existential cross-cultural counselor. In F. D. Harper & J. McFadden (Eds.), *Culture and counseling*. Boston: Allyn & Bacon.

Vontress, C. E. (2005). Animism: Foundation of traditional healing in Sub-Saharan Africa. In R. Moodley & W. West (Eds.), *Integrating traditional healing practices into counseling and psychotherapy*. Thousand Oaks, CA: Sage.

Vontress, C. E., & Jackson, M. L. (2004). Reactions to the multicultural counseling competencies debate. *Journal of Mental Health Counseling, 26*(1), 74–80.

Waldron, Ingrid R. G. (2003). Examining beliefs about mental illness among African Canadian women. *Women's Health and Urban Life: An International and Interdisciplinary Journal, 2*(1), 42–58.

17 Paving the Path of Culture and Counseling: A Conversation with Clemmont E. Vontress

TRACY L. ROBINSON-WOOD

On 27 and 28 July 2008 I interviewed Dr Clemmont E. Vontress in Washington, DC, at the invitation of Roy Moodley, one of the editors of this book. The first session took place in a conference room in the main library on the campus of George Washington University, where Dr Vontress is Professor Emeritus of Counseling. The second session was conducted in the library of his home in Washington. We taped almost four hours of conversation and what follows are selected passages from the interviews. I began by asking Dr Vontress how he started his counseling career.

Clemmont Vontress (CV): When I entered the counseling profession in the fifties, counseling was much different from what it is today. Few people took a degree in counseling. The graduate degree was usually in education with a concentration in counseling, or guidance as it was called then. By the sixties, many universities were offering PhDs in counseling. Among them was Indiana University, where I received my terminal degree. Before then, I became director of counseling in a large, predominantly Black high school in Indianapolis, Indiana. I was hired to set up the school's first organized counseling program. Unfortunately, the school system did not recognize 'counselor' as a job title. Therefore, all of the eight counselors in the counseling department which I directed were teachers, who were only allowed to spend two or three periods a day as counselors.

In graduate school, my interest in culture was an outgrowth of my negative experience in sociology classes. My professors often referred to the 'culturally deprived' or 'culturally disadvantaged.' To me, these labels were euphemisms for African Americans, who were then considered to be a sub-class of the larger society. I was offended, because I recognized that culture is a human necessity. Nobody is deprived of it. Although I disagreed with my professors regarding the nature of culture, I could not express the disagreement.

While still in graduate school, Dr Vontress's major professor did not share his interest in counseling and culture and could not appreciate how or why anyone could be interested in culture and counseling. Undaunted, Dr Vontress found another dissertation topic, graduated, and continued to pursue his interests in culture and counseling.

Tracy Robinson-Wood (TR): What was that like for you to not have your major advisor value your interest?

CV: I was hurt. I felt I was right and I could not tell him he was wrong. He was a very kind professor who was generally supportive. I knew if I did not find another dissertation topic, I would be there forever. However, he told me that everybody knew that 'counseling was counseling.' That is, he could not understand that culture as he understood it would impact counseling in any way. Besides, he respected me as a student and told me that he did not want to see me waste a promising academic future on a topic that would lead nowhere. Not wanting to disappoint him or lose his support, I searched for a topic that he would surely like. That is why I selected a topic dealing with the effects of stress on the test scores of students who responded to test items while being distracted by various stimuli. Although I chose another dissertation topic, my interest in culture and counseling remains my passion to this day.

Dr Vontress's interest in culture and counseling led to his travels to North Africa and West Africa, where he studied culture as it impacts traditional healing. He observed that traditional healers in West Africa relate to, diagnose, and intervene in the effort to help their clients, just as American therapists do. They just do it differently.

CV: I have continued to study culture and to ask questions such as 'How does culture influence human behavior?' 'How does culture contribute to problems in living?' and 'How does culture influence helping theories and procedures?' Although traditional healers in Africa have not codified theories of healing as we have in Western societies, they still can articulate why they do what they do in helping their clients. I have also found that there are various types of healers in most African cultures just as there are in the United States.

TR: Multicultural counseling has expanded to include gender, sexuality, disability, class, and spirituality. Do you think multicultural counseling has departed from the foundation that you initially provided?
CV: I have never used multicultural counseling to refer to models in which culture and counseling are combined. Cross-cultural counseling is not synonymous with multicultural counseling. The latter has stereotypically focused on four groups: Hispanic Americans, Asian Americans, African Americans, and Native Americans. There is a vice president for each of these groups in the Association for Multicultural Counseling and Development (AMCD). I do not see anyone in the Association who is doing anything to change this perception of the focus. As it is presently constituted, AMCD does not incorporate international populations. Conversely, cross-cultural counseling emphasizes culture, period. It does not just focus on these four racially different groups in the United States. Rather, it considers all culturally different people throughout the world. In fact, everybody is culturally different. Culture should take into consideration the way of life of the universal population as well as national groups. All human beings are the same and different at the same time.
TR: Do you think it is possible to discuss culture without talking about ethnicity and race?
CV: No. I do not think so. I believe that it is important for the counselor to first try to understand the client, no matter who that client is. Of course, we are all influenced by various forces external to ourselves. Individuals react to these influences differently. I believe that the counselor should always focus on individual differences. It is anti-therapeutic to do otherwise. Most of all, counselors should not do it in the name of cross-cultural counseling.
TR: Are there cultural groups that have not been paid attention to?
CV: Yes, at least 100 cultural groups from all over the world.
TR: Pedagogically, how does a professor fit 100 cultural groups into a semester course?
CV: I do not agree with the current method of teaching cross-cultural counseling courses in most universities. In most cases, professors use what I call the groups approach. It is one in which they stereotype cultural groups based on race or ethnicity. For example, black people are considered as a single group. No consideration is given to national, regional socioeconomic, or ethnic origin. The same is true of Hispanics. In this country, people of Hispanic origin come from many different countries in the world. You can understand how stereotyping a group

of people based on race or other assumed characteristics may do more harm than good. Yet, this method of teaching is still used in most of our universities today.

TR: So what method do you recommend instead?

CV: I have always recommended that counselor educators who teach cross-cultural counseling courses use a conceptual approach. That is, instead of stereotyping groups, they should use a conceptual approach. Concepts such as assimilation, acculturation, collectivism, individualism, personalism, and the like can be used to help counselors-in-training learn how to adjust their counseling approaches to the individual clients when needed. There are dangers in stereotyping clients. Clients, no matter who they are, must be understood as individuals, not as members of a specific group.

TR: In one of your interviews, you told a story about a young Black man when you were a counselor at Crispus Attacks. I've thought about his confrontation of you when you asked him how he felt about this or that and he exploded with frustration to say that he felt the same way you would feel if you were in his same situation.

CV: This young man's confrontation helped me to recognize that the Rogerian style of counseling was not effective with Black clients. We were taught to preface our inquiries with 'How do we feel' about this or that; so I was doing what I had been taught. The teen was frustrated. I was not really helping him. I was acting on some therapeutic recipe that I had learned in graduate school; and it was not working with my clients. I looked for another way that I could be therapeutic and authentic with my clients. It was a turning point in my professional career. That single experience started my search for another approach that would work with clients similar to that young man. In attempting to recognize them as existential beings, I was led to existential counseling, where I have been ever since.

TR: Do you think that client would have confronted you had you not been like him, a Black male?

CV: I have no way of knowing that. I just know he was frustrated and I would have been too, if someone continued to use that little recipe with me: 'How do you feel?' 'How does it make you feel?'

TR: I appreciate your telling that story. I like to think that this young man would not have had the safety of confronting you if he had not felt that you genuinely cared about him. He knew you were another Black man in the world who was a role model, someone who wanted something better for him. I like to think this was the magic of the encounter.

CV: The safety of being around another person like him?
TR: Well, we know that does not always work. You have talked about this in some of your writings. Sometimes the therapeutic encounter does not work, because the relational quality is missing. I have thought about what makes that therapeutic quality work. I do not think it is because people are of the same gender and race. At the same time, I do not think that gender and racial similarity mean nothing. Sometimes, people may choose to have a therapist of the same race or gender – but it does not mean it's going to be effective. That relational quality is so important.
CV: I agree, but I do not think therapeutic quality is caused by racial or gender similarity. As a therapeutic profession, counseling is designed to help people with the problems of life. There might be security in having a therapist who is different from you. I have had many White clients. I often got the impression that White clients sought me out because of my race. Perhaps they felt more secure, because their therapist was Black. I also got the impression that they were more able to open up to me, because of my race. I recall that when I was growing up, White neighbors would come over to talk to my mother. They would talk with her about almost anything. As a young boy, I was surprised that they spoke so freely with my mother. I wondered if they talked that freely with Whites.
TR: I am not so sure how I feel about that. Historically, Black people have been the holders of White people's secrets without being legitimized and recognized for having that kind of skill and wisdom. All of my patients are White. Most of them are men; and these are good therapeutic encounters, but what does it mean to bring all of who one is into the therapy room? In my case, I bring my blackness and my womanness. I have had men tell me, especially after they have cried bitterly, that they would not do this if I were a man. They felt safe with me, that as a woman I would not judge them.
CV: It may be that we are talking about a phenomenon that is very human. We seem to be more comfortable reporting our deepest secrets to perfect strangers than to friends. I once heard of a man who was flying across the country for an interview for a very important job. En route he sat beside a stranger to whom he revealed some of his deepest secrets, thinking that he would never see the person again, once he arrived at his destination. However, he learned the very next day that the individual to whom he had been so authentic was the person who would interview him for the important job that he wanted so much.

TR: I've interviewed White mothers of non-White children in New Zealand and they talk about all aspects of their lives. Part of their openness to me was related to their knowledge that I would be returning home.
CV: In the case of therapy, your White patients come to you week after week and there is still this sense of anonymity. In general, they think they won't run into you into a restaurant. It's awkward and you don't know how to interact with them when you do. White clients are not as likely to run into their Black therapist in a neighborhood restaurant or drugstore, since Blacks and Whites often live in different parts of the town.
TR: But there are discourses here that White people and Black people have these very separate lives and part of that is true. I am reminded of the first session I had with a Black therapist decades ago. She said to me that if we ran into each other in public, she would not speak to me unless I spoke to her first. She recognized that as professional Black women, we might run in similar social circles.

At this point in the conversation, I reflected on a narrative written by a woman who was biracial. She had been in therapy for years and her therapist was a White man. In her narrative, she stated that the therapist never mentioned race, even though racial issues were core to her suffering. Her story troubled me in that she was in therapy for years, but race was not mentioned. I shared this woman's story with Dr Vontress.
CV: When people come to me for therapy, I invite them to tell me why they have come. I help them with the problem they put on the table. Even though a client may have a multitude of problems, the therapist cannot work on them all at the same time. Although a client may come to therapy with many problems, the therapist helps him or her with the problem defined as the one needing intervention. That is the issue the counselor should work on, at least initially. It is important to recognize that the client has a right and duty to define the problem that brought him or her to therapy.
TR: Even if you detect that the presenting problem is not the real problem?
CV: You can suggest, but you should not force yourself into another area. You may see a relationship between a reported problem and another unannounced problem. For example, I might suggest to my client that there may be a relationship between the reported psychological

problem and the client's inability to find a job. On the other hand, I may find that the client presents a psychological problem that is beyond my treatment ability. In that case, I would tell the client that I believe that he or she needs treatment by someone else. I do not think that counselors should venture into areas beyond their psychotherapeutic ability.
TR: I think this woman needed the assistance of a multiculturally competent therapist. There are lots of reasons clients do not bring up topics: they are embarrassed, are concerned that the therapist cannot hold their stories and problems. Therapists are also reluctant to introduce issues, and although therapists should not force any issue the client is not ready to deal with, we should be leaders in broaching topics about race and other therapeutically relevant topics.
CV: Therapists and clients are often on two different wavelengths, so to speak. Therapists may be reluctant to talk about subjects they cannot handle, for example, sexual orientation. Therefore, they often shy away from the topic. If the therapist cannot relate to a lifestyle, the client can see that the therapist is uncomfortable. On the other hand, the therapist may probe for problems that may not exist. That is the other extreme. In one case the counselor is afraid to explore an issue; in the other case, the counselor may try to give the client a problem, often a reflection of an unresolved personal conflict in the counselor. It may be thought of as projection.
TR: This is dangerous. In the first scenario where the therapist does not want to hear the client talk about gay-related topics, not all clients will stop seeing such a therapist and find another therapist. When clients cannot find good therapists, it makes the client more vulnerable. Among Black gay people for example, the Black community can be homophobic, and racism is found in the White community. Where do Black gay people go with their problems?
CV: Regretfully, psychologists as a group are often perceived to be conservative in terms of acceptance of various lifestyles. Often, we are not as therapeutic to people as we ought to be. After all, we are human. I remember in the early eighties when Black people started developing AIDS. As psychologists, some of us said to our professional colleagues that we had to go out and help people suffering from the malady. However, many therapists were frightened. They were afraid to get involved with something they did not understand.

During the early eighties, Dr Vontress worked at a pastoral counseling center. He and his colleagues were among the first to volunteer to provide psychological services to people who had AIDS. He recalled a training session where several psychologists were in a room with clients who had AIDS. A client moved from one psychologist to another in a circle and talked about his fear of dying. Each psychologist bore witness to the conversation between this client and the psychologists assembled. It was very moving when the client moved in front of Dr Vontress and said, 'I am afraid of dying.'

CV: I said to him, you can help me, for I, too, am dying.

[Dr Vontress and the client embraced and cried together.]

CV: In the training session, relating to clients who were dying of AIDS was too emotionally draining for some psychologists. Many of them had to leave the room. It was too much for them, because they had not gotten in touch with their own mortality.

TR: There are stories too hard for some of us to hear. Sometimes my clients apologize for cursing. I tell them they do not have to make the story pretty so that I can hear it. I am concerned about the patient who needs to tell the therapist, 'I'm dying.' Clients know when the therapists cannot hear what they have to say. I think we have dropped the ball when we limp under the weight of our patients' stories. Some therapists cannot hear patients talk about what they need to talk about.

CV: I agree with you. There are therapists who would rather not see the world as it really is. They are also unable to know who their clients really are. In some cases, they appear to want to go through life wearing rose-colored glasses.

TR: Then why are they in the profession?

CV: Most people go into the profession wanting to help others. However, some of them may not want to get their hands dirty, so to speak. They may even select clients who present with the least challenging problems. When I was in private practice, I did not screen my clients. I saw all clients who wanted to come. I screened out the ones that I felt needed more intense therapy than I was qualified to provide. My challenge was to know when to refer my clients to others who could provide more qualified services than I was able to provide. On the other hand, it is important to recognize clients that you can help. For example, I had a Black male client who consulted me, because he was dying of AIDS. Although I could not help him with his medical problem, I was able to help him with the psychological problems related to the illness. He told me about a psychologically distant father who had rejected him, when he discovered that he was gay. On one occasion, he asked me if I would hug him. I agreed. Soon afterwards he died.

TR: Did you know it was his last hug?
CV: No. And it was hurting to see him in his last days and to know that he had never received the love and respect of his father. I have read about many Black men like my client. I understand that James Baldwin, the great African American writer, was rejected by his father, because his father considered his son to be gay, too black, and too ugly for him to love.
TR: He was brilliant. Did he die of AIDS?
CV: No. I understand that he died of alcoholism.
TR: That is a real problem in the Black community.
CV: It is a real problem for human beings to be rejected by their parents, no matter who they are. Many Blacks, male and female, are rejected by one or both parents. This is a story that is yet to be told and analyzed.
TR: There is so much father absence in our communities.
CV: The family is supposed to be your safety net. And suppose they reject you? Where do you go? Everything that happens in society has an effect on what we do as counselors. However, it is important to realize that we cannot fix all the wrongs and suffering in society. I recall that during the sixties and seventies, some Black counselors became so frustrated by the inequities that they saw in society that they became militant in their role as counselors. They wanted to change the system in order to help directly their clients. Sometimes they encouraged their clients to share their militancy, in order that the clients help themselves. I questioned this approach on the part of counselors. As citizens, we as counselors can and should become activists for whatever cause we choose. However, I do not think that we should be activists as counselors. That is, we should separate our activism from our counseling. We should not counsel clients to be activists, especially if they have no interest in playing such a role. Counselors who allow their activism to intrude on the therapeutic enterprise may be anti-therapeutic.
TR: If counseling is meant to help people with the problems of living, I feel a growing frustration toward counselors and psychologists in our inability or unwillingness to look at ourselves.
CV: Our profession has to work on this.
TR: The multicultural counseling movement has sought to help helping professionals bridge the gap between where we are and where our clients need us to be. My concern about the whole diversity movement is that 'everything is everything.' We each feel like we're human beings and can relate to one another, but at the same time we are not aware of

the things that really trip us up. Where do we go to cleanse ourselves and deal with our issues?

CV: With my research on healing, I see a single spirit cleansing the whole universe and some of these religious groups are some of the most hostile to differences and not only sexual differences. I make a distinction between religion and spirituality, with spirituality being more universal. Organized religion has done more to set back racial equality than to promote it. I have not for a long time been an affiliate of organized religion. However, I am a very spiritual human being. I think that spirituality is a powerful force that unifies people, whereas organized religion often divides us. It contributes to conflict in the world.

TR: So existential counseling is inherently spiritual?

CV: Existentialism relates to all the things that human beings have to consider in living. It can be used in the therapeutic process in building a relationship, in diagnosing, in intervening, and in conducting follow-up. Existential counseling does not encourage the use or memorization of techniques.

TR: Don't counselors need to apply existentialism?

CV: Existentialists neither want nor need a cookbook approach to helping. As a therapeutic approach, it simply consists of one human being helping another. That is the only requirement for helping the other person. In fact, in observing one of my existential counseling sessions, the observer might think that he or she is listening in on a conversation between two friends. It is devoid of therapeutic rituals. As an existential therapist, I have always been cognizant of professional ethics, but I have tried not to be so constrained by that which makes us anti-therapeutic. I have taught graduate courses in professional ethics. Even though we should be aware of ethics, we must be human at the same time. There are times when therapists have to make judgment calls. At the same time, they are protections for service providers and their clients. Therapists who ignore professional ethics often do so at their own peril.

CV: As an existential therapist, in my study of traditional healing in Africa, I found that healers are not constrained as we are. In our attempt to become scientists we have become constrained and are mechanical in our interactions with people.

TR: Years ago, I had a counseling student who said she had no desire to work with men who were sexually abusive. She questioned her limitations. I applauded her interrogation of her self and her willingness to honor her limitations and make a personal judgment call.

CV: There is a category of helpers that is emerging in various parts of the world who are not restrained by professional ethics that we in the helping professions in this country adhere to. They are called philosophical counselors. They are practicing in many countries, including Israel, the UK, and to a lesser extent in the United States. Although not all of them adhere to the same code of ethics that we in psychology respect, some of them have developed their own code of ethics. Most professionals who provide service to the public respect some code of ethics. That seems important.
TR: How do philosophical counselors deal with third-party reimbursement and licensure?
CV: My understanding is that some philosophical counselors are also licensed psychologists. They can receive third-party payment. In the case of those who are not licensed psychologists, their clients must be willing to pay without going through the managed health care system. Certainly, that is a consideration for people who are interested in philosophical counseling.
TR: That introduces class, since not everyone can afford to pay out of pocket, even on a sliding scale.
CV: You are right about socioeconomic status and the ability to pay for counseling. However, traditional healers in Africa are not constrained in the same way that we are. Many of them have organized themselves into professional associations. In those cases, they, too, have begun to establish practice guidelines, in order to protect clients. Since they provide most of the psychological, spiritual, and physical healing in traditional Africa, it is important that the public be protected from charlatans. In general, I have found that healers are able to be much more spontaneous in treating their clients than we are. For them, healing is an art, not a science, as we often perceive our services. Of course, existential counselors try to break away from the scientific model. I try to approach my clients as one human being to another.
TR: Do you think it is possible for counselors to be therapeutic if they themselves have not gone through counseling?
CV: There are many ways to achieve personal insight. Although I have never experienced counseling or psychotherapy in the usual sense, I have had many experiences that have helped me to develop an understanding of myself.
TR: You mean experiences other than one-on-one therapy.
CV: Sometimes talking to a good friend can be therapeutic or going to a good movie or play or having a good psychological and physical

experience, such as jogging, can be therapeutic. I do not think that simply talking to another human being one-on-one is necessarily therapeutic. It all depends on the therapist and his or her state of mental health.

TR: Why do you think so many counselors and therapists are reluctant to consult their own therapist?

CV: I do not know how many counselors in this country consult therapists. Many programs in counseling, psychology, and psychiatry require personal therapy as a requirement for graduation. Some states require periodic therapy for re-certification or licensure. However, of late, I have not seen much literature on the practice. As a therapeutic profession, counseling is designed to help people with the problems of life. People have a lot of problems in society right now, such as the economic breakdown, the disintegration of families, and school dropouts. These and other problems have implications for counseling. That is, one cannot divorce counseling from everything else that goes on in society. Counselors have tried to take up the slack of families, only to find themselves overwhelmed by their efforts. Of course, they cannot make up for all of the failures of social institutions. Counselors should not blame themselves for the breakdown of institutions in society. Counselors have limited resources and abilities. We must know what we can do and what we cannot do to remedy the many problems that our clients bring to us.

In one of his interviews over two decades ago, Dr Vontress stated that Black counselors tended to be more concerned about the relational quality, whereas White counselors were more likely to dig into a bag of tricks toward figuring out how to bend, sit, and speak to get the technique right. I thought of this observation because such reliance on technique came, in my view, from a place of anxiety – about getting it right given how racially segregated people's lives are. Many White counselors in training or those who are seasoned do not have close relationships with Black people. This can translate into multicultural interactions that feel foreign, risky, and uncomfortable. While I was struck at the boldness of his comment, one could argue he was being stereotypical in his observation.

TR: Did you get any flak for making that observation?

CV: Not to my face. That is not to say that I have not been criticized over the years for some of my views. And I welcome and benefit from criticism. I am comfortable with existentialism as a therapeutic approach. It has worked for me. I have tried to tell people how it can work for them. I believe that we are all existentialists. However, we often do not trust ourselves. I am sure that people who have found that existential therapy does not work for them have dismissed my views as impractical, unscientific, or the like.

TR: The current dialogue on diversity and multiculturalism is fragile. Although people are more similar than different, what are your thoughts about focusing on broad similarities related to the human experience as well as attending to differences?

CV: I focus on the similarities first and then, if necessary, on the differences; but many multicultural counselors seem to focus on differences first before they get to similarities. In counseling, I focus on the human being in front of me first. That person is just like me. Then, if the problem calls for it, I may explore cultural differences. In my view, it is wrong to start off the interview with the assumption that the client is somehow culturally different from me.Very often a consideration of cultural difference is inappropriate in a counseling session. It depends on the client's presenting problem. For example, a client in an academic setting may come to consult me about a problem that has nothing to do with his or her cultural difference. The problem may be about not having enough money to pay his or her rent, because he or she has not yet received money from home. That is a problem that any student might have. On the other hand, there are some problems, such as multiple-choice exams, to which some culturally different clients may be unaccustomed and therefore are sources of anxiety for them.

TR: You assert that the current literature focuses on difference first and then similarities. You say you want to focus on similarities and then focus on differences if there is a need to do so. Aren't differences, albeit socially constructed, working in the background or the foreground and waiting for counselors to bring them out of the dark, to name them?

CV: They may or may not be. Counselors should bring them up only when they help to clarify the problem or when they seem to be related to a resolution of the problem. Often, bringing up differences reflects more unresolved issues of the therapist than those of the client.

TR: I had a student from the Middle East once. She thanked me for lecturing on People of the Middle East in my diversity class. There are a lot of Jewish students at my university as there are at universities throughout out nation. This student did not want the Jewish students knowing she was Palestinian. If some students knew who she was, she was concerned their feelings toward her might change. I was mindful of her feelings of alienation. When she came at office hours for academic issues, there were other concerns that sat with her at the table.

CV: And yet therapy evolves as the client gets to know me and trusts me and I have to let it evolve.

TR: You can't control it.

CV: I use the Socratic method as my only major style of counseling.

TR: As you reflect on your life's work, is there any area of it that you are most proud of?

CV: I have never thought of that before. I have written in several areas. They are culture, cross-cultural counseling, Existential counseling, traditional healing, and some other areas to a lesser extent. In looking back, I think that there is a common thread unifying all of them. That thread is the human condition held up to the same light, in order to get a holistic understanding of the condition.

TR: The current landscape of multiculturalism, as well as my own approach to multicultural work, is inclusive of multiple identities: sexuality, class, gender, religion, and disability. Is the addition of these other groups an unwelcome departure from your work?

CV: It is not up to me to say whether the inclusion of other groups in the definition of culture is an unwelcomed departure from my original work. Suffice it to say that it simply does not reflect my conception of culture.

TR: Is there a cultural hopper, in your mind, that should be left alone?

CV: My definition of culture does not include women, gays, seniors, and others that are often included in some definitions. However, I do not speak disparagingly against anyone who defines culture differently. I simply want to make clear that I do not agree with a comprehensive definition of culture in which any and all mistreated groups are thrown into the same 'cultural hopper.'

TR: It is possible that the 'cultural hopper' is rather crowded and has confounded the discussion of culture. This is why I refer to the intersections of spirituality, class, and disability with race, ethnicity, and culture.

CV: Cultural differences should refer not only to racial and ethnic groups here in the United States, but also to cultural groups throughout the world. Culture used to belong to the sociologists and anthropologists. Now other people have taken it over and defined it according to their purposes. This is what happens when a new discipline takes on another discipline's concepts. Many of the current definitions of culture developed by some multicultural writers depart from earlier definitions associated with anthropologists and sociologists.

TR: Is this departure problematic?

CV: There is nothing anyone can do about this departure. However, in our profession, in order for us to communicate with one another and to be therapeutic to our clients, we have to understand what we are talking about. I am not condemning those who choose to define culture in a different way. On the other hand, it is important to know who is a culturally different client. If everybody is culturally different, then nobody is culturally different. If we come to this position, then there is no need for cross-cultural counseling as a sub-specialty.

TR: What is your vision for counseling?

CV: I think that counselors should approach each client as being individually different. We should try to ascertain the unique qualities presented by each client, regardless of race, culture, or ethnicity. Although race or ethnicity may be evident, it does not define the totality of the individual. The same can be said of any other group. I see one world, in which science plays a big part in the way people think and live. In terms of our profession, I see globalism reflected in the DSM and its attempt to diagnose all people of the world in the same way. Although the new edition of the *Diagnostic and Statistical Manual* is in progress, it remains unchanged in terms of its universal perspective. We as cross-cultural counselors are obliged to adhere to its guidelines, in terms of diagnosing our clients from various cultures. I have always advocated for courses in psychology, philosophy, sociology, languages, and the social sciences in general. I also think that a year abroad is a good experience for counselors in training. It is very rewarding for them to feel what it is like to be a foreigner in another land. It enhances the cross-cultural counselor's ability to empathize with culturally different people, especially immigrants.

TR: Thank you, Dr Vontress, for making yourself available to engage in a wide-ranging conversation on your career and ideas about cross-cultural counseling.

Postscript

CLEMMONT E. VONTRESS

I am moved, honored, and enlightened by the content of the chapters written by my colleagues. I am pleased that they have read so many of my works, commented on them, and posited their ideas about the status and future of cross-cultural counseling. Their views will help to determine the substance and direction of this very important speciality of the psychotherapeutic profession, which continues to change rapidly in the United States and other countries. As this profession changes, mentoring becomes increasingly important to its evolution. This is why I am pleased that some of my colleagues discuss it. Their comments highlight the significance of mentoring in cross-cultural counseling. Newcomers need to be systematically socialized into the profession, in order to understand how to integrate culture into therapy. Although there are many definitions of mentoring, for me it is similar to counseling, teaching, and advising. The senior counselor encourages and inspires the junior counselor to be the best that he or she can be. Personally, I have never perceived myself to be a mentor. Rather, I have always enjoyed seeing the other person pursue and excell in his or her area of interest. To see my students developing professional wings and soaring on their own has been the joy of my career. In fact, I believe that each of us knowingly or unknowingly influences others in countless ways. Indeed, we in cross-cultural counseling should consider how mentoring can be institutionalized to ensure the fruition of what Paul Pedersen calls the Fourth Force in counseling.

Assuredly, culture impacts all institutions in society, including psychotherapeutic professions. During the last five decades, the interaction of culture and counseling has come to be known as cross-cultural counseling or multicultural counseling. However, there is little agreement on the nature or therapeutic consequence of the culture–counseling interaction. This lack of agreement exists because several disparate, aggrieved, and alienated groups insist that their members also be considered culturally different clients. The current literature indicates that many professionals in counseling have acceded to their insistence. That is why it is now difficult to institutionalize mentoring in cross-cultural counseling graduate programs. People in the counseling profession must first agree on what therapeutic relationships constitute cross-cultural counseling before they can decide how to assist and inspire newcomers to enter, and make achievements in, the speciality.

The chapters in this book also evoke thoughts about the relationship of the self and the Other. It is a question as old as philososphy itself. Philosophers such as Edmund Husserl (1859–1929), Martin Heidegger (1889–1976), Jean-Paul Sartre (1905–80), and Martin Buber (1878–1965) have considered the problem from an individual and collective perspective. Carl Rogers (1902–87) based his counseling theory on the idea that only the client knows the self. Therefore, the essential work of the counselor is to try to find out how the client perceives his or her own reality. Clients report their perceptions of the world to the therapist, who then tries to confirm his or her correct understanding of them by responses prefaced by such phrases as 'So you feel …' or 'What I hear you saying is …' In discussing existential therapy, I often describe how difficult it is for the therapist as an outsider to understand the essence of the Other, the insider.

The same question may be posed when researchers study groups of people. Can a researcher who is a cultural outsider understand a foreign group or culture? There are historical examples that can be cited that would suggest an affirmative response. Alexis de Tocqueville (1805–59), French political writer and statesman, came to the United States in 1831 and spent several months traveling throughout the country. He returned to France in 1832 and wrote the classic *Democracy in America*, one of the most profound studies of American life. Margaret Mead (1901–78), the American cultural anthropologist, may also be cited as an example of an outsider who studied traditional cultures in the South Pacific and Southeast Asia. She is considered one of the great scholars of the twentieth century.

It may be argued that the self or insider is often unable to see objectively all of her or his own dimensions. The outsider is usually a more objective observer than the insider. When it comes to a Western researcher in Africa, it is indeed appropriate to ask whether the outsider can understand African people, regardless of the methodology used by the outsider. Of course the same question can be asked of African researchers. The continent is so diverse in terms of its terrain, people, and natural resources that it eludes full comprehension. To what extent can a member of one ethnic group understand individuals or groups from another ethnic community? How do religious differences impede the ability to understand the Other, since religion is so much a part of culture?

During my field trips to Africa, I used what may be described as an ethnographic research methodology to learn about traditional healing in three countries. In some ways, my methodology resembled my existential therapeutic approach. Each individual is a separate entity. Although it is difficult for one person to understand the Other, they both share common environments or existential worlds. Therefore, all human beings are more alike than they are different. The same can be said of each country and its people. An outside reseacher who enters a foreign country looking for human commonalities is more apt to understand its people and institutions than one who looks only for cultural differences.

All the contributors to this book have enhanced the counseling profession with their ideas about cross-cultural counseling. I hope that the book will inspire others on all continents to consider what needs to be done to keep alive and enhance the growth of the current excitement about counseling across cultures. Although the therapeutic cultural movement started in the United States, it has now spread throughout the world. That is why therapists in all countries must continue to promote it. To that end, it is important to keep in mind the five cultural rings that I have discussed in my writings. Culture is not a single entity. It consists of many interactive layers of learned and instinctive behaviors and responses.

Even though culture impacts all clients, it is important for counselors to recognize that each person, regardless of cultural background, ethnic identification, or expeiences, is uniquely different from every other human being. The focus on cross-cultural counseling does not mean that counselors should relinquish efforts to ascertain individual differences. These differences transcend culture. They are also physical, psychological, and spiritual. Therefore, it seems tenable to conclude that the most effective counselors are holistic in their attempts to understand and respond therapeutically to the unique needs of each client.

Contributors

Patricia Arredondo, PhD, is Senior Associate Vice President and Advisor for Academic Initiatives and Professor of Counseling/Counseling Psychology, Arizona State University. She is known for her scholarship in the areas of multicultural competencies, organizational diversity management, and Latino psychology. She has served as president of national associations including APA Division 45 Society for the Psychological Study of Ethnic Minority Issues, the American Counseling Association, the National Latina/o Psychological Association, and the Association of Multicultural Counseling and Development. She is an APA Fellow of Divisions 17 and 45 and was recognized as a Living Legend for her contributions to multicultural counseling by the American Counseling Association.

Nancy Arthur, PhD, is appointed as a Tri-Faculty Canada Research Chair and Professor in the Division of Applied Psychology, Faculty of Education, University of Calgary. Her research and teaching focuses on preparing professionals for working in global contexts, including multicultural counseling, international transitions, and career development.

Olaniyi Bojuwoye, PhD, is a professor of Educational Psychology at the University of KwaZulu Natal, Durban, South Africa. He is also a registered psychologist with the Health Professions Council of South Africa (HPCSA). His research interests include traditional healing/mental health delivery services and cross-cultural counseling.

Sandra Collins, PhD, is an associate professor and Director of the Graduate Centre for Applied Psychology at Athabasca University,

Alberta, Canada. She focuses her research and writing in the areas of multicultural counseling, social justice, counseling women, counselor education and supervision, and distance and online learning.

Deone Curling, MEd, is a counselor and psychotherapist at a community health centre for Black women and women of colour in Toronto. She is a doctoral candidate at OISE/University of Toronto. Deone's research interests include Black women's mental health, resilience, race, and culture and psychotherapy.

Jessica M. Diaz, MA, CRC, is a doctoral student at the University of Maryland, College Park. She has presented at a number of local and national conferences on multicultural counseling and has co-authored chapters and journal articles with her mentor Dr Courtland Lee. She is the past president of the Alpha Delta Chapter of Chi Sigma Iota and has served as the student representative for the governing council of the American Counseling Association. Her research interests include multicultural counseling, mentoring of Latino urban high school students, and international counseling.

Lawrence R. Epp, PhD, is a former senior psychiatric therapist in the Johns Hopkins Hospital School Program. He is a past president of both the District of Columbia Mental Health Counselors Association and the Maryland Association for Multicultural Counseling and Development. He is currently a mental health counselor at the Chelsea School in Silver Spring, Maryland, and is on the adjunct faculty of George Mason University.

Farah A. Ibrahim, PhD, is a professor in the Counseling Psychology and Counselor Education program at the University of Colorado Denver. She is a fellow of the American Psychological Association and past president of Counselors for Social Justice, a division of the American Counseling Association. Her research has focused on existential philosophy, assessment of worldview and cultural identity assessment, and incorporating multicultural competencies in doctoral and master's programs in counseling. Her other research areas include Asian American women, psychology of women and worldview, character development among college and high school students, cross-cultural couples counseling, school counseling, counseling Muslims, and cultural competence in a global society.

Courtland C. Lee, PhD, is Professor and Director of the Counselor Education Program at the University of Maryland, College Park. He is the author, editor, or co-editor of five books on multicultural counseling and the author of three books on counseling African American males. In addition, he has published numerous book chapters and articles on counseling across cultures. He is a past president and fellow of the American Counseling Association. He is also a past president of the Association for Multicultural Counseling and Development. Dr Lee is the president of the International Association for Counselling. He is also a fellow of the British Association for Counselling and Psychotherapy. He is the former editor of the *Journal of Multicultural Counseling and Development* and currently serves as a Senior Associate Editor of the *Journal of Counseling & Development.*

Ronald Marshall, PhD, is a senior lecturer at the University of the West Indies in the Department of Behavioural Sciences, St Augustine Campus. His research interests focus on the social and psychological problems of minorities, health behaviour and health care access in the Caribbean, and changing aspects of the family.

Roy Moodley, PhD, is Associate Professor in Counseling Psychology at the Ontario Institute for Studies in Education at the University of Toronto. Research and publication interests include traditional and cultural healing; multicultural and diversity counseling; race, culture, and ethnicity in psychotherapy; and masculinities. Roy co-edited *Transforming Managers: Gendering Change in the Public Sector* (UCL Press/Taylor and Francis, 1999); *Carl Rogers Counsels a Black Client: Race and Culture in Person-Centred Counseling* (PCCS Books, 2004); *Integrating Traditional Healing Practices into Counseling and Psychotherapy* (Sage, 2005); and *Race, Culture and Psychotherapy: Critical Perspectives in Multicultural Practice* (Routledge, 2006).

Paul Pedersen, PhD, is a visiting professor in the Department of Psychology at the University of Hawaii. He has taught at the University of Minnesota, Syracuse University, and University of Alabama at Birmingham, and for six years at universities in Taiwan, Malaysia, and Indonesia. He has authored, co-authored, or edited 40 books, 99 articles, and 72 chapters on aspects of multicultural counseling and international communication. He is a fellow in Divisions 9, 17, 45, and 52 of the American Psychological Association.

Tracy L. Robinson-Wood, EdD (Harvard), is a professor in the Department of Counseling and Applied Educational Psychology at Northeastern University. Previously, she was a professor in the Department of Counselor Education at North Carolina State University. Tracy teaches courses in research, research design, multicultural psychology, and diversity. She is author of the textbook *The Convergence of Race, Ethnicity, and Gender: Multiple Identities in Counseling.* Her research interests focus on the intersections of race, gender, class, and culture in psychosocial identity development. She has developed the Robinson Resistance Modality Inventory (RRMI) and is conducting empirical research on ethnically diverse Black women, resistance, coping, and racial identity development. She is a Licensed Mental Health Counselor and see clients at a private agency in Massachusetts.

Pasty Sutherland, MEd, is a counsellor and psychotherapist, and a researcher at the Centre for International Governance Innovation (CIGI) in conjunction with the University of Waterloo, Ontario, Canada. She is also a doctoral candidate in Counselling Psychology at the University of Toronto. Her research and publication interests span areas of critical multicultural counseling and psychotherapy, traditional and cultural healing, and transgenerational trauma.

Rinaldo Walcott, PhD, is an associate professor at the Ontario Institute for Studies in Education at the University of Toronto. He is the author of *Black Like Who? Writing Black Canada*, as well as the editor of 'Rude: Contemporary Black Canadian Cultural Criticism.'

Valerie Watson, PhD, has worked as a teacher, lecturer, and trainer in secondary and higher education and in the voluntary sector. She has a personal and particular research interest in ethnicity, race, and culture as it relates to counseling and counselor education. Her completed thesis examined the training experiences of Black counselors in England. Currently, Valerie is a counselor in the counseling service at the University of Nottingham.

Carmen Braun Williams, PhD, is Assistant Vice President for Diversity at the University of Colorado, Associate Professor Emerita in Counseling Psychology at the University of Colorado Denver (UCD), and a licensed clinical psychologist. Prior to her administrative appointment,

Dr Williams served as associate dean of the School of Education at UCD. Her research is in cultural competence in psychotherapy and racial identity. Dr Williams received her doctorate in clinical psychology in 1980 from Pennsylvania State University.

Index